organization

space

The MIT Press   Cambridge, Massachusetts   London, England

organization

space

LANDSCAPES,

HIGHWAYS,

AND HOUSES

IN AMERICA

Keller Easterling

© 1999 Massachusetts Intitute of Technology

9-13-02

This book was set in Janson and Rotis Semi Sans by Graphic Composition, Inc.

Printed and bound in the United States of America.

Library of Congress Cataloging-in-Publication Data

Easterling, Keller, 1959–
    Organization space : landscapes, highways, and houses in America / Keller
Easterling.
        p.   cm.
    Includes bibliographical references and index.
    ISBN 0-262-05061-7 (hc : alk. paper)
    1. Space (Architecture)   I. Title.
NA9053.S6E18   1999
710—dc21   99-40790
                                                                          CIP

Contents

Acknowledgments

Many students at Columbia University, in seminars and studios, helped cultivate the ideas in this book. Colleagues and friends who read this manuscript, particularly Richard Prelinger and Michael Sorkin, already have my thanks. The Graham Foundation, The New York Foundation for the Arts, The National Endowment for the Arts, The MacDowell Colony, and the John Nolen Research Fund provided support for this book and for related projects. The following libraries provided archival material: Benton MacKaye Papers, Dartmouth College Library; Division of Rare and Manuscript Collections, Cornell University Libraries; Avery Library, Columbia University; the National Archives and Records Administration; and the New York Public Library. Historians and historical societies at Greenbelt, Maryland; Greendale, Wisconsin; Greenhills, Ohio; Kingsport, Tennessee; Levittown, New York; Mariemont, Ohio; and Norris, Tennessee also provided archival material. I would like to thank my friends Jordan Crandall, Susan Jonas, Andrea Kahn, Brian McGrath, and Ray Gastil for their support. Melanie Kiihn, Elise Lau Carranza, Ashley Schaffer, Phu Hoang, and William Taylor assisted me in various research efforts. I also thank Roger Conover, Melissa Vaughn, and Jean Wilcox at MIT Press for their careful attention to the manuscript. This book was written for Monty Graham.

Introduction

Architects are accustomed to resolving spaces according to aesthetic or geometric principles. This book, however, is interested in organizational expressions of spatial arrangements as well as the sites or agents of change within those organizations, and it argues that some of the most common and powerful means of altering space might be best described in this way.

The design professions have encyclopedias full of specific nomenclature related to form and geometry; yet unlike geology, biology, music, or mathematics, architecture has few common terms to describe spatial organizations with active parts, temporal components, or differential change. For instance, biological terminology must express relationship and duration or characterize systems that evolve, "learn," or adapt over time. Geologists study not only artifacts, but processes like fluvial activity, glaciation, and erosion, developing descriptions of watersheds or ice flows that incorporate temporal markers and elastic boundary conditions. Military protocols describe changing groupings over time with a language that can accommodate such fluidity. In communication and computational networks, timing and storage space are one and the same thing and so cannot be expressed as absolute spaces or objects. Rather, technologists who work with these environments use the term *network architecture* to refer to the powerful protocols organizing interplay, adjustment, and timing among ecologies of circuitry.

Architects are typically more fluent in descriptions of activity and relationship that result in artifacts or forms within conventions that favor the designation of site as a single entity. We are most comfortable with nouns rather than verbs, with artistic products that have representational currency, and with organizations that can be optimized. In the early twentieth century, architecture pursued a fascination with activity by equating it with motion or stylizing motion as speed within a bachelor's world of fast cars, airplanes, and forms representative of dynamism. We have also traditionally codified the activities of building within master plans and modular systems. When the profession was intrigued with active organizations in the 1960s and 1970s, these organizations were often seen holistically as ecologies for which a comprehensive pattern could be determined—returning a fascination with activity and relationship to a fascination with geometry. Though new electronic infrastructures and computational equipment vividly model the operatives of active organizations, the late twentieth-century interest in network interplay often appears to be scripted by an unconscious revival of midcentury desires for cybernetic or recursive organization. The architect with new computational tools is often more attracted to the visuals or behaviors of software environments than to the invisible network architecture behind the screen. Our work with these tools thus sometimes reinforces a rather conventional notion of site surrounding the elaboration of an object representing organization. We rarely define sites in a way that will permit exploration of organizational or network architecture, in part because we rarely define sites in multiples. Even in urban sites we often simply reframe the boundaries to include a larger set of adjacent areas, returning the site to a single unit and placing it under the purview of urban design or planning.

To truly exploit some of the intelligence related to network thinking, an alternative position might operate from the premise that the real power of many urban organizations lies within the relationships among multiple distributed sites that are both collectively and individually adjustable. This discussion transfers intelligence from many different models of active organization to an understanding of spatial environments. It pursues a fascination with simple components that gain complexity by their relative position to each other. For instance, it is possible to understand sites as separate agents that remotely affect each other—that is, the way one can affect point C by affecting points A and B. It is also possible to describe the amplification of a simple move across a group of separate agents, or to describe their parallel or serial sequencing. This architecture is not about the house but rather about housekeeping. It is not be about triangles and tauruses or motion trajectories, but about timing and patterns of interactivity, about triplets and cycles, subtractions and parallelism, switches and differentials. Architecture, as it is used here, might describe the parameters or protocols for formatting space.

Organizational expressions perhaps inform our understanding of some very familiar development formats that typically resist conventional architectural analysis. For instance, the process of assembling residential formations often resembles agricultural production in that large numbers of houses are executed simultaneously in uniform fields, and the logistical format or protocol of that process is the chief determinant of spatial and material consequences, not the appearance of the suburban house. Here organization does not merely facilitate architecture. It is the architecture or the logistical software for spatial production. Though ageographic, the generic specifications for assembling offices, airports, highways, and many different kinds of franchises are also explicitly calibrated according to protocols for timing and interactivity. These protocols, whether generic or idiosyncratic are the dominant architectures in our culture of development—architectures, privileging not the formal, morphological attributes of building, but rather a repertoire of operatives affected by time, patterns of connectivity, and changing populations of multiple components. These are the new inventions and gizmos— the management styles, the production sequences, or networking protocols— that make space in America and around the world.

Though spatial economies may be most complex when they are diverse, circumstantial, and incomplete, architects, managers, and planners have often sought comprehensive control over even distributed spatial systems like infrastructure networks. We have often fixed a complex ephemeral activity within a particular kind of morphology, procedure, or aesthetic attempting not to adjust but to determine the aesthetics and technics of the system as a totality. The traffic-engineered interstate highway, for instance, was designed as an inflexible and totalizing system segregated from interaction with other transportation modalities and valued as a smooth system of neutralized equivalence. Like mass-produced housing, the more neutral, uniform, and quantifiable, the more bankable. Even the newest communication-information networks are often discussed as smooth systems of integration and connection with less emphasis on the differentiation of the network (e.g., the "information highway"). Technocracy, traffic engineering, cybernetics, or environmentalism—a few of the twentieth-century persuasions that appear in this discussion—have all toyed with unifying theories of complexity or appeared to long for some kind of comprehensive understanding of the organizations they studied. Just as the design professions have valued successive models of intelligence and geometric models of organization, so generic spatial formats, are usually introduced with enthusiastic claims of optimization—claims that are always overturned within the comedies of the marketplace. The ultimate generic product streamlined to travel unimpeded from manufacture to market becomes an unattainable goal since the generic can always be made yet more generic through some new and, ironically idiosyncratic, wrinkle in retail psychology or some new, supposedly more efficient distribution format.

In the same way that many organizations change or grow as a result of their own eccentricities, the production of spatial commodities is fueled by mistakes and risks within the inevitable anarchy and unpredictability of the market place. These are the market's jokes or implausible details that are extreme if only to be real. Although we think of these eccentricities as tactical, ephemeral, and untraceable, they are also caused by deliberate inventions that find some way of tripping the lock and entering the marketplace, even if only for a short period of time. They are also not necessarily small and discrete like wild cards, since, they often have the power to shift the rules of a larger game. Eccentricities are often amplified within an organization so that an effective intervention may not involve comprehensive control but partial or tactical adjustment. Tactical sites have larger powers. Generic spatial production, for instance, amplifies small adjustments by way of its own banality. When a small desire meets large volumes of consumers, or a dumb component is multiplied within a banal or repetitive environment, it has the power to gradually reconstitute an organization. Repetitive housing, for instance, critiqued for its monotony, potentially amplifies a small fitting or detail. Similarly, transportation redundancies might be valued since they present opportunistic sites for installing intelligent switching between networks. This material looks for sites that temporarily interface a wave of consumption to recondition or overwrite a space. The discussion looks for elements that are accident-prone or inventions born in eccentric conditions, with the assumption that the world grows or learns by these accidents, and whatever remains eccentric to a culture's boundaries and brackets is more likely to cross-reference its intelligence. These eccentricities or wild cards—which are constantly creating volatility, difference, and conflict within development organizations—are smart in their own way, and they are the subject of this book. They produce space by adjusting organization. They are the sites of organization space in America.

Perhaps in these sites, architects return to find a previously obscured opportunity and an expanded repertoire for their formal skills and aesthetic inclinations. If the most powerful sites are improvisational and responsive to the circumstantial changes of anarchical organizations, they are also suggestive of an active and inventive practice of architecture within some of the most common development protocols in America.

The book's three parts visit the organizational territory of landscapes, highways, and houses in America. The material looks opportunistically for eccentric episodes in the history of these development organizations that prefigure our contemporary interests and confound the notion that cultural intelligence is successive rather than coexistent. It looks for practitioners who ventured into the architecture of organization and for alternative proposals that would have arranged our most familiar environments in a different key. The argument often uses these eccentric issues, events, or careers to interrogate a larger organization or to cross-reference and encapsulate historical material.

Each of the three parts references a midcentury period when new infrastructure technologies associated with electricity, automobiles, and electronics were reformatting the country. Engineering was gaining power as a political tool. Planning was a dangerous word, associated not with ineffectual bureaucracy but with political and economic reorganization. The federal government was inventorying the country's natural resources, industrial capabilities, and population migrations, and practitioners from many disciplines became government associates, conducting experiments to reengineer infrastructure networks and redirect protocols for consumption, distribution, transportation, and exurban development. These unusual practitioners, who today might be too easily labeled "planners," were often architects and designers who were working in the organizational strata of American space.

The discussion is not designed to provide an architectural or planning history. Nor does it intend to provide a general characterization of American infrastructure organizations. Since the episodes are only considered for what they offer to a discussion of organizational architecture, the research is in no way part of a prescriptive program involving revival or reform. None of the practitioners are heroes of the story, even though some appear in all three parts of the book as members of a cast of characters involved in the development of land, highways, and residential infrastructures during this century. The material also references early the twentieth-century technocracy movement, midcentury systems analysis, and the sentimentalism associated with the postwar environmental movement, but these more positivistic ideologies only serve to critique our own persistent desires for comprehensive control and recursive structure in complex organizations.

The episodes are designed to defamiliarize familiar environments by identifying those sites that have the power to divert or rearrange them, and so they are chosen because, whatever their approach, they identify an unorthodox way of siting adjustment within a larger organization. The material is continually drawn to inventions that pursue a simple fascination across several disciplines to find a cultural loophole within the dominant development formats. These sites of invention, the wild cards in the organization, remain the object of the discussion. Echoes among the parts hopefully disrupt the category distinctions of land, highway, and subdivision since the most interesting practitioners were involved with all three, and each of these environments borrowed organizational protocols from the other. There are no organizational typologies. Houses, cars, and their attending spaces were treated as products; land was a utility; and highways were landscapes. The material favors events that engage or critique our current fascinations and form a resonant suite of articles in an ongoing discussion—one that necessarily visits territory outside the contents of this book.

Part I looks at the infrastructure prototypes of Benton MacKaye (1879–1975) to interrogate a number of prewar episodes that were critical to the formatting of land and infrastructure in America. MacKaye's terrestrial, fluvial, and automobile infrastructures were specifically designed to be utilities and to operate interdependently with existing rail, highway, and electrical infrastructure. Though he made many proposals about altering infrastructure space in America, he was not trained within the design professions but rather in the earth sciences and so expressed spatial attributes in organizational rather than formal or geometric terms. At a time when new networks associated with hydro-electricity and automobiles were being used as a means of galvanizing politics around very deterministic or technocratic principles, MacKaye expressed these technologies, for instance, as geological models that registered space against time and activity. MacKaye's practice lay outside of the prevailing career patterns and disciplinary boundaries. Perhaps as a consequence, his work contacted many different players and events of the time, and so he is a useful touchstone. In addition, his practice is important to this discussion because, while he dealt with physical sites, he also constructed virtual sites or persuasions in his writings that positioned the practice itself as a tactical site of spatial production and adjustment.

Part II looks at those rare moments in the history of national highway systems when they were perceived as differential or intermodal networks. The interstate highway system was conceived as a frozen shape that neutralized interplay among various species of network and carrier. It was a dumb network with dumb switches. Both before and after the interstate was legislated however, independent designers, private interests, and municipalities proposed highway systems based on alternative organizational protocols. Some treated the highway as another of America's machines or gadgets that could be tooled to handle more complex activities. In other proposals, the highway mimicked or borrowed an organizational repertoire from railroads, airports, or the surrounding landscape. Still others designated sites of intermodal exchange in the roadsides, intersections, or urban terminals of the system. There were also persistent ambitions to merge the highway with computers or other electronic technologies that would shape it into an automated, self-regulating network. This discussion looks at applied network technologies, but it also uses the terms of network architecture to extend an understanding of interchanges, parallel transportation networks, and roadside rights-of-way as sites for building intelligence into several transportation systems simultaneously.

Part III looks at the power of small components and logistical adjustments in large repetitive fields of residential fabric. It uses the subdivision, to examine the commodification and distribution of space according to a product model. Residential property has perhaps always been a commodity, but the discussion goes to a pivotal point just prior to the most familiar midcentury wave of suburban growth when the new technicians of "subdivision science" arrived in Washington to lobby for their various approaches to organizing residential space. Just when these earnest planners thought they could establish scientific controls over the subdivision, the rules of the game shifted, and the government effortlessly appropriated their attempts to optimize sub-urban formats. The subdivision turned, while still in their hands, into something entirely different and much more powerful as the government systematized and mobilized home-building enterprises into the nation's flagship post-Depression industry under the guidance of the Federal Housing Administration. The episodes look at a comparative set of organizational expressions attending the subdivision at this juncture. Residential fabric has typically been arranged in generic networks that achieve varying degrees of neutrality and differentiation as a consequence of many logistical variables. Some subdivisions examined here were either differentiated by timing or by some intermediate organizing agent. In other subdivisions, the critical sites of adjustment were the repeated components or fittings of the house and lot within their distributive markets of consumption.

The familiar environments discussed in these episodes were often viewed through a cultural persuasion that partially obscured their organizational constitution. Landscapes, highways, and houses have throughout their history been used as economic indicators and as instruments of employment, banking, and commercial production. Yet their promotion was reduced to simple slogans or broad cultural abstractions. These persuasions or coercions, most of them loyal to the cults of aesthetics or technology, associated development products with, for instance, freedom, technological positivism, psychological well-being, or patriotism. Terrestrial landscapes have consistently been associated with visual beauty, spiritual reverie, and environmentalism. The suburban housing product was associated with patriotism and contentment, and the interstate highway with freedom or "elbow room." Both the campaigns of persuasion and their critics have referenced exhausted ideologies like the "American dream," and the "open road." Homogeneity, kitsch, boredom, and mistreatment of women are required topics in critical discussions of America's generic space, but the critiques may be uninformative precisely because the persuasions that adhere to these environments often do not correspond to the operatives controlling them. For instance, architects have continually tried to administer aesthetic makeovers to the midcentury "organization man." Meanwhile, a new orgman, born into and heir to that logistical environment, writes the software for contemporary residential and commercial formations as well as for the new virtual organizations of the office and factory.[1] Some cultural scripts may neutralize the complexity of the environments discussed; yet, ironically they also often reveal something about the organizations they fail to control or describe. The spin or the campaign as well as the logistics of these organizations may provide some of their most powerful and pliable sites of adjustment.

Each of the book's three parts also generates its own species of discussion and merges architectural languages with other languages of process and models of interplay. Both the text and the practitioners discussed here use many different kinds of models from, for instance, geology, mathematics, and electronics to conceive and articulate organizational protocols. Some abstract terms are particularly durable in this discussion as a means of mapping or recording interplay as well as articulating adjustable organizational protocols. They enrich an existing language of site and are used artistically rather than scientifically to highlight the activity and exchange within an environment. These terms include the following: *remote, redundancy, parallel, differential, switch, governor, partition, function, summation,* and *subtraction.* There is no glossary, however, and no attempt to define the terms, but rather to compound their meanings and to use them as markers of active process.

For instance, it might appear easy enough to apply geological terms to discussions of landscape and network operatives to an overtly networked system like the highway, but considered abstractly, "network" describes not only something that is organized like a web, such as a grid of streets or highways, but an organization of multiples that may act independently or in concert. Electronic network intelligence relies on smart and flexible patterns of switching between heterogeneous components and multiple scales of activity. Multiplicity, differentiation, and diversity are understood to strengthen a network, and the smarter the system the more its operation runs counter to conventional notions of efficiency. Redundancy and parallel networking among computers multiply pathways and circuits, increasing the supply of material for trial and error, thus increasing the speed of problem solving as well. The amount of switching is one indication of the degree of that intelligence. While a digital switch might model a binary, on-off arrangement, a mechanical model might extend the understanding of switch to include amore continuous process of translation or modulation like a mechanical differential or governor. A fluvial model may be useful in expressing flow or elastic boundary. A mathematical expression like function may be useful in describing an organizing agent that establishes interdependence among variables or expresses one variable as a function of another. A repeated fitting like a standardized detail may reconstitute an organization in batches as a kind of summation across similar elements. That summation may generate an influence greater than the sum of its parts. Even subtraction is a useful organizational expression. In the design professions, subtraction is not generally regarded as a constructive tool and is often associated with the *tabula rasa*, demolition, or the preparation of ground to receive an authorized design intervention. Subtraction in an environment of exchange, however, may be a positive rather than a negative means of negotiating space or removing obstruction. These terms circulate through the book so that an expression of network architecture may be used to describe a landscape ecology, or a geological term may be used to describe a highway network.

The book is organized as an assemblage of multiple texts of different types that operate in parallel. It was written after publishing two research efforts in new media formats and borrows some of its organizational structure from these formats. Some texts are critical. Some texts provide general background information that will be very familiar to scholars and students in the planning and design professions. Some text assumes a tighter focus to present an anecdote, biography, or critical detail. There are several strategies for reading this book. The first article in each part looks at dominant perceptions of landscapes, highways, and residential formations and introduces an eccentric career, issue, or historical moment against which to reexamine these formations. The final articles leave the historical examination to cross-reference contemporary models of active organizations and to identify potential sites of adjustment within generic development protocols. The articles in between contain more detailed historical examples and are often accompanied by a layer of text that provides background, quotes, and other anecdotal information. The illustrations provide another layer of information often featuring comparative proposals for national organizations and networks. The hope is that the parallel texts will allow readers for instance, to read the first and last articles in each part as an essay or to read selectively throughout, as deeply or as lightly as they wish.

Notes

1. In a chapter entitled "The Orgamerican Phantasy" from *The Tradition of the New* (1959), Harold Rosenberg nicknamed Whyte's organization man "The Orgman." David Riesman's *The Lonely Crowd* or A. C. Spectorsky's *The Exurbanites* joined Whyte, Rosenberg, and others in describing what was considered to be a character type of the postwar period.

Part 1

1.0 TERRESTRIAL NETWORKS

Environmentalism and even the words "environment" or "ecology" are often associated with a kind of piety about the conservation and protection of animals and plants as well as a holistic understanding of ecological terms. America's endangered beauty is a kind of palliative, inspiring spiritual reverie and aesthetic appreciation of landscape scenery. Bioenergetics is the privileged ecology, and technology is a threat to nature. The environmental movement recognizes turn-of-the-century conservationists as their true predecessors and usually traces a continuous history between the ideologies of conservation and the emotional messages of the midcentury ecocrisis. This material, however, looks at some instructive intervening episodes in which the design of landscape was considered together with the design of technological networks—each borrowing attributes of the other.

The infrastructure prototypes of one practitioner, Benton MacKaye, are exceptional artifacts of this intervening period. MacKaye articulated organizational expressions for both technological and terrestrial networks and looked for sites of adjustment in their combined protocols. He is best remembered for his conception of the Appalachian Trail, which though typically regarded as an attractive nature preserve, was, as MacKaye originally conceived it in 1921, a terrestrial infrastructure network that would reorganize the entire eastern seaboard. Perhaps colored by the customary sentiments surrounding the appreciation of landscape, MacKaye has often been rendered as the solitary Thoreauvian thinker or the quintessentially rugged nature lover. His career was much more unusual, however, and his personality much more eccentric than these profiles would suggest. He considered himself to be an engineer, an artist, and a special technician of what he called "geotechnics." For MacKaye, geotechnics, a hybrid discipline of his own making, fused into

1.0.1 Benton MacKaye, MacKaye papers, Special Collections, Dartmouth College Library.

one the seven words "geography, forestry and conservation, engineering, colonization, regional planning, and economics."[1] He was a self-proclaimed "regional planner," when planning was a new endeavor, and though it would typically become the task of committees and official agencies, MacKaye fashioned this "imaginative vocation" for a single practitioner.[2] Throughout his career, MacKaye designed national and international infrastructure prototypes that, like the trail, were large linear land organizations, incorporating political and economic instructions while also acting as transportation and utility networks (figure 1.0.1).

MacKaye's combination of artist and engineer distinguished his position from that of many of his contemporaries in the technocracy, back-to-the-land, or environmental movements, yet he was associated with many of the key players in those movements. In addition to being a member of the Technical Alliance, a group that spearheaded the technocracy movement of the 1920s and 1930s, he was also a member of the Regional Planning Association of America (RPAA), another influential political group interested in using the new infrastructures of hydroelectricity and automobiles to sponsor distributed networks of community. As a technician-planner for the Tennessee Valley Authority (TVA), MacKaye was also part of federal efforts to organize infrastructures, and he would later be among those who helped initiate the environmental movement.

During the interwar period, new technologies, new materials, and their effects on production and employment were causing enormous upheavals in both urban and rural populations. As in any one of this century's "technocrazes," public policy privileged engineering expertise and quantifiable means of problem solving even in response to social issues. For instance, leaders of the technocracy movement proposed to replace the government-elected officials with engineers who would rationalize the faltering economy by managing resources, electrification, and commerce. The RPAA, though not as extreme as the technocrats, stridently condemned metropolitan power centers, claiming that they dictated illogical patterns of settlement and industry. President Hoover, himself an engineer, but one of a slightly different stripe, valued some of the same methods of fact-finding and rationalizing the "economic machine"; he believed these efforts would be best directed by traditional capitalist programs, however, with the federal government only serving as a clearinghouse of expertise. Later, many public projects like the TVA involved the regulation of both terrestrial and technological infrastructure such as hydroelectric waterways and farmland networks. New Deal philosophy often paired traditional values and nostalgic social programs with new technologies and scientific expertise. Fueling the romance with both rationalism and traditionalism, these new technologies, it was proposed, would organize the planning macrostructure in such a way that the traditional microstructure of small-scale work, craft, and family could return, accompanied by the value-laden, romantic story of "the land" and its soulful methods of work and craft. Though that might have been the story, these reform ideologies also served as sentimental political promotion for conservative business motives.

MacKaye's approach was also different from planning practices that evolved within the design professions, since his training in forestry and earth sciences offered models for sites and spatial interventions that were ecological in nature, that is part of some interplay or exchange. He treated a site as a set of interdependent parts within which small shifts in balance or orientation had enormous effect. He once wrote that with planning, "the final thing planned is not mere area or land, but movement or activity," and the most unusual aspect of his practice was his method of identifying site in not only the spatial, but the temporal and procedural protocols of development and economic exchange.[3]

When MacKaye graduated from Harvard College in 1900, and from Harvard's School of Forestry in 1905, the last frontiers of the West were being settled, and among the important issues for his generation of young intellectuals were the politics of land use as well as the new tools and advances of modern technology. "Physiography," which he described as the study of "land forms in action," was a new concentration within geological studies at the time. It focused on the dynamic terms of geology through the study of fluvial activity, erosion or glaciation, thus departing from a method of study that previously focused on the classification of artifacts.[4] Applying intelligence from geological, particularly fluvial systems, MacKaye's national and international terrestrial networks proposed to revalue and redirect other infrastructures while also reconfiguring exurban development. Technology was another nature, and the industrial landscape a kind of "wilderness," or a fluvial system that could be diverted or constrained. He used words like "levee," "watershed," or "river system" to describe the behavior of his infrastructures and their interactivity with patterns of migration and commerce in America.[5] Levees and watersheds were like special partitions that, not unlike partitions of digital space, were not about merely subdividing space, rather they often served as radial or linear points of translation or regulation in an organization. As organizational expressions, the fluvial models described activity rather than form and they allowed him to consider a more elastic condition of boundary as well as the continual activation of currents or flows of activity over long durations.

While the design professions typically tried to frame the boundaries of an organization and control the territory inside those boundaries, MacKaye often adjusted organizations by indirect or remote activation of sites. Natural ecologies often changed dramatically by way of some small intruder or foreign influence. The relative placement of the components, not the components themselves defined the constitution of the organization. MacKaye also used subtraction within an organization to alter its constitution with the awareness that, in a terrestrial ecology, subtraction was often part of some reciprocal exchange or might even produce growth within connected sites.

Examining a site in ecological terms also often meant highlighting the rules by which it operated, and MacKaye's interventions often occupied the rules and protocols governing the organization, as well as the spin or the virtual frameworks that colored perceptions of it. He discovered that an organization could be reconstituted by inverting a single protocol within this immaterial strata of the site.

MacKaye was among the first to use the word *environment*, but for him, environment was an expanded site with physical, temporal, and virtual strata. He crafted a set of virtual sites within cultural paradigms and persuasions, developing, primarily through his writing, a means of shifting or inverting perceptions to introduce new values and protocols for development. The approach involved a kind of noninvasive means of altering the landscape by changing attitudes about it, and MacKaye treated the practice as simply another practical and resourceful means of cultivating the landscape. Designing an adjustment to the landscape often involved the identification of a dormant existing condition that might be shifted into a new more effective position, so that the projects involved not holistic prescriptions, but partial reversals or adjustments with radiating but not entirely predictable influence.

The practice involved what MacKaye called "visualizing," and while it was influenced by American pragmatist philosophers like Emerson and Thoreau, it also strongly resembled Sir Patrick Geddes' interpretations of Henri Bergson in its reliance on the use of memory and eidetic perceptions. Theatrical craft, however, with its methods of storing experience in visual and corporeal memory may have been the chief influence. MacKaye was brought up in New York City and New England within a family of free-thinking dramatists, inventors, and scientists. His father Steele MacKaye (1835–1894) was an actor, writer, producer, manager, and inventor of the theater who staged giant spectacles and pageants with elaborate stage machinery. Many details of the MacKaye family life verged on a kind of Yankee Dada, where eccentricities were treated as completely serious, almost commonplace, and all in a day's work. Perhaps as a consequence, MacKaye considered the merger of technical and artistic practices to be second nature. Given the power of environmental sites to adjust cultural perceptions, the artist working alone could intervene. In the same way that a tiny antigen in a biological system could have extensive

Let us take the case of the civil engineer in "planning" an efficient railroad grade across a mountain range. His first job is to record or map the topography and thus to visualize the environment in question. Somewhere in this there exists already some particular line across the mountain range that marks a grade more efficient than any other line across said range. The engineer proceeds to find that line already fixed by nature; he does not contrive or invent some line to suit his fancy. Thus the engineer visualizes the potential railroad grade there already within the actual terrain. From this case we should say that planning is discovery and not invention. It is a new type of exploration. Its essence is visualization—a charting of the potential now existing in the actual. . . . And what is the thing that is planned? Is it an area, or a line

merely, or is it something else? It is something else. The engineer plans for something more than a line across the mountain; he plans for movement of freight and passengers. And so with planning generally: the final thing planned is not mere area or land, but movement or activity.[6]
—Benton Mackaye

effects, so MacKaye's "imaginative vocation" could be a tactical site of spatial production and adjustment. One could argue that both MacKaye's practice and his infrastructure prototypes were wild cards within the prevailing organizations of development.

The following episodes begin in 1921 with MacKaye's first article proposing the Appalachian Trail. Together they examine infrastructure prototypes and proposals, including the trail, limited access highway networks, hydroelectric networks, and proposals for new national political partitions. The episodes also look at the projects of two government agencies with which MacKaye was either directly or indirectly involved: the Natural Resources Planning Board and the Tennessee Valley Authority.

[Steele MacKaye] was perhaps a forerunner of what might be called the 'statesman-dramatist.' He was not interested in writing a play which did not image social forces. He made these forces stand forth—as do wind and rain and sunlight. His *Paul Kauvar* set forth the cyclone of the French Revolution. His Drama of Civilisation set forth, in the Indian brave and in the cowpuncher, the racial forces contending for a continent. His World Finder (with the super-stage technique of his Spectatorium) visualised the greatest of the Earth's migrations.

Can prophecy be dramatised as well as retrospect? That is what interests the regional planner, who is concerned with equipping regions for future human living. I believe that prophecy can be drama-

Steele MacKaye

Steele MacKaye fused into one giant, impossible vision the most ambitious manifestations of the engineer, entrepreneur, and dramatist. His theatrical productions were overscaled historical pageants or epic spectacles with gigantic moving stage tableaus, weather, fire, and changing atmospheric light. When not directing plays, he also designed and patented a folding chair for the theater, worked on the invention of a new railroad coupling, and pursued an interest and investment in photosculpture, a process by which a machine would make three dimensional objects from photographs. He was the first American to play Hamlet in London and a founder of the Madison Square Garden, Lyceum, and St. James Theaters in New York City.[7]

When Benton was a child in New York City, Steele MacKaye produced the *Drama of Civilization*, an indoor version of Buffalo Bill's "Wild West Show" staged as a kind of time-line of American westward expansion. One of Benton MacKaye's biographers, Paul Bryant wrote that even in his 80s Benton could "still describe with a glowing eye, the entrance of the wagon train and the sweep of the prairie fire across the Garden's [Madison Square Garden] stage."[8] But Steele MacKaye's ultimate invention was the "Spectatorium" that was planned for the World's Columbian Exposition. Its 70 by 100 foot stage was to house many of Steele MacKaye's other devices for light and scenery. Lighting devices like the "luxauleator," the "nebulator," the "illumiscope," and the "colourator," were designed to simulate changing effects of the daytime sky and thus create a "mechanical duplication of nature." Illuminated texts would pass across the stage. Even ocean battles could be waged on floating stages. These electromechanical versions of theatrical tools pushed the theatrical form toward a kind cinematic reality or one similar to virtual reality simulations of today's computer era. Ironically, the financial failure of MacKaye's theater occurred at the same time that motion picture film projection was becoming popular.[9]

Steele MacKaye was the son of a prominent businessman, and he recognized no obstacles to the simultaneous pursuit of business, engineering, and art, though he often struggled between the dueling habits of mind associated with these endeavors.[10] While he had a sense of order that would sometimes lead him to regiment his life in peculiar ways, Steele MacKaye was also a grand thespian of flamboyant character. His affectations were disciplined, even righteous. An actor, he believed, was a responsible cultural practitioner. In the difficult position of being the initiator of new ideas on many fronts, he was never able to enjoy any financial stability and was usually struggling against failure. In 1927, one of Benton's brothers, Percy, wrote a two-volume memoir of his father entitled *Epoch*. The book was written not as a single text, but as an almost encyclopedic assemblage of his father's achievements, related in Percy's own voice and interspersed with other texts, lists, and illustrations related to events and personae that contributed to the intellectual history at the turn of the century. Percy managed to mention William James, Thomas Edison, Oscar Wilde, Henry David Thoreau, David Belasco, Cecil B. de Mille, and scores of others with whom Steele MacKaye associated.[11] In a way the book was a model of the catholic and inclusive epistemology that was shared by all the children.

Benton MacKaye later recognized that his father's theatrical productions approached a scale of operation that could no longer be contained by the stage but rather approached the scale of larger environments outside the theater. Benton's stage was the larger environment of the enveloping outdoors—the surrounding medium of immaterial culture and material civilization.[12] Later in his career he would write of geotechnics, as his father had written of the theater, "geotechnics consists of emulating nature."[13]

tised. I believe that my father thought it could be; that he was a pioneer in seeing the theatre (and all dramatic activity) as a sort of focusing lens—a telescope, whereby the public mind can look into perspective, and be enabled to vision, not alone the actuality of the past, but the potentiality of the future. Such, to my mind, is the aim of the visualiser—whether statesman, regional planner, or dramatist: to focus the people's vision.[14]
—*Benton MacKaye*

But already we may speak of the body as an ever advancing boundary between the future and the past, as a pointed end, which our past is continually driving forward. Whereas my body, taken at a single moment, is but a conductor interposed between the objects which influence it and those on which it acts, it is on the other hand, when replaced in the flux of time, always situated at the very point where my past expires in deed.[20]
—Henri Bergson

. . . in the outlook tower Geddes showed me a whole series of "time charts" he and his colleagues had once worked on, attempting to represent the flow of historic events in colored streams, widening, thinning, sometimes blending. And he himself when going over his graphic chessboard with me once even speculated on the possibility of creating a kind of four-dimensional chess in a box, composed of graphs whose movements through space would enable one to express changing relationships in time.

But how impossible it is to express time in such spatial terms! It is only in the symbols of language and music, or—as Henri Bergson saw—in motion pictures that the flow of liv-

Sir Patrick Geddes

Benton MacKaye and Sir Patrick Geddes have remained minor historical characters, perhaps more interesting for their failures to achieve the kind of cultural power that, it could be argued, was achieved by Lewis Mumford. Coincidentally, Mumford often served as a kind of public representative for the two. Both MacKaye and Geddes proposed eccentric schemes, often wrote in florid, romantic tones, and sometimes conceived of history and ecology in positivistic and nostalgic terms. Both maintained a mental state that was constantly cross-referencing a number of disciplines, paradigms, and associations. Both were pragmatists who valued learning and experience over orthodoxy but were simultaneously straining under their own desires for a clear epistemological framework.

As Geddes' protégé, Mumford has usually been credited as the conduit of a prescient philosophy that espoused the integration and adjustment of new technologies like automobile and electrical networks in relation to terrestrial ecologies. As Mumford was absorbing and disseminating Geddes' teachings, however, MacKaye was developing, independently, a philosophy and practice of regional land planning that was distinctly American and strikingly similar to that of Mumford's mentor. Geddes, in fact, christened the term "geotechnics" for MacKaye's science.

MacKaye first met Geddes during Geddes' visit to New York in the summer of 1923. Mumford had set up an itinerary that included appearances at the New School and meetings with his new RPAA colleagues at the Hudson Guild Farm in New Jersey. MacKaye later wrote:

I shall never forget my first walk with Patrick Geddes (later Sir Patrick) the sandy bearded Scot of Edinburgh, Dundee, Dunfermline, Dublin, Montpelier, Bombay, Indore, Jerusalem, Tel Aviv—with the whole epic of civilization visioned from his famed Outlook tower at Edinburgh.

This was springtime in 1923 at the Hudson Guild Farm in the New Jersey highland. Geddes, 'Jack of all trades and master of city planning,' proved a fast walker for a sexagenarian though his tongue outdid his legs. But first he had asked me about my work and so had to listen as I recounted adventures in conservation under Gifford Pinchot and in regional planning (under nobody). I had delved back to geography under professor Davis when Geddes rounded on me in the path.

'None of those!' he caught me up—'Not conservation, not planning, not even geography. Your subject is geotechnics.'[15]

As evidenced by his expansive, nonlinear monologues, Geddes valued the ephemeral qualities of thoughts born in speech, and he privileged experience and conversation as the real time precipitant of mental activity. Geddes said he was "like the cuckoo who lays its eggs in other people's nests," because he effected much of his publishing through conversation. His works ranged so broadly from botany to city planning to experimental photography that they did not lend themselves to compilation or publication within any customary format. Mumford wrote that Geddes' books were like notes written "on the margin of his thinking," and that they were only a faint reflection of, "his massive practical grasp, his astonishing breadth of scholarship, his relentless confrontation of reality."[16] These writings, chief among them *Cities in Evolution* were in constant flux among any one of his subjects and a thousand other paradigms and associations. Geddes's theories also cross-referenced the thinking of geographers, historians, and philosophers including Marsh, Spengler, Nietzsche, Reclus, Le Play, and Kropotkin.

Geddes and MacKaye shared the use of higher elevations as vantage points for surveying and planning. Geddes had his Outlook tower, and MacKaye had his Appalachian mountain top. Both considered "seeing" to be more than simply the faculty of vision. "Survey then plan" was Geddes watchword. From new French geographers Elise Reclus and Paul Vidal la Bache and the French sociologist Frederic Le Play, Geddes borrowed an instrumental technique for mapping the landscape—the valley section. The valley section indexed the various strata of flora, fauna, and minerals present in the landscape, and Geddes mixed a sectional and a panoramic view in his visual

ing experiences through time can be symbolized.[21]
—*Lewis Mumford*

surveys. But survey involved not only inventorying the components of a landscape but understanding the relationships among these components over time. The landscape, as viewed from his "outlook tower" on Edinburgh's High Street was a kind of crystal ball for reading both past and future. The view was overlain with history and imagination in a vast "synoptic" implosion. Geddes' view of the landscape expanded upon repeated surveys and over the depth of time lent by historical information. This perceptual practice reflected his admiration of French philosopher Henri Bergson. For Bergson the mind was a function of time and experience—an expanding whole within a temporal continuum. The practice also referenced the work of American pragmatists like William James and John Dewey.

Geddes was, however willing to declare a provisional unity in his thinking sufficient to make prescriptive pronouncements about the past, present, and future of the environment. By the middle of the nineteenth century, geographical studies examined not only terrestrial activity but also man's manipulation in the environment. For Geddes, the nineteenth century, or the "paleotechnic age" (a term he borrowed from Kropotkin) was marked by land abuse and a pursuit of the machine, and he hoped to nurture an evolution from the "gloom of paleotechnic inferno" to the "neotechnic eutopia."[17] Many of his writings resembled Kropotkin's with their claims that profit motives, overproduction, and specialization created perverse patterns of distribution that unfairly favored only one sector of society.

Some of Geddes' inventions and gadgetry were telling accompaniment to his philosophy. In experimental photography, for instance, he attempted to alter views with overlays, touch-ups, and erasures. His "thinking machines" were another prop for exercising this thought. Paper was folded into thirty-six squares and each square was assigned some aspect of culture. Circulating across the folded paper generated a cycling network of associations where adjacencies suggested new pairings and triads. The machines were particularly interesting because he developed them at a time when he had temporarily lost his eyesight and so devised a way to review his thinking through tactile mnemonics. Geddes even talked about the possibility of a "four-dimensional" thinking machine that would incorporate temporality and animate the framework into a series of changing connections.[18]

Geddes' summer-long visit proved difficult for Mumford as he discovered a paradox in his master's behavior. Mumford appeared to Geddes to be an eager protégé who could organize and disseminate ideas, and during the visit Mumford sat for hours listening to Geddes as he pontificated in muffled tones. Finally the young protégé found it difficult to reconcile Geddes' apparent intentions with his attraction for unifying theories, or worse, his illusion that the structure of his own mind reflected that unity. Equally distressing to Mumford was that while Geddes shunned the existing authorities of knowledge, those communicating through what he called "verbalistic empaperment," he was capable of positioning himself as a rather overbearing authority whose monologues were suspiciously tautological. Although the potential of Geddes' methods was perhaps stunted by self-reflexive or totalizing tendencies, the breadth of his conversation was so far ranging that individual moments like the walk with MacKaye at Hudson Guild Farm proved to be extremely valuable.[19]

Notes

1. Benton MacKaye, *From Geography to Geotechnics*, ed. Paul T. Bryant (Urbana: University of Illinois Press, 1968), 40.

2. Percy MacKaye, *Epoch: The Life of Steele MacKaye, Genius of the Theatre in Relation to His Time and Contemporaries*, vol. 1 and 2 (New York: Boni and Liveright, 1927), 474.

3. Benton MacKaye, "Regional Planning and Ecology," *Ecological Monographs* X (July 1940):349.

4. Paul T. Bryant, "The Quality of the Day: The Achievement of Benton MacKaye" (Ph.D. diss., University of Illinois at Champaign-Urbana, 1965), 52–56. Two of MacKaye's teachers at Harvard were Nathaniel Southgate Shaler and William Morris Davis. MacKaye would later credit both William Morris Davis and the British biologist-geographer Thomas Henry Huxley as the initiators of the study of "physiography." *Physiography: An Introduction to the Study of Nature*, London: Macmillan and Co., 1877, a seminal book by Huxley, studied the Thames basin, by relating the characteristics of the region to the changing effects of tides and atmospheric conditions, thus departing from a previous method of study that focused on the classification of artifacts. Davis too addressed the dynamic terms of geology by examining fluvial activity, erosion, and glaciation. Bryant wrote of Nathaniel Southgate Shaler, "Shaler was a student of Agassiz and learned from him the naturalist's approach to science, the discipline of close observation, the importance of detail, and above all the significance of relationships. This concern for relationships, for interaction and process, Shaler carried beyond his purely scientific work into a consideration of science's place in society and its influence upon the character of men." Bryant, "The Quality of the Day," 52.

5. MacKaye used the term "river system" in Benton MacKaye, "The New Exploration: Charting the Industrial Wilderness," *The Survey Graphic* 65 (1 May 1925): 154, 153;

and Benton MacKaye, "The New Northwest Passage." *The Nation* 122 (2 June 1926): 603. He used "watershed" and "levee" in many of his publications. He also used the word "flow" throughout his work to describe economies, population migrations, and distribution patterns in addition to fluvial movements.

6. MacKaye, "Regional Planning and Ecology," 349.

7. Bryant, "The Quality of the Day," 9, 11, 10; and Percy MacKaye. *Epoch: The Life of Steele MacKaye*, vol. 1, 122–123. Paul Bryant's unpublished dissertation is the best book-length biographical text on Benton MacKaye—one that had the advantage of personal interviews and correspondence with him.

8. Bryant, 12.

9. Larry Anderson, "Yesterday's City: Steele MacKaye's Grandiose Folly," *Chicago History* 16 (3, 4) (fall and winter 1987–88): 105, 110–111.

10. Bryant, 8. To distinguish himself from his father, for instance, Steele MacKaye added the "e" to the family's surname to regain the Scottish pronunciation.

11. Ibid., 15–16. Bryant writes, "[Percy MacKaye] . . . sometimes magnifies fleeting contacts into important connections and sometimes mentions important names when they have little bearing on his father's career."

12. Bryant, 15, 17–18; and Percy MacKaye, *Epoch*, vol. 2, 467–469.

13. Benton MacKaye, "Geography to Geotechnics." Serial publication in *The Survey:* 1. "Global Law," 87 (June 1951): 268.

14. Benton MacKaye in Percy MacKaye, *Epoch*, vol. 2, 475.

15. Benton MacKaye, *From Geography to Geotechnics*, p. 22.

16. Philip Boardman, *Patrick Geddes: Maker of the Future* (Chapel Hill: University of North Carolina Press, 1944), 155, ix.

17. Peter Hall, *Cities of Tomorrow* (Cambridge: Basil Blackwell, 1988), 143–45. Peter Hall has demonstrated that the terms paleotechnic and neotechnic were Kropotkin's own, and he notes that Kropotkin met both Howard and Geddes. Pyotr Kropotkin, *Fields Factories and Workshops* (London: Thomas Nelson and Sons, 1898), 350; and Patrick Geddes, *Cities in Evolution* (New York: Oxford University Press, 1950), 48.

18. Novak, 360–363.

19. MacKaye proposed to the group that perhaps *geotechnics* might be a more provocative term than "regional planning." Several of the RPAA members were skeptical of the new title, however, though Mumford used it in some of his later writings. In a later compilation, *From Geography to Geotechnics*, MacKaye told, with typical modesty and candor, a story about his reluctance to use the term in relation to his work of the 1920s and 1930s because he could not find it in the dictionary. In the 1940s, MacKaye finally found geotechnics in the dictionary defined as "the applied science of making the world more habitable." "I swallowed a howl I lest I should break the library edict of 'silence.' My inhibitions over the years evaporated. The name was now respectable. Once in the dictionary it could be employed in all companies—and with a definition better than my own. And so, at long last, the *name*. Meanwhile, during those years and under various names, I had been working on the *thing*." Bryant, 24.

20. Henri Bergson, *Matter and Memory* (New York: Humanities Press Inc., 1979), 88.

21. Lewis Mumford in a previously unpublished biographical essay on Patrick Geddes entitled, "The Geddesian Gambit," ed. Frank G. Novak Jr., *Lewis Mumford and Patrick Geddes: The Correspondence* (London: Routledge, 1995), 363.

1.1 SUBTRACTION INVERSION REMOTE: APPALACHIAN TRAIL

MacKaye's Appalachian Trail proposal was simple. A footpath following the crest of the Appalachian ridge would travel from Maine to Georgia as one continuous trail 2,000 miles in length. Though it was only a footpath, Mac-Kaye characterized the proposal as a "transportation project," because by its placement, the trail inverted the conventional hierarchy of transportation and development infrastructure. Typically, long-distance rail or highways formed the main transportation trunks, with primary, secondary, and tertiary streets leading to pedestrian networks. Conversely, in the trail arrangement, a footpath was the dominant infrastructure that would organize streets and rails. Branch lines of the trail and special railways would extend this landscape into thirty-six of the largest nearby metropolitan areas. The mountain ridge became the central spine of development, replacing the tall buildings of the metropolis and reversing its dominant pattern of concentric growth. An infrastructure of land or "super national" forest and a network of compact communities and industries would crystallize around the footpath to replace the suburbs. The interstate geological formation of the Appalachian ridge would function as a kind of public utility or reservoir of natural resources, organizing transportation and hydroelectrical networks while locating industry and community. The trail idea proposed no master plan but rather an ordering principle for a new economy. It would broadcast a field of influence and a new mechanism for the migrations of population as well as the economies of production and distribution (figure 1.1.1).[1]

MacKaye first conceived of a long-distance trail while camping through the White Mountains when he was nineteen and later returned to the idea while working for the government in Washington. He worked for the Department of Forestry under Gifford Pinchot from 1905–1918 and for the

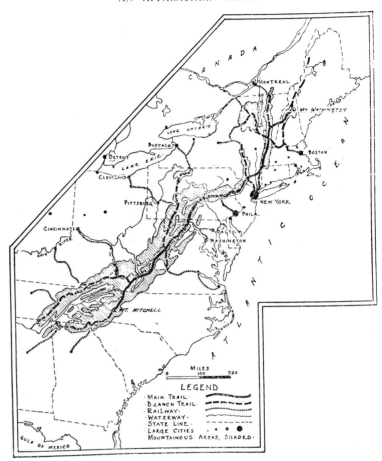

1.1.1 Illustration accompanying Appalachian Trail project showing parallel railways and waterways. Benton MacKaye, "An Appalachian Trail: A Project in Regional Planning," *Journal of the American Institute of Architects* IXX (October 1921): 7.

Department of Labor from 1918–1919. MacKaye was a member of a new profession of foresters and planners who often envisioned their role not as a segregated specialization but as an interdisciplinary advocacy. Under Pinchot, MacKaye was given responsibility for a large number of America's public land preserves, and he worked on a bill to manage land conservation and fuel extraction in Alaska. While working for the Department of Labor, he began to formulate ideas linking forestry to other economies of employment and settlement that were published in a report entitled *Employment and Natural Resources* (1919). Influenced by the postwar plans of several countries to colonize unsettled lands as a means of housing and employment for returning veterans, the report proposed a group of permanent encampments for work and/or recreation with an Appalachian trail at their center. It recommended a reorientation of labor toward working the land, making it both a preserve and an employment resource, and it featured the trail as the means for just such a reorientation of resources. The mountain landscape would supposedly also act as a cultural tonic for returning veterans as well as a means of organizing depressed rural and logging industries.[2]

During the 1910s and 1920s, MacKaye was a member of several intellectual cadres interested in reforming legislation. While in Washington, he belonged to a group of journalists, activists, and government workers who called themselves, the "Hell Raisers." The group composed and promoted legislative reform addressing, among other things, the organization of electricity, land, and other natural resources.[3] Their radical political leanings were reinforced by association with the Communist Party and the programs of the Soviet Union. During this time MacKaye, for instance, studied Russian and considered going to the Soviet Union as a "volunteer technician." MacKaye, together with Frederick Ackerman, Charles Whitaker, and Stuart Chase, fellow "Hell Raisers," was also part of the Technical Alliance for a time.[4] While Ackerman continued to be a leader of the technocracy movement, MacKaye and Chase felt somewhat alienated from the scientific determinism espoused by the group and its leader, Howard Scott. Chase, an economist and admirer of Veblen, later wrote, "Scott was a difficult man to work with—a real Napoleonic type."[5] The two turned their attentions instead to a new group of intellectuals called "Whitaker's group," which would later be called the RPAA. When the RPAA formed, there was some question about whether it should be a larger organization or a "small group of technicians."[6] Like the Technical Alliance, they were intellectuals attempting to effect policy changes in much larger organizations. Though the RPAA remained a loose aggregate of professionals pursuing separate prototypes, the group also developed a collective platform concerning the systemic management of resources and the emerging pattern of new infrastructure networks.

MacKaye's work, and the Appalachian Trail in particular, were critical to the formulation of the RPAA platform. MacKaye wrote an article about the trail in 1921 for the *Journal of the American Institute of Architects,* where Charles Whitaker was then editor. The article got the attention of two other "Whitaker's group" members, Clarence Stein and Lewis Mumford. After meeting MacKaye, Stein thought the trail idea was a provocative means of expanding the agendas of a committee he was chairing for the American Institute of Architects, the Commission on Community Planning.[7] Mumford was later introduced to MacKaye in 1923 as the RPAA was forming. The trail idea was so well aimed and it represented so many of both the community building and land management goals of regionalists, that it helped to galvanize the RPAA in its early days. It became a kind of trope of regional planning efforts.

More interesting than its association with any one platform or critique, however, was the character of the Appalachian Trail as an organization. As in geological models, the Appalachian organization was analogous to the ruts and divides caused by glaciation and glacial flow. Like a continental divide, watershed, or levee, it contained and shaped reciprocal exchange and activity along its length. MacKaye would later extend this fluvial model by likening the trail to a kind of levee that contained and shaped development. The trail was governed by additional organizational protocols as well. It was also a linear subtraction along the crestline of a mountain range, an "open way" that had the power to rearrange priorities in an industrial economy.[8] Finally, the trail was immaterial. It was a void or a line of force, not a construction. This largely invisible physical alteration, however, effected a simple but radical reversal in the flows of commerce and population migration. Without vastly changing the physical arrangements, but reversing the protocols of its use, this "supertrail" remagnetized and recentered development in the territory through which it passed, remotely affecting areas some distance from the spine. It would format industrial and urban patterns, changing them from a series of concentric nodes to a more evenly distributed network straddling a spine. The entire network also multiplied intelligence and connection through parallelism and differential connection between different species of network.

It was not a single trail but a "cobweb" of trails that would cover the mountain and recircuit all the existing transportation networks, creating new branches and circuits.[9]

Among the most important qualities of the trail's organization was its power as a partial or tactical intervention. The footpath, though scaled to the body within a single section, when extended for hundreds of miles became a powerful mark or divide in the land. And while there was a direction of travel, there were no fixed termini. The trail also traveled through similar crestline terrain at its interior, but it organized vastly different terrain at its periphery. The tactical placement of a single detail, repeated or extended, would have enormous radiating effect. Since the sites were constituted within patterns of connection and process, population flows, transportation and utility networks, and other distributive protocols, small adjustments were potentially very effective within the larger organization. Even though the Appalachian Trail was mammoth in size, it initiated a process of systemic though not necessarily comprehensive changes, and after attaining a gigantic length, the network relationships were no longer simple.

In the years following the Appalachian Trail article, MacKaye continued to mine the prototype for more meaning. He treated this special kind of line and the large land organizations it was intended to adjust as a heuristic device to discover more about the workings of the land. He studied it in panorama and cross section, and he studied its effect on labor, resources, and population migration. In 1922, MacKaye wrote that the Appalachian Trail was "deeply calculated to interest not only architects and landscape architects but foresters and all others of the genus 'engineer.'"[10] MacKaye proposed that reconditioning the industrial and terrestrial landscape could only be directed by the "composite mind of several engineers."[11] Hydroengineers, foresters, silviculturalists, and economists, for instance, were all technicians in this endeavor. MacKaye considered land-based engineering and natural resource planning to be on a par with those forms of engineering which were later to be privileged in America, namely those related to commerce and defense. He considered his own practice of Geotechnics or "regional engineering," as he called it, to be a kind of composite form.[12]

As the new field of electrical and automobile networks became critical layers in the Appalachian organization, they materialized a network of associations MacKaye had projected for the trail. Rather than considering these networks as alien, he conceived of these emerging technologies as part of an inclusive ecology. Highways and hydroelectrical grids operated on an almost geological scale, thus expanding the industrial ecology into an environmental realm beyond the scale of the machine metaphors and motion studies used by technocrats. As a by-product of fluvial activity, electricity could be understood as an energy abstraction as well as a terrestrial activity. In another article about the trail, entitled "Appalachian Power: Servant or Master? [*The Survey Graphic, March 1924*]." MacKaye calculated, in horsepower, the units of potential energy available through coal and water resources along the Appalachian spine. He borrowed terms like "quanta" used by technocrats, but used them to refer not only to units of energy but to units of culture. A unit was equal to 1 percent of the total horse power resources from carbon and water in the area and corresponded to one of the labor recreational settlements he planned for the Appalachian Trail. The new networks were also recalibrating the framework of place and potentially locating industry independent of the metropolis. MacKaye said of the new electrical grid, "The factory need not go to Niagara, Niagara can go to the factory, that is within a radius of some three hundred miles." MacKaye wrote of a net overlaid on the Appalachian spine whose interstices were anchored by the development of natural resources in specific locations. The hydroelectric grids materialized a network of relationships that were already latent in the landscape (figure 1.1.2).[13]

The trail fueled MacKaye's fascination with the interactivity between urban and rural regions, and he used it to model an understanding of congestion on a city street as a consequence of sites that however remote, were reciprocal and consequential rather than discrete. Using cross-sections of the New England plateau, he traced the flow of material from the "source" to the "mouth" from the "sphere of 'origin' to the sphere of 'distribution'; from the simple to the complex. . . ." The various diverse tributaries of production contributed to giant confluences like New York, which MacKaye likened to another kind of Niagara. "Let us understand that traffic congestion on State Street and subway congestion at 'Park Street under' are resultants of activities taking place in Dakota and Texas, in New York and Charleston, as well as in Somerville."[14] "Here the strands are woven on a continental scale," MacKaye wrote of his new exploration. "Some day, of course, we shall have to enter Boston. But on the same day we shall have to enter New York and Chicago and San Francisco (and perhaps even Liverpool and Hong Kong). For these are all in the sphere of distribution. They are nerve centers of a continuous flow that is continental (intercontinental) in its vastness (figure 1.1.3)."[15]

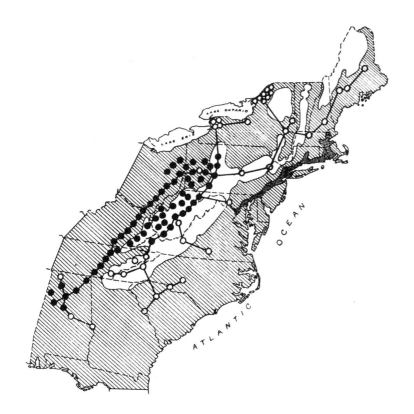

1.1.2 Illustration accompanying "Appalachian Power: Servant or Master." The caption reads, "Each Circle marks the center of one percent of the continuous potential horse power from coal and water within the area shown: The 61 black circles are centers of coal power, and the 39 white circles of water power. The super-populated belt is shown in dark shading; the Appalachian Mountain belt is unshaded." Benton MacKaye, "Appalachian Power: Servant or Master," *Survey Graphic* (March 1924): 619.

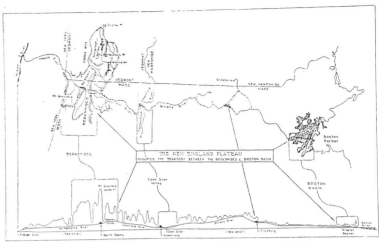

Cross-section of New England: a part of the "Atlantic Border Empire"

1.1.3 Cross-section of New England included in "The New Exploration: Charting the Industrial Wilderness." Benton MacKaye, "The New Exploration: Charting the Industrial Wilderness," *Survey Graphic* 54 (1925): 155.

As MacKaye continued to develop the trail prototype, he began to position the Appalachian Trail as a piece of this global infrastructure. It would filter and reroute east-west rail and vehicular freight potentially developing new global ports or at least making the global ports of the large cities more efficient. These rearrangements and consolidations of continental infrastructure systems would together become part of a renovated global system. MacKaye wrote, "A number of world-scale industrial enterprises have been achieved, or projected—the Panama and Suez canals; the Trans-Siberian and Cape-to-Cairo railways; continental systems of giant power; industrialization of agriculture. These things suggest an unconscious groping toward a controlled integration of world industry (figure 1.1.4)."[16]

In 1927 MacKaye even proposed a new type of atlas, charting activity rather than territory within industrial infrastructure. This "World Atlas of Commodity Flow" would survey global requirements, resources, and lines of travel by air, ocean liner, and rail. The atlas would support not only the rearrangement of global infrastructure and transportation routes but also the formulation of new protocols for the economies of distribution among coun-

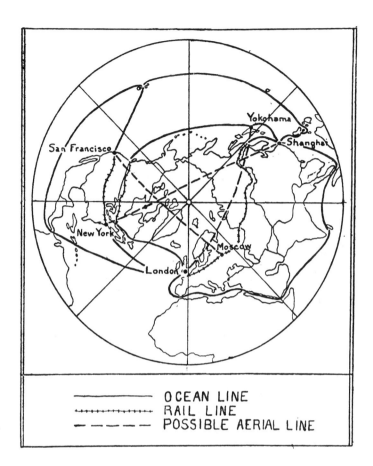

1.1.4 Projected "Lines of World Communication" from "Industrial Exploration," a serial publication in *The Nation.* Benton MacKaye, "Charting the World's Commodity Flow," *The Nation:* I, 125 (July 20, 1927): 72.

tries. MacKaye set out a seemingly impossible mission for the atlas that rivaled the absurd ambitions of the technocrats. It proposed to chart the world's physical and psychic requirements, measuring the need for food, clothing, and shelter as well as the need for culture and beauty. It would correlate between population and the fact that most people "eat wheat for breakfast" or that "cotton is a universal garment," and it would also measure the world's potential resources in horsepower.[17] Given the breadth of the project, it was perhaps no surprise that MacKaye found no funding for the project. In a letter to Geddes in 1925, Mumford wrote that MacKaye had not yet found the financing for his "world atlas of *potential* commodity flow" and was therefore "elaborating the more general and social points of his thought."[18]

Jessie Hardy Stubbs

While in Washington and associating with the "Hell Raisers," MacKaye lived in a cooperative household, not coincidentally nicknamed "Hell House." In 1917, he married the prominent suffragette, Jessie Hardy Stubbs. Stubbs was an antiwar activist who led disarmament campaigns and conferences. She outlined a book entitled *The Sexual Revolution*, which proposed to illustrate, in part, a political and economic world where the most powerful roles were controlled by women rather than men.[19] In 1918 Stubbs had a severe nervous breakdown, and though she recuperated temporarily after a trip to the country, she continued to suffer from headaches and anxieties. She committed suicide in 1921, and MacKaye retreated to Shirley, Massachusetts, to the homes of friends and later to New York City.[20] He rarely spoke of his marriage again.

Technocracy

The technocracy movement of the 1920s and 1930s initiated the practice of using engineering as a tool of political policy. Early technocracy theory grew on the one hand from a socialist critique of capitalism, one fueled by post-World War I and Depression era economies, but the movement was also prompted by the very persuasions that were partly responsible for these economies—Taylorism and Fordism. Thorstein Veblen led the movement initially. His ruminations about the fallacies and affectations of capitalism, published in *The Engineers and the Price System* (1921), hinged on a critic of those business structures that generated inflated profits and wasteful distribution. A better leader, Veblen argued, was the engineer. The engineer already embodied the ethic of the worker and could scientifically rearrange the doomed business system. The worker-engineer could more easily ascend to a position among the political elite, and a system based on units of energy, rather than an artificial system of prices, would provide more equitably for everyone. The book and Veblen's New School (New York City) discussion group inspired one of its members, Howard Scott, to form an offshoot group, the Technical Alliance. Scott was a self-styled technocrat and village bohemian who dressed in a kind of engineer's costume—a soft shirt, red tie, red handkerchief, and large leather jacket. While influenced by Veblen, he led his own charge as the head of several organizations and journals, including the Technical Alliance, of which he was "chief engineer."[21]

By 1933, the technocracy movement had received some of its strongest criticism and some of its most significant praise. Though it had reached the peak of its popularity, the group was also on the verge of a divisive split. Howard Scott joined with Walter Rautenstrauch's Committee on Technocracy at Columbia to work on the *Energy Survey of North America*. Scott published a kind of manifesto in the January, 1933, issue of *Harper's Magazine*. It was one of the few statements from the group to make procedural proposals, describing, among other things, a new currency of energy units.[22]

Scott was the most visible member of the group. His technological determinism overshadowed the group's attention to social issues, and his public stance alienated other members of the Committee on Technocracy like Rautenstrauch and Ackerman.[23] Rautenstrauch thought the engineer would supply a quantitative method to a political structure, not replace that structure by declaring engineers as the only capable elected officials. The technocracy movement split into a more radical faction led by Howard Scott, Technocracy Inc., and a more reform-minded group, the Continental Committee, established by Ackerman and led by Harold Loeb.

As the leader of Technocracy Inc., Scott replaced his engineer-as-bohemian costume with a kind of uniform, a gray suit and blue tie. Together with one of his devotees, Columbia geophysicist M. King Hubbert, he wrote the *Technocracy Study Course*, further elaborating the group's platform and eventual plans. As outlined in the *Harper's Magazine* article, "energy certificates" would replace currency, and a corporate syndicate headed by a "technate" would replace the existing political hierarchy. The technate would even be served by electronic machines that would help sort and tabulate the massive amounts of data necessary for the governing engineers to accurately direct production.[24] The same technologies that threatened labor would be used to maintain a self-regulating economy. The promise of technology's own self-organizing, self-regulating economy, however, relied on a perpetually forthcoming effort in comprehensive information collection. Once the necessary data had been compiled, technology and production would finally become rationalized and predictable.

Loeb, leading the Continental Committee, was a friend of Scott's in the Greenwich Village days. While Scott adopted the style of the engineer-as-bohemian, Loeb took up the habits of the more common literati-as-bohemian. Loeb conducted a study entitled *Plan of Plenty* that led the Continental Committee away from technological positivism and toward a program to adjust existing economic mechanisms in a way that resembled the Keynesian approach of New Deal bureaucrats. The committee was more inclusive in its membership as well. For instance, it was supported by Stuart Chase who had been articulating a similar contention in his books of the previous ten years and who had been alienated from the more radical proposals of Scott.[25]

In the ensuing years, some of the technocrats' proposals were incorporated into a less radical attitude toward the superiority of engineering, but one that still favored quantifiable approaches to problem solving. Influenced by technocracy theories during the New Deal period, a generation of young practitioners sought opportunities for the application of engineering intelligence through planning. The survey, inventory, and report would become a standard practice of policymaking in Washington.

Notes

1. Benton MacKaye, "An Appalachian Trail: A Project in Regional Planning," reprint *Journal of the American Institute of Architects*, 19 (October 1921): 1–8; and Benton MacKaye, "Great Appalachian Trail from New Hampshire to the Carolinas," *New York Times*, Sunday, 18 Feb. 1923.

2. Benton MacKaye, in the introduction to *From Geography to Geotechnics*, ed. Paul T. Bryant, 5.

3. Biographer Paul Bryant wrote that their ". . . efforts ranged from arousing indignation over a Maryland law permitting flogging of criminals to proposals for eliminating private profit in the munitions industry, from federal control of water power to the granting of suffrage to women." Bryant, 90; and Lewis Mumford in the introduction to *The New Exploration: A Philosophy of Regional Planning* (Urbana: University of Illinois Press, 1962), xii. Reprinted from 1928 version.

4. Bryant, 34–36; and Larry Anderson, unpublished biography of MacKaye. Courtesy of the author.

5. Stuart Chase, "My Friend Benton" in "Benton MacKaye: A Tribute by Lewis Mumford, Stuart Chase, Paul Oehser, Frederick Gutheim, Harley P. Holden, Paul T. Bryant, Robert M. Howes, C.J.S. Durham," *The Living Wilderness* 39 n., 132 (January/March 1976):18.

6. Minutes of the Regional Planning Association of America, 7 June 1923, are quoted in *Planning the Fourth Migration: The Neglected Vision of the Regional Planning Association of America*, ed. Carl Sussman (Cambridge, MA: MIT Press, 1976), 17.

7. John Ross, "Benton MacKaye: The Appalachian Trail," in *The American Planner: Biographies and Recollections*, ed. Donald A. Krueckeberg (New York and London: Methuen, 1983), 203–5.

8. Benton MacKaye, *The New Exploration: A Philosophy of Regional Planning* (New York: Harcourt, Brace and Company, 1928), 179.

9. Benton MacKaye, "Progress Toward the Appalachian Trail," *Appalachia* 15 (December 1922):244.

10. Ibid.

11. Benton MacKaye, "Appalachian Power: Servant or Master," *Survey Graphic* 51(1 March 1924):618–19.

12. MacKaye, *The New Exploration*, 34–5.

13. MacKaye, "Appalachian Power: Servant or Master," 619; and Robert W. Bruere, "Giant Power—Region-Builder," *The Survey Graphic* 54(1 May 1925):161–64.

14. Benton MacKaye, "The New Exploration: Charting the Industrial Wilderness," *The Survey Graphic* 65 (1 May 1925):155, 156.

15. Ibid., 194, 156.

16. Benton MacKaye, "Industrial Exploration," serial publication in *The Nation*: "II. Charting the World's Requirements," 125 (27 July 1927):92; and "I. Charting the World's Commodity Flow," 125 (20 July 1927): 72; and Benton MacKaye, "II. Charting the World's Requirements," 92. The article was weakest when it was prescriptive about the need to, among other things, "untangle" metropolitan "bottlenecks," but it was most significant in its proposal to explore "parallel (and competing) lines of commodity flow."

17. Benton MacKaye, "Industrial Exploration," serial publication in *The Nation*: "II. Charting the World's Requirements," 92.

18. Frank G. Novak Jr., *Lewis Mumford and Patrick Geddes: The Correspondence* (London: Routledge, 1995), 232.

19. Larry Anderson, unpublished biography of MacKaye.

20. MacKaye to Katherine Menhenharr, April 25, 1921, Benton MacKaye papers,

Dartmouth College Library. Bryant does not mention MacKaye's wife in his biographical work. A scrapbook of Stubbs life can be found among these MacKaye papers.

21. Thorstein Veblen, *The Theory of the Leisure Class*, reprinted by Mentor Books, 1953 (original publication 1899); and William E. Akin, *Technocracy and the American Dream: The Technocrat Movements, 1900–1941* (Berkeley: University of California Press, 1977), 34.

22. Akin, 65–66, 80–96.

23. Allen Raymond, *What Is Technocracy?* (New York: McGraw-Hill Book Company Inc., 1933), 100–119. One critic, journalist Allen Raymond, wrote a series of articles about the movement and published a book entitled *What Is Technocracy?* that raised further questions about the mythical figure of Howard Scott. For instance, did Scott ever receive a doctor's degree, and why was he referred to as "Dr. Scott" while at Columbia? Scott himself told Raymond that he was called "Dr." because it was simply customary to call associates of the university "doctor" or "professor." Had he been an "engineer and technician" on the Muscle Shoals project in Alabama? No one on the project could remember Scott at first, save one witness who remembered him as a peculiar character who carried a gun and gave the impression of being a German spy. When his position of "equipment engineer" was investigated, it led only to reports of his incompetence on the job and the reasons for his being fired. In some cases Allen did not question but simply repeated the apocryphal stories about Scott's allegedly fraudulent behavior, and he tactfully stopped before seriously compromising reports from reputable figures that, despite his eccentricities, Scott had a massive grasp on his subject.

24. Akin, 101, 137–140.

25. Ibid., 116–130.

1.2 FRAMEWORK: *TERRA INCOGNITA* AND ENVIRONMENT

As MacKaye applied his infrastructure ideas to not only continental but global networks, he began to develop not a physical prototype but a cultural persuasion or script that could be used as a tool to reconstitute infrastructure organizations. An article in 1925 and a subsequent book in 1928, both of which were titled *The New Exploration,* articulated the notion that technological systems had their own ecologies that could be adjusted by new physical as well as perceptual "frameworks."[1] Effecting change did not necessarily involve physical restructuring. MacKaye's method of "visualizing," as he would call it, allowed him to highlight the protocols of activity and exchange within an environment, which were often pliable and filled with new sites and opportunities. The article and book developed an argument that gently dismantled some of the prevailing methods of organizing land by revealing new territory within them—territory that MacKaye sometimes called *terra incognita* or *environment*—territory essentially discovered within a new arrangement of perceptions.

Even the earliest Appalachian Trail article made way for the new organization by adjusting perceptions about the history and economy of the eastern seaboard. MacKaye usually began an article or book by placing his reader in an extreme spatial or temporal location. For instance, in the 1921 article, he placed the reader on the trail at a high altitude and likened their range of vision to that of a giant. He wrote, "Let us assume the existence of a giant standing high on the skyline along these mountain ridges, his head just scraping the floating clouds. What would he see from this skyline as he strode along its length from north to south?" Both as a forester and a mountaineer, MacKaye had walked along the Appalachian ridge and surveyed the surrounding land from its peak. Even though at any one position the trail section was small, its length and height enlarged an individual's experience by extending the body's visual range. From the giant's vantage point, MacKaye also inventoried the natural resources of coal, water, and woodlands as well as the psychic, recreational resources along the whole length of the crestline. He imagined that the cartoon giant enlarged not only the visual but the temporal frame of reference as well, enabling a view of several historical periods at once from the time of Indian settlements and Daniel Boone to the industrialization of large metropolitan areas.[2]

The giant, though clownish and typical of MacKaye's often elementary sometimes even corny writing style, nevertheless demonstrated a very real mental faculty. For MacKaye, physical passage through the landscape by, for instance walking or riding, provided a mnemonic structure to store and index memory and experience. Movements of the body exercised the mind and stimulated memory and understanding. MacKaye's theatrical family moved from New York City to the colonial town of Shirley, Massachusetts, when he was nine years old. Less interested in quoting the bard and grooming himself as another of the family's esthetes, MacKaye was fascinated instead with the humor and slang of common parlance and the outdoor world of the town. As a teenager, he devised "expeditions" through the woods of Shirley that he numbered and recorded in a book. Biographers, friends like Mumford, and MacKaye himself have perhaps romanticized these walks as formative boyhood events. Most were short and sketchy, but they represented a much more expansive practice that MacKaye's brother Percy would later call "expedition nining" after one of the favorite walks.[3] "Expedition nining" outlined a very specific mental craft. Features of the land, flora, and fauna acted as mnemonic devises to prompt stories and geological sagas that were intertwined with literature and autobiography. Like acting techniques that use mental and physical cues and rhythms to construct, store and release an entire virtual world, MacKaye's childhood expeditions allowed him to store experience in both the walking body and the landscape. Landscape was found within the mind, but that landscape could also be understood as mind and experience. The world was mind, and this virtual space could be cultivated by repeated perceptions that were stored and cross-referenced with knowledge from history, geology, and other cultural endeavors.

The trail was a long gigantic spectacle, and like Steele MacKaye's massive theatrical extravaganzas, it was intended to recreate rather than represent an experience—one that also, magically, expanded into temporal realms outside the present. Like MacKaye's own expeditions, perceptions involved more than simply visual contact with the scenery. Passage along the trail enveloped the individual in a motion picture experience and a script that was consciously compiled, stored and reconstituted. The high altitude enlarged views, while the narrow path collapsed many historical epochs into a single body and a single moment. The view from the mountain panorama summoned the larger history of human migrations, geological eras, and biological cycles. The Appalachian Trail was the "longest marked path in the world paralleled by the age-old, greatest of all Indian Trails—The Great Indian Warpath—which formerly extended from the Creek territory in Alabama north into Pennsylvania, the lowland or valley counterpart of the crest-line Appalachian Trail."[4] A carefully placed vantage point and a simple set of narratives that manipulated the temporal framework of the experience adjusted the most instant and immaterial layer in the landscape organization—the cultural persuasions that influenced its perception.

Terra Incognita

In the 1925 article, "The New Exploration: Charting the Industrial Wilderness," MacKaye claimed that his adjusted vision of the land revealed new territory within it. Contained within a special issue of *Survey Graphic,* one that served as a print manifesto for the RPAA, the article ostensibly contributed to the group's ideas about network regionalism. Among articles articulating the group's antimetropolitan platform, MacKaye's produced an unusual portrayal of the industrial landscape. In the article he introduced his proposals within a kind of fast-forward pageant of global history that collapsed time from Mesopotamia to the present and criss-crossed the globe from Siberia and Sumatra to the Hwang-Ho Valley. Speeding through discoveries and explorations by da Gama, Magellan, and Peary, using expressions like "iron horse" or "westward ho!" and mentioning Daniel Boone and the Egyptians in the same breath, he concluded the saga with the voyages of Peary, Amundsen, and Scott and their discoveries of the North and South Poles. Though these discoveries marked the end of the planet's terrestrial exploration, MacKaye described an "interchange" where this final discovery delivered the explorer to a new uncharted territory. Man "in dispelling one wilderness ... has created another," MacKaye wrote. "For the intricate equipment of civilization is in itself a wilderness. He has unraveled the labyrinth of river and coast line but has spun the labyrinth of industry." The grids for electricity and automobiles as well as a collection of other lines of flow for goods and population migration formed a "surface web," "a working thing; a rough hewn organism—a system" whose "physiology" resembled "that of a river system." This "industrial wilderness" or "wilderness of civilization" was a kind of geological formation, read not for its shape but for its recording of change and movement. The "incognito of industry" that MacKaye would later call the "*terra incognita*," lay as the undiscovered territory within the successive flows of population and development.[5]

Like the "open way" of the Appalachian Trail, the *terra incognita* was neither vacancy nor *tabula rasa*; it was neither cleared nor raised but rather found. It was a site constructed through the subtraction of dominant development patterns. Despite the actual dominance of these industrial forces in the landscape, MacKaye reversed their position to be the negative field, the dumb network, within a landscape cultivated by more diverse agents of culture. The "new exploration" of this *terra incognita* was to discover a more "efficient framework" that lay below the "surface web." The process of discovery involved selecting, reframing, and revising within the layers and remainders of both active and obsolete industrial infrastructure.[6] Unlike specifically formal proposals, the operatives of adjustment involved deflecting, diffusing, or reframing and crafting new adjacencies or relationships among multiple parts.

Environment

In 1928 MacKaye published his best known book, *The New Exploration: A Philosophy of Regional Planning.* The book compiled all of his ideas and prototypes of the 1910s and 1920s and, like Chase's *The Tragedy of Waste* or Mumford's *The Golden Day,* it attempted a large holistic synthesis of cultural trends and a more general "philosophy" of regional planning that sometimes grew strained under the weight of more comprehensive pronouncements. Most of *The New Exploration* outlined a catechism of the basic tenets of MacKaye's regional planning philosophy. Like Geddes and the other members of the RPAA, he charted a chronology of developmental periods that he described as "flows." He identified an "outflow" of early settlement and exploration on foot and horseback, a "reflow" of railway settlement and industrialization, the "inflow" to urban areas, and the "backflow" to the suburbs caused by extreme densities associated with the skyscraper. The book reinforced MacKaye's opposition between indigenous and metropolitan culture as well as his distinctions between urban, rural, and primeval lands.[7] MacKaye's romance with primeval wilderness and his moralizing about what he called "metropolitan invasion" further polarized his position on metropolitan versus indigenous culture. Casting regional planning as a global effort, he wrote of a technology of "world integration"—a "terrestrial lacework"—with networks for not only for commerce and communication but also for land-based exchange and ecological balance.[8]

Perhaps what remains as one of the most provocative aspects of the book was MacKaye's merger of engineering and what he called the "art of developing environment," not only making a more subjective art form critical to an engineering approach, but treating a specific kind of artistic contemplation as a means of cultural production. MacKaye considered: "(1) Material resources (soils, forest, metallic ores). (2) Energy resources (the mechanical energy resident in falling water, coal seams, and other natural elements). (3) Psychological resources (the human psychological energy, or happiness, resident in a natural setting or environment)." The latent power of the environment as mined and "converted" by the artist was considered to be like the latent power in waterfalls and dams. It was, like electricity, an "outward flow" of energy.[9]

The narrative of the book itself demonstrated MacKaye's craft for constructing sites from psychic material. It began by placing the reader, again, in several high altitude vantage points, one of which was the tallest building in Times Square. From the interior of the metropolis, MacKaye surveyed the flows of traffic and the concentric organization commanding undeveloped land at the urban periphery. The reader was then led below to the street and under the street surface to the subway to observe the currents from a regional and global "watershed" of commerce surrounding New York City. The reader's position was then shifted to the summit of Mount Monadnock, New Hampshire, which MacKaye called the "Fujiyama of New England." Mount Monadnock afforded the view of an entire region, one penetrated by the paths of early settlers, divided into the jurisdictions of states and villages, and criss-crossed with roads and rail lines. With typical histrionics, MacKaye wrote, "a million details—a little section of the world. . . . We pronounce it all 'beautiful,' and then decide that it is time to be going home. But wait! Let us tarry awhile—till we *see* the things we look upon. Let us lay down the field glass and take up a stronger telescope—the eye of the imagination. . . . Let us *visualize* once more."[10] For MacKaye the vision was of two "worlds." In the

There is one *terra incognita* not yet touched. And that is the world itself. This is not the world of continents and natural harbors; it is the world of railways and of seaports. It is not the world of intricate mountain fastnesses but the world of metropolitan fastnesses.[16]

−Benton MacKaye

Let us, from the top of the Empire State building and via the airplane of the imagination, take cosmic flight in search of the perspective to see this problem whole.
We head outward toward the moon and then look back. What a meager object planet earth becomes—a little round cheese with yeast working here and there is small blotches that we dub "America," "Europe," "China"! The yeast appears to rise and fall in alternate war-like spasms and depressions. We go far enough away to get a truly cosmic view; then come in closer to study the surface in detail.
We find the "cobweb" of earthian industrial civilization, a matrix of tiny streams—a veritable blood system—whereby the earthians somehow make a living. Each stream is an article of need. We pick out three of them—silk, flour, nails—elements respectively of clothing, food, shelter. We follow their paths around the planet.[17]

−Benton MacKaye

Don't confuse environment with beauty: don't confuse

metropolitan world, the city controlled the natural world in the distance. From Mount Monadnock, the land was the resource that issued instructions for shaping commerce. Its water and minerals fueled industry and agriculture and sanctioned development of Boston far off in the distance. Mount Monadnock was the negative of the metropolitan world. From Mount Monadnock, the metropolis did not establish the commanding order, rather, the land's latent resources appeared to organize the metropolis.

"Visualization" was a "psychological conversion" of the land's resources. "Visualizing" involved a larger abstract reappraisal of the environment that incorporated ideas about knowing through seeing and seeing through thinking. Intellectual understanding was deepened through a kind of enhanced perception—enhanced not through powers of magnification but through powers of time. MacKaye proposed looking long enough to see, in time lapse, the activity changing a slowing animating landscape—to see not the still but the motion picture. The practice engaged the mind and the body in summoning multiple scenarios over time. MacKaye consciously shaped these motion pictures and memories into a virtual space within which understanding and interplay were multiplied without conscious control. This space was the environment. It was a kind of "common mind." Quoting Thoreau, MacKaye referred to the environment as "the very atmosphere and medium through which we look."[11] More importantly, with the creation of this motion picture, his own contemplative process joined the protocols of industrial production, and he could express an economy in quantities of "psychic resources."

Throughout the book, MacKaye distinguished his art from aesthetics or planning practices and from the work of "'general appreciators'" or "amateur, landscape makers," instead likening the practice to a fusion of military and theatrical techniques. The "appreciators" were "found in the ranks of such movements as those for establishing national parks and forests, and for the eradication of city slums." They were "fighters against specific evils," and MacKaye, in contrast, saw the environment as a larger political and economic stage.[12]

MacKaye described military strategy as "one kind of regional planning." He wrote, "It is the charting and visualizing of deliberate, coordinated action over an extended territory." Military strategies also prepared for unforeseen contingencies that unfolded over time.[13] The military analogy was significant. MacKaye conceived of his gigantic brand of landscape operation as something like a massive mobilization of the country's resources during war time, and MacKaye often proposed his infrastructure project in relation to wartime efforts or postwar employment. As he hinted in the first Appalachian Trail article, landscape, the armies of men needed to develop it, and the scale of the endeavor might even be a psychological substitute for the dramatic and emotional release associated with war. MacKaye argued that the "lure of the scouting life" could rival that of the military; it only needed to be "dramatized" in a way that was equally "spectacular."[14] As a virtual project, MacKaye also thought that the effort to build such a trail would be pliably merged with other projects concerning forestry, community building, highway development, and water control or dam building efforts, making it possible to adjust an economy by adjusting a virtual as well as physical site.

The theatrical analogy was equally significant. The planner who prepared as an actor prepared for theater pursued a very different craft from that of the planner as engineer of optimal conditions. The actor prepared by storing in the mind and the body emotional tropes related to event, activity, and duration. Those moments were assembled like small motion pictures that reconstituted the material of a script as well as its subtexts and alternative scenarios. The planner or environmental artist would deliberately use mental-temporal space to develop multiple iterations of the plan. "Every deliberate action—big or little, good or bad, military or industrial—starts in the mind. It must be conceived and rehearsed in the realm of thought before it can take place in the physical. It must be *created* before it can be *done*."[15] Often, for MacKaye, these rehearsals involved the ability to see cultural protocols in an inverted form—to see the negative of a dominant development format. This altered perception was not a prelude to making, but was itself the conversion of resources and the production of space.

the total source with any part thereof. Environment is outward influence; it is literal and mental atmosphere; it is a permeating medium of life.[18]
—*Benton MacKaye*

And the art itself is ready at hand awaiting its realization. It is a synthesis of various amateur efforts of the naturalist, the photographer, the local historian, the folk-player, the civic leader. This synthesis is gradually moulding itself into a distinctive form of culture— it has been called "outdoor culture": it is the art of developing environment. The flow of water over Niagara Falls possesses a potential mechanical power which the engineer can develop and convert to man's needs; this same flow over Niagara possesses a potential spiritual power which the artist can develop and convert to human ends.[19]
—*Benton MacKaye*

1.2

We rest our case on the findings of the aeroplane observer.... He sees the industrial structure in physical terms. Money and price, the laws on the statute books, the property lines on surveyor's maps, the findings of the learned economists are beyond his purview. He sees land, mines, waterways, mills, machinery, houses, and men. He sees them moreover not as a single aerial photograph, but as an aerial motion picture—with sufficient time element to note movement and change.[36]

—Stuart Chase

The sight of a New England village green after a long absence brings a mist to my eyes. This is where I was born, my homeland, the place I love. The Alps look cold and bleak beside the White Mountains of New Hampshire. One signboard on the Mohawk Trail hurts me more than a hundred on the Rocky Mountains..."[37]

—Stuart Chase

Although its members are known in some quarters for their advocacy of public housing and their important experiments in community and neighborhood design, the group's greatest collective contribution has been almost totally ignored: the members sought to replace the existing

Network Regionalism

When planning historians have profiled the RPAA, they have usually included a few remarkable plot lines. The RPAAs membership referenced many professions and disciplines, among them architecture, finance, forestry, and economics. Charles Whitaker was primarily responsible for gathering the group together during April of 1923 in Clarence Stein's office in New York City.[20] Though its numbers expanded from time to time, MacKaye, Mumford, Stein, and Wright formed a core group.[21] Many of the members brought experience from positions in Washington during World War I. Mumford brought a familiarity with the New York publishing world and a seven-year correspondence with Sir Patrick Geddes. The group met informally, found some consensus and produced, with relative ease and speed, two of the most significant residential prototypes of the twentieth century, Sunnyside, in Queens, New York, and Radburn, New Jersey. Though often remembered for their residential prototypes, the RPAA also addressed larger organizations of industry and infrastructure and attempted to forge an expanded role for planning within the nationwide economies of distribution and settlement. The president of the United States admired them, and some of their ideas contributed to the blueprint of the New Deal's regional and residential planning. Their vision relied on the complexity and variability of community at a point when America endorsed a standardized, generic form of community making. In hindsight, many of their principles and prescriptions have appeared to some to be well suited to address midcentury planning problems. Neglect of their work during the postwar period has often been characterized as a missed opportunity. In fact, the RPAA has often been portrayed and has often portrayed itself as a group of mistreated heroes.

The RPAA argued that the concentric urban growth pattern should be replaced by a "network of cities of different forms and sizes, set in the midst of publicly protected open spaces permanently dedicated to agriculture and recreation." Mumford would later call this network, the "metropolis in a new constellation," saying, "this is the organic type of city that the technology of our time, the electric grid, the telephone, the radio, television, fast transportation, information storage and transmission, has made possible"[22] The *Survey Graphic Re-*

gional Planning Number (May 1925) and and a film entitled *The City* (1939) served as manifestoes for the group.

The cover illustration for the *Survey Graphic* issue dramatized the major contention of the RPAA. With a split image, it juxtaposed a congested city like Pittsburgh against an image of a father, daughter, and baby strolling through a healthy landscape that contained a vernacular cottage and a hydroelectric dam. The group often used both historical and technological imagery within a mixture of reportage, metaphor, and allegory to form their persuasions. Most of the RPAA members contributed articles to the issue that dramatized the evils of the metropolis and argued that new infrastructure and housing were instruments for rearranging and recalibrating developmental patterns. Mumford's article, "The Fourth Migration," attempted to demonstrate the historical inevitability of the RPAA's approach by tracking three migrations of population from the city to the West and then back to the city via different infrastructure networks. He claimed that new automobile, airplane, and commercial infrastructures would initiate a "fourth migration" that might operate centripetally or centrifugally, thus either reinforcing the metropolitan structure or defining distributive networks of decentralized industry.[23] Stuart Chase contributed an article entitled "Coals to Newcastle" that outlined wasteful distribution economies in America. Many of the other articles intensified the group's entrenched position against the evil powers of the metropolis.

By the late 1920s, the RPAA was among those groups anxious to lobby the New Deal government about their approach to regional planning. In 1931 they invited the then governor, but soon to be president, Franklin Delano Roosevelt (FDR), to a round table on regionalism held at the University of Virginia (UVA). Chase, MacKaye, Mumford, and Wright spoke at the round table. Mumford's talk argued for deriving a "common meaning" for the notion of regional planning.[24] Other groups, most notably the Regional Planning Association (RPA), also used the term "region" but used it in reference to metropolitan regionalism and a reprise of City Beautiful planning that was anathema to the RPAA's goals.[25] MacKaye discussed his concept of "liquid planning."[26] Chase delivered a rather giddy speech in which he claimed that "a combination of Russia and a certain October 29th," had initiated the new "planning pandemonium." Given the success of

centralized and profit-oriented metropolitan society with a decentralized and more socialized one made up of environmentally balanced regions. Even today, the idea is radical.[38]

—*Carl Sussman*

experiments Chase had witnessed as a trade-union delegate to Russia during World War I, the American economy, with its wasteful land boom practices and severe depression, looked bleak by comparison. Chase could and did say, "I told you so." His book *Tragedy of Waste* had forecast these problems, though he gave some credit for new planning concerns to the "astute propaganda" of his colleagues in the RPAA. Since intelligentsia in all fields were cooking up five-year plans, Chase also proposed his own plan for "economic regions," saying the "great task of master planning is to bring purchasing power into alignment with the growth of the technical arts. . . . It means tinkering with the credit system, tinkering with wages, tinkering with hours of labor."[27] The plan was later echoed in his book *A New Deal* (1932), from which came the nickname for FDR's New Deal administration. In the book, Chase aligned with an increasingly accepted Keynesian approach, setting out the basic tenants of FDR's New Deal as: "A managed currency. The drastic redistribution of the national income through income and inheritance taxes. A huge program of public works."[28]

At the UVA conference and during the presidential campaign, FDR spoke of the need for an experiment in regional-national planning that might also generate employment. Many assumed that the Muscles Shoals project was a likely candidate for this planning test case. As part of the National Defense Act of 1916, the government had constructed some nitrate plants at Muscle Shoals, Alabama, and disposal of the properties was a lingering issue. Many proponents, from RPAA members to Henry Ford to Howard Scott, had ideas or affiliations with the Muscle Shoals development.[29] Senator A. E. Morgan fought for and eventually directed legislation in which not only Muscle Shoals but the entire Tennessee River watershed would become a supranational water control project under the newly formed TVA. The TVA focused on hydroelectric power and water management to renew agricultural areas while preserving and enhancing cultural activities. Though there was much theorizing about the preservation of existing regional culture, the activities of the TVA both renovated and disrupted the settlement of thousands of people.[30]

Mumford expressed disappointment that he and other RPAA members were not given significant jobs in TVA. The TVA's administrative triumvirate was southern and pursued three different reflections of New Deal liberalism, which occasionally led to crossed directions from the board. Several administrative jobs went to local or regional personnel. For instance, Earl Draper who headed the division of Land Planning and Housing, had worked on southern suburbs and, under John Nolen, the planned town of Kingsport, Tennessee. TVA historian Walter Creese quotes a conversation between A. E. Morgan and Draper in which Morgan expressed a desire to hire people who were aware of local conditions and would not be controlled by a "clique or a group that is preconceived in the notions of what has to be done . . ."[31]

Among the different visions of America's future exhibited at the 1939 World's Fair, Futurama and Democracity were perhaps the most notable. In the Science and Education Building, however, the chief attraction was yet another vision of the future, the film manifesto of the RPAA entitled The *City*.[32] With narration by Lewis Mumford and music by Aaron Copland, *The City*, reiterating the party line, portrayed the evils of the metropolis and the virtues of small communities molded from the region. Filmmaking suited the RPAA's methods, in that it presented a world formed from the selective documentation of existing conditions. *The City* contrasted the slums of Pittsburgh and the hectic pace of New York City with the tranquility, order, and good sense of Radburn and the greenbelt towns. These new towns were populated by children on bicycles or mothers tending to babies and allotment gardens. They were associated, however, not with the socialist collective, but rather with the American colonial small town. Shirley, Massachusetts, MacKaye's hometown, so clearly outlined the civic and cultural functions of the RPAA paradigm that it became a kind of mascot for the group and the star of *The City*.

MacKaye and several of the RPAA members like Mumford, Stein, and Chase indulged in quite of bit of sentimentality about the New England small town during their careers. Avoiding associations with laissez-faire capitalism that created towns like "Zenith," the RPAA referred instead to an American urban form with origins in the eighteenth century but which remained largely intact in the 1920s and 1930s—the typical colonial New England town. They referred to the political and ecological position of these towns as compact, largely agricultural, communities cultivating and taking instruction from the natural resources, and geologic presence of the land. *The City* patiently observed women baking pies and the simple technologies of the water-wheel miller, the blacksmith, and the farmer. MacKaye and Chase were both New Englanders, and *The New Exploration*, was itself a kind of hymn to the New England small town. MacKaye claimed that the small settlement generated a true cosmopolitanism and that the metropolis generated a kind of "standardized exotic" as inauthentic and artificial as its own money-based economy. MacKaye wrote in *The New Exploration*, "Cosmopolitanism adds to the world's variety: metropolitanism adds to the world's monotony." By taking cues from the specialties of the landscape and soils as they change from area to area, the towns would contain more variety than the great monolith of the metropolis.[33]

The nostalgic Yankee moralizing, however, was mixed with hopes of a bright new "neotechnic" society. The film also showed cars and townless highways moving efficiently through the country, and airplanes taking off as the narrator read, "Science takes flight at last for human goals. . . ." The group often used airplane views or motion picture metaphors to take a more comprehensive look at the landscape or animate exchange and activity within it, while at the same time associating with twentieth-century technological advances. As Stein and Mumford were in Shirley filming *The City*, however, Stein wrote to MacKaye, "The other thing which is lacking and, I am afraid, will be somewhat difficult to secure, is any scenes of the community itself. As soon as one tries to gather a crowd of people these days, one gets a whole lot of automobiles in the foreground. Although we are not going to pretend that this is a colonial village in colonial times, somehow or other, we have the fear that the thing will seem a little out of character if there is too much of the automobile age."[34]

Showing the old city and the new, Mumford's narration claimed, "You take your choice. Each one is real. Each one is possible. Order has come—order and life together. We've got the skills. We've found the way. We built the cities. All that we know about machines and soils and raw materials and human ways of living is waiting. We can reproduce the pattern and better it a thousand times. It's here! The new city. Ready to serve a better age. You and your children—the choice is yours"[35]

Notes

1. Benton MacKaye, "The New Exploration: Charting the Industrial Wilderness," *The Survey Graphic* 65 (1 May 1925): 153.

2. Benton MacKaye, "An Appalachian Trail: A Project in Regional Planning," reprint *Journal of the American Institute of Architects*, 19 (October 1921): 4.

3. Bryant, 16, 19–30.

4. MacKaye, "An Appalachian Trail," 4.

5. MacKaye, "The New Exploration," 179, 153, 154. Benton MacKaye, "The New Northwest Passage," The Nation 122 (2 June 1926): 603; Benton MacKaye, "Industrial Exploration," serial publication in *The Nation:* "I. Charting the World's Commodity Flow," 125 (20 July 1927): 71. MacKaye used the word incognito in *The New Exploration* and *terra incognita* in "The New Northwest Passage" and "Charting the World's Commodity Flow."

6. MacKaye, "The New Exploration," 154.

7. MacKaye, *The New Exploration: A Philosophy of Regional Planning* (New York: Harcourt, Brace and Company, Inc., 1928), 56–94.

8. Ibid., 20.

9. Ibid., 50–51.

10. Ibid., 50.

11. Ibid., 213–214, 212, 205 (MacKaye quoting Thoreau), 213.

12. Ibid., 212.

13. Ibid., 153.

14. MacKaye, "An Appalachian Trail," reprint, *Journal of the American Institute of Architects*, 19 (October 1921): 8.

15. MacKaye, *The New Exploration, 1928*, 152.

16. MacKaye, "The New Northwest Passage," *The Nation* 122 (2 June 1926): 603.

17. MacKaye, "End or Peak of Civilization?" *The Survey* 47 (1 October 1932): 441.

18. MacKaye, "Tennessee—Seed of a National Plan," *Survey Graphic,* 22 (May 1933), 254.

19. MacKaye, "To Keep Malignant Growths Off Our Highways," *Boston Evening Transcript*, February 21, 1928.

20. Frank G. Novak Jr. *Lewis Mumford and Patrick Geddes: The Correspondence* (London: Routledge, 1995), 172; and Stuart Chase, "My Friend Benton" in "Benton MacKaye: A Tribute by Lewis Mumford, Stuart Chase, Paul Oehser, Frederick Gutheim, Harley P. Holden, Paul T. Bryant, Robert M. Howes, C.J.S. Durham," *The Living Wilderness*, 39 n. 132 (January/March, 1976):18.

21. The charter members included engineer and architect Frederick Ackerman (1878–1950) Frederick Bigger, builder and financier Alexander Bing, John Bright, writer and economist Stuart Chase, forester and regional planner Benton MacKaye, writer Lewis Mumford (1895–1990), architect Clarence Stein (1882–1975), journalist and editor of the *Journal of the American Institute of Architects*, C. H. Whitaker (1872–1935) and architect and planner Henry Wright (1878–1936). Housing experts Catherine Bauer (1905–1964) and Edith Elmer Wood (1871–1945) as well as Tracy Augur and Clarence Arthur Perry were among those who were later involved. Carl Sussman, ed. *Planning the Fourth Migration: The Neglected vision of the Regional Planning Association of America*, Cambridge, MA: MIT Press, 1976, 2, 7.

22. Lewis Mumford, Statement before the Senate Subcommittee on Executive Reorganization, Friday, April 21, 1967, MacKaye papers, Dartmouth College Library, manuscript copy, 9, 3.

23. Lewis Mumford, "The Fourth Migration," *The Survey Graphic* 54 no. 3 (1 May 1925): 130–33.

24. Lewis Mumford, "Regional Planning," Institute of Public Affairs. *Round Table on Regionalism* (5th Session: 1931: University of Virginia) July 6–11, 1931, 199. Portions of this conference are reprinted in Sussman, 197–215.

25. The Regional Planning Association, begun in 1921 under the philanthropic sponsorship of the Russell Sage Foundation, was developing another type of regional plan that it later published in 1929. Both groups used the term "region" but used it to define different goals. Whereas the RPAA proposals represented a radical reversal of urban centrality with roots in the Garden City tradition, the Regional Plan Association proposal represented a late chapter in the City Beautiful tradition. Charles Dyer Norton, the young man who proposed the New York project, was Daniel Burnham's son-in-law, a trustee for the Russell Sage Foundation, and an active proponent of Burnham's plan for the City of Chicago in 1909. The regional plan for New York City and its environs would, like the Chicago plan, propose a metropolitan organization of the region's infrastructure, suburbs, and parkland. The final plan completed in 1929 after a decade's work produced ten volumes. The RPA contributed an article to the *Survey Graphic* regional planning issue in 1925, but shortly after the publication of the RPA's larger final report, Mumford and Thomas Adams, the project's director, engaged in a public debate in the pages of the *New Republic* in 1932. For the RPAA, the most egregious error of the RPA was of course, that it invested the city with even more power rather than divesting that power to smaller centers of population. Some have argued that while the RPAA got the attention of FDR, its antagonism of the RPA alienated them as potential New Deal personnel since Delano administered the New York project as well as the National Resources Planning Board, one of the main New Deal planning agencies. Regional Plan Association, "New York Today—and Tomorrow?" 139; and Carl Sussman reprinted the debate between Adams and Mumford in *Planning the Fourth Migration: The Neglected Vision of the Regional Planning Association of America.*

26. Benton MacKaye, "Cultural Aspects of Regionalism," *Round Table on Regionalism* (9 July 1931), 1–7.

27. Stuart Chase, "The Concept of Planning," *Round Table on Regionalism*, reprinted in Sussman, 209, 210, 212, 216.

28. Stuart Chase, *A New Deal* (New York: MacMillan Company, 1932), 192, 213–241.

29. Roscoe C. Martin, ed., *TVA: The First Twenty Years.* (Knoxville: The University of Alabama Press and the University of Tennessee Press, 1956), 3; and Allen Raymond, *What is Technocracy?* (New York: McGraw-Hill Book Company Inc., 1933).

30. Phoebe Cutler, *The Public Landscape of the New Deal* (New Haven: Yale University Press, 1985), 136; and Michael McDonald and John Muldowny, *TVA and the Dispossessed: Resettlement of Population in the Norris Dam Area,* (Knoxville: University of Tennessee Press, 1982).

31. Walter Creese, *TVA's Public Planning: The Vision, The Reality* (Knoxville: University of Tennessee Press, 1990), 248. Creese sites Jordy's "A Wholesome Environment," 25–26; also in Creese, 253, Draper interviewed, 30 December 1969, Oral History Project, The John Willard Brister Library, Memphis State University, Memphis, Tennessee.

32. Wurts, Richard, Appelbaum, Stanley, et. al, *The New York World's Fair 1939–1940* (New York: Dover Publications, 1977), 3, 89.

33. MacKaye, *The New Exploration*, 59, 60, 76; Benton MacKaye. "Outdoor Culture: The Philosophy of Through Trails," *Landscape Architecture*, 17 (April, 1927): 167, (reprint p. 5); Benton MacKaye, *The New Exploration*, 63, 71.

34. Stein to MacKaye, 26 August 1938, Benton MacKaye papers, special collections, Dartmouth College Library.

35. *The City*, Presented by American Institute of Planners through Civic Films, Inc., produced by American Documentary Films, Inc. (1939). Directed and photographed by Ralph Steiner and Willard Van Dyke. Narration by Lewis Mumford, music by Aaron Copland.

36. Stuart Chase, *The Tragedy of Waste* (New York: Grosset and Dunlap, 1925), 24–25.

37. Stuart Chase, "Coals to Newcastle," *Survey Graphic* 54, no. 3 (1 May 1925): 212.

38. Carl Sussman, ed., *Planning the Fourth Migration: The Neglected Vision of the Regional Planning Association of America* (Cambridge, MA: MIT Press, 1976), 3.

Though MacKaye articulated a philosophy of regional planning in *The New Exploration*, his TVA career involved actual prototypes. The dams, waterways, hydroelectric easements, and highways of the TVA were all systems that directly related to his fluvial models for active organizations. In fact, since the UVA round table on regionalism MacKaye had begun to characterize his particular approach as "liquid planning." Unlike solid planning, the components of liquid planning were active. A decorative landscape fixed by an aesthetic pattern was an example of solid planning, whereas a field of crops, as a rotational organization, was an example of liquid planning. Highways, railroads, and ports were also examples of liquid planning, since their shape or position was less important than the flow of goods among them. MacKaye described the "iron web" of civilization as a circulatory system, the strands of which were "hollow" and, like "veins," carried the "vital *liquid* element."[1]

In 1932, just months before Franklin Delano Roosevelt was elected to the presidency, MacKaye joked in a letter to his friend Clarence Stein, "How can he [FDR] run the country unless the RPA tells him how?"[2] The RPAA was thought to have been influential in shaping the New Deal blueprint as well as national planning experiments like the TVA. But in the early days of the New Deal, the RPAA was just one group among the many planning enthusiasts to arrive in Washington. There were many authors of the TVA legislation. Technocracy and futurism, sampled as ideology or style, colored the more romantic or nostalgic renderings of back-to-the-land sentiments.[3] Like river control and dam building projects of the 1920s, the TVA would be host to all of the sentiments and politics associated with these often conflicting notions of engineering and reform.[4]

Finally, MacKaye was the only charter member of the RPAA who was given a position in the TVA, and while he was disappointed that most of his colleagues were not involved, he was delighted with the job. At the TVA, a collegial atmosphere of thinkers and planners concentrated in a few buildings created a kind of miniature District of Columbia in Tennessee and a global experiment in planning. MacKaye received visitors like A. E. Morgan, Henry Wright, Raymond Unwin, Stuart Chase, David Cushman Coyle, Clarence Stein, and a group of younger colleagues who gathered around him for study and entertainment. He wrote to Stuart Chase, "We've got a crowd of bully boys and girls down here—worthy of the HR [Hell Raisers]—suffragette days in Washington. . . . I was given the little chore of laying out a regional plan for the whole Tennessee Valley—a plan for a plan; this constitutes my job; I have the best job in the TVA and the best job of my life . . ."[5]

Among the TVA bureaucrats, there were plenty of conflicting notions concerning both valley and national planning. Some of the national planning schemes were colored by technocracy theories and others by traditional utopian ideologies. Characterizing the two minds of the TVA, MacKaye jokingly complained to Chase about both the "landscape artichokes" who were interested in "esthetics and beautification" as well as the "hard-boiled engineers [men of the type of our friend Howard]." The "esthetes" appeared to be unaware of the many different kinds of problem solving involved with the economy of a region. The "he-men" heroes of engineering unwittingly aligned themselves with the "industrial captains" as "practomaniacs" who regarded many critical aspects of culture as superfluous.[6]

MacKaye avoided the aesthetic, technical, and planning cults by concentrating on "liquid planning" and developing organizational expressions for activity within organizations. He developed two specialized types of partition, *watershed* and the *wayside*, that appeared again and again in his TVA writings. These partitions were not about simple subdivisions of space or demarcations of territory but rather about designating an active boundary. A watershed, for instance, marked not only edge but also relative concentrations of program or radiating effects from some discrete but generative feature of the site. It could be elastic or inelastic, porous or solid, and it could directly or indirectly alter the constitution of an organization. Different from a region bounded by "fixed lines," a watershed was a planar fluvial system that modeled a "sphere of influence" or an area radiating from a point of activity.[7] As the area adjacent to the roadway, the wayside too was an active boundary that affected a larger organization. The part of the wayside that was right-of-way was truly *terra incognita*, a ribbon of land bounded by statistical, mathematical, and legal formulations of traffic engineers that lay adjacent to and even connected every different watershed and landscape of the region. Though it was a neutral or unexplored territory, it could be designated in ways that affected all the surrounding land as well as the experience of driving on the roadway. MacKaye also merged the repertoires of watershed and wayside to create a special tool for repartitioning the country into new political jurisdictions.

Wayside

In the first hundred days of FDR's administration, when it appear that a pilot national planning project might involve water problems in the Tennessee River Valley, MacKaye pursued a public conversation with the New Deal administration by publishing not only an outline scheme for the Tennessee Valley but an approach to understanding watershed and valley systems across the nation. In articles like "The Challenge of Muscle Shoals," [*Nation* 1933], "The Tennessee River Project: First Step in a National Plan" [*New York Times* 1933], and "Tennessee—Seed of a National Plan" [*Survey Graphic* 1933] he applied his models of fluvial dynamics not only to water but to electricity, highways and population migrations. The "'stream control' was of two kinds: the stream of water in the rivers, and the stream of development along the highways."[8]

The highway was a strong liquid planning prototype and one of MacKaye's most effective and politically popular planning instruments. It was a continental-intercontinental intervention that affected commercial as well as recreational traffic. Moreover, highway building was becoming increasingly prominent within the national agenda. In the years just before his tenure at the TVA, MacKaye published several proposals for the limited-access highway as a terrestrial infrastructure, among them: "Townless Highways" [1930], "Roads Vs. Shuttles" [1931] and "Cement Railroads" [1932]. Like the Appalachian Trail, highways and parkways were, along with railroads, units of regional organization. MacKaye's latest liquid planning prototype, the "townless highway," proposed a wide easement or wayside as insulation from development. Access would only occur at specialized interchanges that would eliminate grade crossings. Distinct communities would be developed some distance from the roadway. Like most limited-access highway proposals, MacKaye proposed to separate the two directions of traffic, making it possible

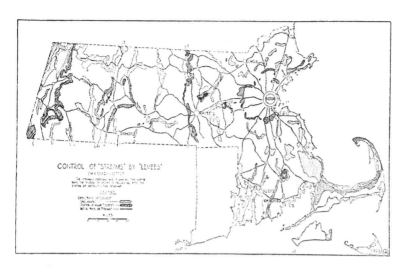

1.3.1 Control of "streams" by "levees." The openways crossing and flanking the motor ways: The system of levees interlocking with the system of metropolitan streams. Benton MacKaye, *The New Exploration: A Philosophy of Regional Planning* (New York: Harcourt, Brace and Company, 1928), 194.

to use not only the two waysides but the very large central area as a means of organizing and accumulating land for a terrestrial network.[9] The townless highway was just another of MacKaye's specialized linear prototypes. He wrote to Clarence Stein in 1929, that the townless highway idea was the "complement in a sense of 'an Appalachian Trail'. One follows the primeval crestline or main 'dam' across the metropolitan 'stream'; the other follows the 'stream' itself (figure 1.3.1)."[10]

MacKaye was also particularly interested in addressing those forms of transportation that, like waterways, airways, and "landways," crossed long distances without interruption. Both railroads and the limited access highways were examples of these "specialized landways." The wayside, as part of this right-of-way, was "a strip of public land devoted to movement," one physically and legally insulated from grade crossing and commercial access. MacKaye considered the wayside to be a critical conduit between towns and wilderness or recreation areas. He recognized that crafting wayside space involved crafting the law that changed uses and perception of the space. He wrote that a "cordon sanitaire" or "some other tightly woven brand of 'legal

In thinking up schemes for Roosevelt I find myself going back to the visualization that I tried to popularize last winter in my 'Open Door' article, in which housing, highways, and wilderness areas were placed in one great flying wedge—highways being the 'center rush'.[26]

—*Benton MacKaye*

[From his post at the TVA, MacKaye wrote to his friend Stein about visits from "people whom I've casually known in the whirl of New York and Washington" and one particular banquet for Sir Raymond Unwin which characterized the atmosphere of the TVA.] An enormous crowd filled the lobby—all of them of course eager to see this particular big man from across the seas [Sir Raymond Unwin]. Many of our friends were in the swirl and we joshed and gurgled among them. Any man who had a wife had her along. And there were many singleites of each gender. Harvey and I went floating through the human sea. Somebody suddenly took my arm. Who could it be—among all the many good friends there present? Was it of TVA or Knoxville?—'carpet bagger or cannibal'? Was it lady or gent? I turned—it was Sir R. I presented Harvey to him and the three of us rolled on arm-in-arm. Later we parted—Sir T. and Henry and the other visitors to the speakers table, Harvey and I and merry spontaneous crew to one of the side tables where we frisked and bellowed softly and all but threw the biscuits at each other while the waiter brought on the soup, the ice cream, the salad, and—finally the steak. You see it was a PLANNING dinner. Henry and Sir T. made the principal speeches—both accompanied

fence' must be strung between the stations of each side of the road."[11] While at the TVA, MacKaye wrote sample legislation for amendments to the two Federal Aid Highway acts. For MacKaye, the legislation would create a nationwide system of highways with broad rights-of-way and limited access, bypassing cities. The creation of a national highway system automatically meant the parallel formation of a diverse national network of wayside landscapes.

Watershed

MacKaye also merged the ideas of watershed and wayside in the creation of national planning partitions. In the *New York Times* article MacKaye had written before arriving at the TVA; he discussed the Tennessee Valley as a system that was part of a larger "intermountain" area made up of the Mississippi basin and the Appalachian Valley. He proposed building a highway in the intermountain "lane" formed by the valleys running from Lake Champlain to Tennessee. This highway was to act like a levee that would not only control water but contain and format development along its length. He then extended the vision to imagine a series of belts and valleys across the country that could be related by similar conditions and viewed as a new "public domain," or political jurisdiction, and he described these river and valley systems as "lanes of national development."[12] MacKaye posed the provocative challenge, "Question, is this dream of President Roosevelt's to come true in a piece of true statescraft—or in one more real-estate adventure? Is the word 'Tennessee' to join company with 'Florida'? (figure 1.3.2)."[13]

The TVA presided over a area that crossed state boundaries to assume the apolitical shape of a watershed, one which was roughly the size of Ohio. Throughout his career, MacKaye was interested in political organizations like the TVA that recognized boundaries other than those related to territorial acquisition or the conveniences of geometrical property survey. The shape of a region or the external boundary criteria depended on an emanating generative activity and was often an elastic condition. The region's organization might have both centripetal and centrifugal influence on populations and goods. In his TVA writings, MacKaye treated each of the industries, from milk to timber, as a kind of watershed, and later he would even use the term "traffic shed" to describe changing transportation volumes. All these different "economic watersheds" coexisted in a system that constantly differentiated not only the borders of the region, but its internal workings.[14] In 1937, after leaving the TVA, he began using this special idea of watershed as an organiza-

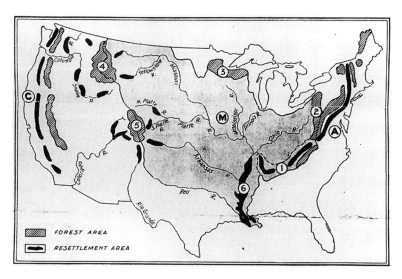

1.3.2 Lanes of national development as mapped in article, "The Tennessee River Project: First Step in National Plan." a) Appalachian Valleys, b) Mississippi Basin, c) Columbia-Sacramento Valley, 1) Tennessee Valley 2) Pittsburgh-Alegheny Area, 3) Minnesota-Wisconsin Forest Area, 4) Columbia-Yellowstone Area, 5) Colorado-Platte Area, 6) Lower Mississippi Area. Benton MacKaye, "The Tennessee River Project: First Step in National Plan," *New York Times* (16 April 16, 1933):3.

tional expression for new national political partitions. Rather than considering the whole of the country as a palette to be subdivided, he focused first on internal mechanisms or generative centers that would command a surrounding order or organizational field with its own variable boundaries. These fields or areas were often larger than a single valley or watershed and often more like a valley system whose boundaries might be related to not only fluvial but agricultural or geological features as well. MacKaye devised a scheme based on the watersheds of seven major river valleys in the country, a scheme he called the "seven little TVAs," and he later devised a similar scheme based on some of the TVA studies, called "the new thirteen," which divided the nation into thirteen regions (figure 1.3.3).[15]

MacKaye's proposals for new national frameworks independent of state boundaries were perhaps influenced by similar studies being conducted in Washington by the National Resources Committee (NRC).[16] The NRC was established to make qualitative and quantitative appraisals as well as future plans for regional development, public works, population distribution, and

alternately by looks of deep wisdom and flashing bursts of laughter. . . . If ever I write my memoirs the starred chapter thereof I'm living right now in these nights and days. And the only way to tell you thereof is to turn this letter into a Memoir and stop the living for the writing. So come on down and live it with me and tell the dear Aline we only need her smile to make the blueprints *live.*[27]
—*Benton MacKaye*

There's a lot of guff about aesthetics and beautification; and nonindustrial planning is

THE NEW THIRTEEN

1.3.3 "The New Thirteen" a hand-drawn scheme for a federation of regions. Benton MacKaye, *Geotechnics of North America*, unpublished manuscript, Benton MacKaye papers, Dartmouth College Library.

yet in the hands of the 'landscape artichokes' who would cope with the problem of life's setting and background in terms of planting pansies. But 'the flowers that bloom in the spring, tra-la, have nothing to do with the case.' On the other hand, the hard-boiled industrial engineers (men of the type of our friend Howard) are too high and mighty to think on the thing—human sensibility—that the whole damn show is all about; they as well as the industrial 'captains' themselves, are what my old brother James use to call 'practomaniacs.' They are merely grown up men who

housing among other things.[17] The NRC produced several hundred of the most lucid and thorough surveys and plans of the country's resource potentials. In 1935, the NRC published one of its most notable reports, *Regional Factors in National Planning*, that proposed to repartition the nation into regional planning jurisdictions. The NRC consulted a variety of bureaucrats, intellectuals, and planners of the day, and while reflecting a liberal direction, the NRC sought a broad political base and aligned with other New Deal agencies in its recommendations to regulate the economy through consumption and insurance. The NRC (also called the National Planning Board, National Resources Board, National Resources Committee, and the National Resources Planning Board) was sanctioned by executive power and shuttled under the umbrella of several different pieces of legislation. It was renamed and reorganized under various jurisdictions to avoid controversy when "planning," particularly national planning, was a politically sensitive notion.[18] Toward the end of the 1930s, an increasingly conservative congress was suspicious of the power and the political leanings of advisory groups close to the president. By the late 1930s and early 1940s, these kind of planning activities were often associated with socialistic proposals and the board or committee was abolished.[19]

Ostensibly, the study, *Regional Factors in National Planning*, only reviewed an existing "interstate cooperation movement." Interstate metropolitan agencies like the Regional Plan of New York and its Environs, the New England National Resources Board, and the Pacific-Northwest National Resources Board, were examples of this type of cooperation. The report included a map of ten valley authorities other than TVA that had been proposed in Congress as of 1935. In the seventy-fourth Congress, "over a dozen" bills were introduced proposing various regional development authorities, and the report treated these as precedent for a new national organization.[20] Since New Deal power structures already appeared to threaten the balance of powers between federal and state governments, the National Resources Committee portrayed itself as a coordinator of intergovernmental cooperation that would only further decentralize power rather than create a new political authority.[21]

The report assembled a remarkable series of maps that reorganized the nation around jurisdictions other than states. These jurisdictions were often defined, not by territorial boundaries but by organizational expressions for activities related to land or commerce in the region. The report studied the implications of defining regions by "indefinite areas," by "static elements" such as "geological features," or by a "dynamic entity." For instance, generative centers might define a field radially and "elastic boundaries" would be responsive to fluctuating conditions of population and economy.[22] Most of the study's conclusions were compiled into a series of five maps. The first mapped regions centered on "major metropolitan influence," where subnational centers generated a flexible field to absorb and regulate the region's changing conditions. A second map showed the country organized around cities that would serve as convenient administrative centers. A third map, based on groups of states, and a fourth based on a "single function" such as agriculture or water problems were discouraged. The fifth and final map in the series was based on composite regional problems. These composite regions were, in a sense, the resultant of multiple overlays mapping physical, sociocultural, and economic features. The five maps supported the committee's final designations of twelve regions. Shortly thereafter these planning ideas began to be implemented, and by 1936 every state except Delaware had a planning board. There were also plans for other river valley authorities like the TVA for the Missouri, Mississippi, Red, and Arkansas Rivers (figure 1.3.4).[23]

like to play tin engine and choo-choo car. We might say 'the hammers that clang in the spring, bang, bang, have nothing to do the case.'[28]
—*Benton MacKaye*

Meanwhile the example of the physical sciences has corrupted the arts of economics and sociology. Merely because a few billion dancing molecules can be described by a mathematical formula, and their behavior predicted within certain limits, the illusion has arisen that the economic and social behavior of man can be treated likewise. A pseudoscience is one that collects a series of verifiable facts, such as bumps on the skull, and derives conclusions therefrom that have nothing to do with the case. The value of a statistical collection of facts can be easily exaggerated. There are too many other loose facts that failed to get into the collection. This is a big world, and a pailful of small facts has no more scarcity value than a pailful of sand on the beach. Hence the pseudoscientific aroma of economics and sociology as currently practiced. Nobody but God can possibly know enough to design a social or an economic order in the way in which an engineer designs a bridge.[29]
—*David Cushman Coyle*

1.3.4 Diagrams from National Resources Committee. *Regional Factors in National Planning and Development.* (a) Possible planning regions based upon major metropolitan influence; (b) possible planning regions based upon administrative convenience; (c) national resource board planning districts based upon group-of-states arrangement; (d) national resources board water resources regions based upon a single function; (e) possible planning regions based upon composite planning problems. U.S. National Resources Committee. *Regional Factors in National Planning and Development* (Washington, D.C.: U.S. Government Printing Office, 1935), 158, 160, 162, 164, 165.

International Highway Networks and Partitions

After his retirement to Shirley, Massachusetts, MacKaye continued to sketch and map giant plans for linear infrastructure prototypes and national systems of watersheds and partitions, working very diligently, but for no one in particular. He was interested not only in the way that these new infrastructures could reconfigure national jurisdictions but also in the way they might establish international and intercontinental linkages. As early as 1926, in an article entitled, "The New Northwest Passage," MacKaye mapped an intercontinental infrastructure system between the world's two largest producers, North America and Asia. In MacKaye's plan, Roald Amundsen's 1924, trans-Arctic air and ocean route from New York to Peking provided the initial mark around which to develop a linear network of intercontinental infrastructures with possible landing stations near the North Pole as well as rail linkages to other major global cities like Berlin Paris, Moscow, London, and San Francisco (figure 1.3.5).[24]

In retirement, MacKaye also designed an Alaska-Siberia highway that would crystallize around logging and defense installations. Since, by the 1950s, the chief focus of America's highway building efforts would be the interstate highway system, alternative highway approaches became increasingly rare. In 1942, however, there were proposals in Congress for highways linking various North and South American countries. One congressional measure proposed a highway across Canada linking Alaska with the lower forty-eight states. MacKaye extended the idea by proposing that the North American section of the road might form the eastern leg of a longer military highway from Edmonton, Alberta, to Irkutsk, Siberia. The Alaska-Siberia-Burma Road, as he called it, was consistent with military strategy toward both the Japanese and the USSR. Knowing the Alaskan and Siberian terrain and studying the locations of military bases, MacKaye devised a route sympathetic to construction and defense as well as a practical scheme for the highway's execution—one that organized the experience and effort of many groups, including foresters, loggers, and military personnel over a period of time sufficient to construct and then manage the road (figure 1.3.6).[25]

As a complex global instrument of physical, economic, and political reorganization, the Alaska-Siberia highway was the kind of problem MacKaye had trained himself to address. Though he was not able to influence legislation, the highway plan was an interesting reprise of MacKaye's radical Washington

Suppose the government of the state called the "United States," instead of laying out the land of Louis in rectangles and in shapes resembling extinct animals, had followed the policy of LaSalle in his fictitious career of continental planner. In what wise would little Tommy be obliged now to relearn his geography lesson pertaining to the map of U.S.A.? ... He would look hereon in vain for those eight and forty cockeyed daubs of varied colors. Instead, he would discern a bakers dozen or so of ample sized forms, bounded by barriers between flows of water and of traffic. A careful count might reveal thirteen of them.[30]

—Benton MacKaye

In January of 1891, I recall my brother Benton, at the age of twelve, reading aloud to some of the family the Constitution of his "Cosmopolitan Organisation": a world-scheme for the abolition of all national barriers and prejudices. In his after-career (since his R.M. degree in Forestry at Harvard) during constructive planning in government conservation of our natural resources and in editorial writings, Benton MacKaye has developed from his boyish thought on "Agri-

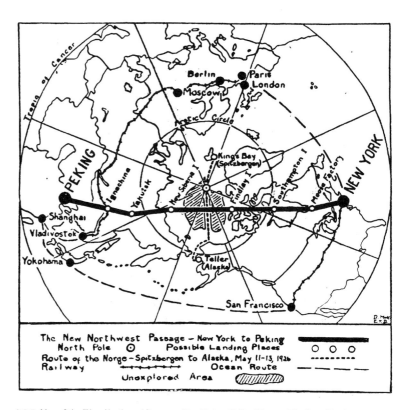

1.3.5 Map of the "New Northwest Passage—New York to Peking." Benton MacKaye, "The New Northwest Passage," *The Nation*, (June 2, 1926):603–604.

culture" and "Cosmopolitanism" a comprehensive philosophy of Land Use in its natural and Human ramifications, conceived as a problem of super-engineering—his "New Exploration," some aspects of which he has glimpsed in articles by him published in the *Survey*, the *Nation*, and other journals.[31]
—*Percy MacKaye*

days when Russia was a fascination among his group of left-wing activists. The road cross-referenced many of MacKaye's previous prototypes. Like the Appalachian Trail, it aligned the highway with larger continental and geological features and linked it to employment, community, and large-scale military mobilization programs. It was also linked to his proposals for new land-based political jurisdictions, which, like watersheds, would have elastic boundaries. For MacKaye, however, the artistry and engineering involved not the shape of the roadbed or the landscaping of the roadside but rather the organizational architecture. He was interested in establishing new political, economic, and employment affiliations that would rearrange the prevailing protocols for public infrastructure building.

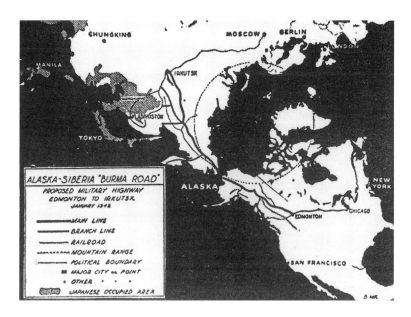

1.3.6 Plan for an Alaska-Siberia-Burma Road. Benton MacKaye, "Alaska-Siberia Burma Road," *The New Republic* (March 2, 1942):292–294.

Notes

1. Benton MacKaye, "Cultural Aspects of Regionalism," *Round Table on Regionalism*, (9 July 1931), 1, 1–7; and Benton MacKaye, "End or Peak of Civilization?" *The Survey* 47 (1 October 1932): 441.
2. MacKaye to Stein, September 24, 1932. MacKaye, on this occasion, referred to the RPAA as the RPA.
3. MacKaye to Stein, 27 May 1933; MacKaye to Stein 30 May 1933.; Stein to MacKaye 6 June 1933.
4. Paul Conkin, *Tomorrow a New World: The New Deal Community Program* (Ithaca: Cornell University Press, 1959).
5. MacKaye to Chase, 20 July 1935.
6. Ibid.
7. MacKaye, "What is a Region in Planning?" TVA office memorandum to Tracy Agur, October 1934 (revised 26 October 1935).
8. MacKaye, "Tennessee—Seed of a National Plan," *Survey Graphic* 22 (May 1933): 53.
9. MacKaye, "The Townless Highway," *The New Republic* 62 (12 March 1930): 93–5.
10. MacKaye to Stein, 10 October 1929.
11. MacKaye, "Motorway Legislation: Dual-Transport vs. Mono-Transport," office memorandum to Tracy Augur, head planner from Benton MacKaye, regional planner, 19 February 1936, 5, 11, 16, 11.
12. MacKaye, "The Tennessee River Project: First Step in a National Plan." *New York Times*, 16 April 1933, 3.

13. MacKaye, "Tennessee—Seed of a National Plan," 253, 252, 294.
14. MacKaye, "What is a Region in Planning?"
15. ("Seven Little TVA's") sketch in Benton MacKaye papers, Dartmouth College Library. "The New Thirteen" in Benton MacKaye, *Geotechnics of North America*, unpublished manuscript, MacKaye papers.
16. MacKaye met with National Planning Board representatives while he was at the TVA.
17. Marion Clawson, *New Deal Planning: the National Resources Planning Board* (Baltimore and London: Johns Hopkins University Press for Resources for the Future Inc., 1981), 43.
18. The NRC was legislated by the National Industrial Recovery Act of June 16, 1933 as part of the Public Works Administration. In June of 1934, the NRC was replaced by a National Resources Board that would consolidate various long-range planning efforts into one group under the direct jurisdiction of the President. In 1935, the name of this group was changed to the National Resources Committee, and its legal base changed from the now unconstitutional National Industrial Recovery Act to the Emergency Relief Appropriation Act of 1935. In 1939 the group was changed yet again under a presidential reorganization scheme to be the National Resources Planning Board, dropped its cabinet members and had to go to the Congress rather than the president for appropriations; and John Hancock, "The New Deal and American Planning: the 1930's" in *Two Centuries of American Planning*, ed. Daniel Schaffer (Baltimore, Johns Hopkins University Press, 1988), 201–203.
19. Clawson, 225–236; Walter Creese, *TVA's Public Planning: The Vision, The Reality* (Knoxville: University of Tennessee Press, 1990), 324–336; Alan Brinkley, *The End of Reform: New Deal Liberalism in Recession and War* (New York: Alfred A. Knopf, 1995), 66–72; Jordan A. Schwartz, *The New Dealers: Power Politics in the Age of Roosevelt*, (New York: Vintage Books, 1994), 20–21; and Clawson, 52–71.
20. U.S. National Resources Committee, *Regional Factors in National Planning and Development* (Washington, D.C.: U.S. Government Printing Office, 1935), 107.
21. Ibid, 115, 113.
22. Ibid, 140–141, 155, 18, 165. MacKaye, too, used the term "elastic" to describe the boundary conditions of regions modeled after watersheds.
23. Ibid, 155–77.
24. MacKaye, "I. Charting the World's Commodity Flow," 72; and MacKaye, "The New Northwest Passage," *The Nation* 122 (2 June 1926): 603.
25. MacKaye, "Alaska-Siberia-Burma Road," *The New Republic*, CVI (March 2, 1942): 292–294.
26. MacKaye to Stein, 15 November 1932.
27. MacKaye to Stein, 28 September 1934. MacKaye refers to Aline MacMahon, Clarence Stein's wife and a Hollywood film actress. MacKaye's underlining.
28. MacKaye to Chase, 20 July 1935.
29. David Cushman Coyle, "The Twilight of National Planning," *Harper's Monthly Magazine*, 171 (October 1935): 559.
30. Benton MacKaye, The New Thirteen: Whither State and Region in American Federalism," from *Geotechnics of North America: Viewpoints of its Habitability*, unpublished. Manuscript dated April 1953 MacKaye papers, Dartmouth College Library.
31. Percy MacKaye, *Epoch: The Life of Steele MacKaye*, vol. 1 and 2 (New York: Boni and Liveright, 1927).

1.4 SITES

MacKaye was an inventor of organizational protocols, an artist whose medium involved not only physical sites, but also those temporal, virtual, and procedural sites that have generally remained unexpressed in the fields of design and planning. His prototypes might be characterized as linear networks or partitions that incorporated both transportation and utility programs as well as instructions for cultivating land and translating between land, community, and industry. He tinkered with organizations by subtracting pieces from them, reversing their governing protocols or reconditioning their distributed components by means of both remote and direct agents of change. These adjustments were reliant on carefully selected positions in space and within a culture of thought. Planning only involved highlighting or adjusting an existing condition within which there were several optional contingencies. Similarly, MacKaye's infrastructures had no definite boundaries but rather a repertoire of possible behaviors that could change over time. A site of intervention, understood to be part of an ecology, need not attempt comprehensive control over the organization to affect it. MacKaye's interventions were wild cards, usually involving partial or tactical adjustments that would have some radiating effect within the organization.

Just as MacKaye understood his sites of intervention to be distributed, tactical, or remote, so he also conducted his practice with a light touch. His work lay outside the boundaries of any single profession. He did not fit the model of an heroic figure in either the technocracy or environmental movements. He did not become a well-known New Dealer, and he never achieved the fame of some of his RPAA colleagues. Clarence Stein and his wife, actress Aline McMahon, were great friends to MacKaye and had often helped him with money on occasions when the lack of disciplinary boundaries proved to be less than lucrative. Stein once called him "the most disinterested man I ever met."[1] He followed the verbs rather than the nouns in culture. He was interested in neither the leading role or the chorus of the play, but the *mise-en-scène*. Although MacKaye's infrastructure prototypes were clearly explained within his writings, his eccentric practice may have been less clearly delineated even in his own mind. This practice, itself a kind of wild card, shared organizational attributes with his infrastructure prototypes and often involved the same kind of perceptual tricks and inverted cultural scripts about positions of power in culture.

Although he often talked about increased economic efficiency, MacKaye was not intent on using his infrastructure prototypes to optimize organizational structure, a desire that appears to have underwritten so many cultural endeavors of the twentieth century. At some point in this century, for instance, technocrats and environmentalists have both pursued models of holistic or self-organizing systems with recursive structure. The technocrats claimed that technology could be self-regulating if tools like computers would compile enough data to reveal its most efficient ecology. Environmentalists have portrayed the planet as a single self-regulating organism whose balance may be upset by man's extremes. Technological potentials inspired visions of heroism among the technocrats and sent the environmentalists into crisis. The midcentury cybernetics conferences that investigated the possibility of automatic or self-balancing systems in biological and technological ecologies contributed to both movements. Their discussions mixed models between a broad range of disciplines from anthropology to neurophysiology to computational networks.[2] The late twentieth-century preoccupations with new technologies have often revived a rather narrow range of ideas from these researches. The possibility of circular, self-organizing systems of interactivity, artificial intelligence, predictability, and optimization within complexity are among those inherited fascinations. The received agenda perhaps even obscures a broader project of cybernetics—which was to characterize interplay and organization in many different environments and systems.

Fascinated with biological systems, Ian McHarg, a more recent proponent of a position similar to that of MacKaye and Geddes, used in his book, *Design with Nature*, images of nautilus shells, snowflakes, bees, and other organic organizations to discuss the growth of cities as a process that generated "natural" patterns.[3] MacKaye was, however, not interested in idealized biological patterns or recursive organizational systems. He might be more easily identified not with the positivistic ideologies surrounding cybernetics, but with its broader goals and its rather unusual personnel. For instance, MacKaye's eccentric practice often resembled that of Gregory Bateson. Like MacKaye, Bateson was interested in ecological expressions or organizational architecture. He broadly applied cybernetics' most abstract principles to analysis of tribal behavior in New Guinea, a digital language for dolphins, or processes of addiction and fellowship in Alcoholics Anonymous. In fact, Bateson's work and cybernetics in general may be most interesting not for their content and certainly not for their holistic views but for the way in which they prompted cross-environmental and interdisciplinary modeling of ecological relationships and ideas.

Though MacKaye played a role in the midcentury environmental movement as a cofounder with Aldo Leopold (1886–1948) of the Wilderness Society, he did not site his work within a cultural conflict. He carried the antimetropolitan flag, but his practice relied on elementary and subtle craft rather than an entrenched position. The careers of Leopold and MacKaye form an interesting parallel. Leopold also studied forestry, worked with Gifford Pinchot, and based some of his thinking on Thoreau. Like MacKaye, he was among the first to use the word *environment*. The environmental movement however, was characterized more by Leopold's approach to ecology and environment than MacKaye's. Leopold's philosophy sponsored an emotional concern for the preservation and protection of animals and plants, and his sentiments were expressed with a kind of literary poetic. Leopold gave the name "wilderness area or trail" to prototypes like MacKaye's linear landscape infrastructures, and these terms survived to influence legislation.[4] *Sand County Almanac*, published a year after Leopold's death, became one of environmentalism's "sacred texts." Leopold is remembered as kind of "patron saint." He has been described as "the Moses of the New Conservation impulse of the 1960s and 1970s, who handed down the Tablets of the Law but did not live to enter the promised land." Wallace Stegner described him as "an American Isaiah."[5] MacKaye noted that Leopold made "one of the very few contributions thus far to the psychology of regional planning," but both the moral and psychological spiritualism associated with the environmental movement's appreciation of landscape were very different from MacKaye's environmental art, which was about exploring an industrial wilderness and often finding opportunity even within what would appear to be an opposing force.[6]

Although the eccentricities of MacKaye biography have made him attractive to scholars, these eccentricities also resist some of culture's favorite treatments of personality. The environmental movement was predisposed to recall MacKaye's role as a conservationist and preservationist rather than a technician and an artist. The greenway movement, organized to preserve abandoned infrastructure corridors for recreational trails, has adopted MacKaye as a kind of mascot. A younger generation of environmentalists has been interested in the part of MacKaye's practice that celebrated the phenomenal, revelatory world of communion with nature. MacKaye was proposing ingenious, provocative, and even radical revisions of both terrestrial and technological ecologies, but the speculations of this kind of terrestrial technician did not fit the more comfortable personae of the Yankee naturalist.

MacKaye has also often been analyzed as a "Mumford influence," since Mumford was remembered as the chief cultural proponent of neotechnic cooperation between terrestrial and technological forces. Mumford designed his career to satisfy the requirements of a cultural critic and author with a broad social and political program, and he did not split his time between writing and designing prototypes. MacKaye's choice to write a major book like *The New Exploration* no doubt owed something to Mumford's influence. A new edition of MacKaye's *The New Exploration* was published in 1962 during the incipient years of the modern environmental movement. In the introduction, Mumford, typically effusive, wrote that the book should have "a place on the same shelf that holds Henry Thoreau's *Walden* and George Perkins Marsh's *Man and Nature*." He went further to liken MacKaye's voice not only to Thoreau, "but Davy Crockett, Audubon, and Mark Twain."[7] Mumford was always generous in his estimations of MacKaye and often couched his public critiques in praise. Stopping just short of apologizing for MacKaye's extremes, he often tried to clarify and realign MacKaye's views to make them more presentable, while at the same time associating himself with some editorial aspect of MacKaye's various publications.

When MacKaye retired to Shirley, Massachusetts, in 1945, Mumford encouraged him to write an autobiography of geotechnics. *Geotechnics of North America: Viewpoints of Its Habitability*, MacKaye's final opus, was written in the ensuing twenty years and finished in 1965 when he was eighty-six years old. He worked from a drafty room in a small house, a room with books, a stuffed bird and all of his charts and drawings of new national organizational schemes. While its writing style expressed the flavor of his experi-

Let no one misread my friend's character or his life mission. Though no small part of MacKaye's thought was devoted to preserving and properly utilizing wilderness areas, as the base of all other parts of the human heritage, he never thought of the wilderness as the last refuge of despairing hermits, who might

ence, it was not an autobiography but rather an exegesis on the philosophy of geotechnics or a descriptive version of what MacKaye had previously called the "World Atlas of Commodity Flow." With somewhat quaint titles like "The Quadruped Economy (Food and Paw)" or "From Ice to Iroquois," the book attempted a simple understanding of land planning from its inception. Though the style served MacKaye's purpose of relaying profound paradigm shifts by way of simple language and situations, here, the elementary tone also accompanied somewhat elementary concepts.[8] Mumford read the manuscript and wrote back a long and affectionate letter to his friend saying that after several readings, he considered it to be unpublishable, largely because of its breadth. It was a retelling, Mumford said, not only of MacKaye's personal experience, but of the history of the continent, a history that was for the most part already "in the public domain." The manuscript needed editing, a job for which neither Mumford nor Stein could volunteer. Mumford suggested that copies of the book be distributed to a selection of libraries. Though *Geotechnics of North America* was never published, a compilation of new and previously published articles entitled *From Geography to Geotechnics,* did, in some ways, function as the autobiography Mumford had previously suggested.[9]

Only practice with actual sites and prototypes appeared to relieve MacKaye of his tendency to search for totalizing frameworks within which to map global history. This epistemological juggling as evidenced by his everexpanding outlines and classifications was perhaps symptomatic of a mind that was ironically unwilling to finalize those kinds of determinations. In any event, the historical material was, in some sense, not intended to relay history as would a historian, but rather to condition the reader's perceptions for his own idiosyncratic continental saga. Finally, with an extreme form of resourcefulness, MacKaye sited his prototypes in this organizational territory and in doing so retooled and recircuited some of the most powerful development protocols in America.

wish to escape from the complexities and mischiefs of civilized life. He was never a mere simple-lifer, still less an antiurbanist. Like Thoreau, MacKaye appreciated the communal values of the New England villages, and even better than Thoreau he appreciated the culture of cities. So far from believing that man's three major environments, the primeval, the rural, and the communal or urban, were mutually exclusive, MacKaye held rather that they were complementary, and all three were necessary for man's full development. MacKaye was all these things. If MacKaye's work, aside from the A. T., was often too far off the beaten track to gain public attention, still less to win popularity, this was because he himself was opening fresh trails, though sometimes covering his footsteps by using old-fashioned terms, obsolete data, or testimony drawn from the great teachers of his youth, whose names are hardly known today even by scholars.[10]

—Lewis Mumford

Notes

1. Clarence Stein wrote a letter of recommendation on MacKaye's behalf to TVA's director of unemployment, C. L. Richie, 7 October 1933.
2. Influenced by midcentury fascinations with biological systems, Ian McHarg—a more recent proponent of a position similar to that of MacKaye and Geddes—used in his book, *Design With Nature,* images of nautilus shells, snowflakes, bees, and

other organic organizations to discuss the growth of cities as a process that generated "natural" patterns.

3. Ian McHarg, *Design with Nature* (Garden City, N.Y.: Natural History Press, 1969).

4. MacKaye, *The New Exploration*, 203. This characterization of wilderness survived to influence important pieces of legislation like the 1946 Bill for Wilderness Belts, The Wilderness Act of 1964, and The National Trails System Act of 1968.

5. John L. Thomas, "Lewis Mumford, Benton MacKaye, and the Regional Vision," in *Lewis Mumford Public Intellectual*, eds. Thomas P. Hughes and Agatha C. Hughes (New York: Oxford University Press, 1990), 66–99; Philip Shabecoff quoted historian Donald Fleming and Stegner in *A Fierce Green Fire: The American Environmental Movement* (New York: Hill and Wang, 1993), xiii, 90, *n. 28.*

6. MacKaye, *New Exploration*, 203.

7. Lewis Mumford in the introduction to Benton MacKaye, The *New Exploration* (Urbana: University of Illinois Press, 1962), vii.

8. MacKaye, *From Geography to Geotechnics*, unpublished manuscript, Benton MacKaye papers, Darthmouth College Library. Pictures of MacKaye's study in Shirley can be found in the MacKaye papers.

9. Mumford to MacKaye, 2 November 1970, MacKaye papers Dartmouth College Library.

10. Lewis Mumford in Stuart Chase, Lewis Mumford, and others, "Benton MacKaye: A Tribute by Lewis Mumford, Stuart Chase, Paul Oehser, Frederick Gutheim, Harley P. Holden, Paul T. Bryant, Robert M. Howes, C. J. S. Durham," *The Living Wilderness*, 39 n 132 (January/March, 1976), 17.

Part 2

2.0 DIFFERENTIAL HIGHWAYS

The history of the interstate highway is contained within our amnesic recollections of the recent past, and its dominance over all other transportation
formats in America has perhaps obscured our ability to see it as an adjustable
and differential network. Many highway histories have treated the interstate
as a predestined event in a patriotic saga. A pilgrim put one foot in front of
another or a cow strode beyond the pasture for the first time, and soon, the
rutted trails were paved with concrete, the wagon wheels faded to pneumatic
tires, and these and other abstractions of movement evolved inevitably into
the federal government's version of the limited-access highway. The more
contentious histories have usually taken an entrenched position against the
villainous collusion between federal agencies and private automobile interests, pointing out a kind of conspiracy within companies like General Motors
to not only dominate but eliminate all other forms of transportation, particularly interurban rail. Other histories have treated the interstate as yet more
evidence of the long-standing tradition of using engineering expertise to
galvanize legislation.

Though justified by claims of reasoned expertise, the history of highway
networks proceeded by illogical steps. For instance, specifications for the system were designed for a long-distance network but were applied to an intercity network. In addition, the primary reason for routing the highway through
the city involved the increased revenues to be gained from higher volumes
of urban traffic, but as the costs of the highway escalated, it became clear
that the majority of those costs were due to urban mileage. The highway was
also understood to be an evacuation facility for the urban areas in times of
war, yet it had the adverse effect of concentrating population in those urban
centers. Highways were projected to solve some of the city's traffic problems,

but most of them increased commuting time. Since cars were sold to thousands of Americans before there were adequate roads to accommodate them, in a sense, the vehicle and its infrastructure were sold separately, and the highway network was routed in relation to the distribution of automobile products in urban areas. The forces that facilitated legislation of the Interstate highway system eventually merged with the agendas of commerce and defense, and for all the claims of pioneering individualism, for all the pictures of Conestoga wagons used in its promotion, the interstate was one of the most centrally controlled and bureaucratically directed chapters in American history, it policies remaining largely the same over a period of decades. The legislative history was protracted over fifty years, but the extent of change after passage of the Interstate Highway Act in 1956 was massive and rapid. The interstate was the largest public works project and the most prominent national network to be built in this century. As perplexing as these now familiar historical curiosities was the lack of coordination and integration between the highway and other adjacent transportation networks and landscapes. The following episodes look at eccentric proposals for national highway systems that treated the highway as a differential or intermodal network capable of translating between carriers and infrastructure formats.

Using statistical models, traffic engineers designed the interstate as a response to vehicle populations. Engineers derived formulas to handle variable loads at different times of the day, but the equations always yielded the highway as a fixed register of dynamic equilibrium or movement at a particular speed. Traffic engineering principles determined everything from the dimension of the highway to the turning radius of the driveway, and they also governed the hierarchy of tertiary, secondary and, minor streets. Even minor streets were sized for large phantom vehicles moving at top speeds. Not only was the organization of the highway network contingent on vehicle populations, but the design of the roadway itself was engineered to be viewed from a static position inside the vehicle. Similarly, while early highway designers saw the road as a means of accessing a diverse set of regional landscapes by car, it was eventually designed as a hermetic system that created its own channel of surrounding traffic-engineered landscape contours. The highway was legislated as an intercity network, yet it was not specialized to interface with the complexities of the city, and was simply designed to pass uninterrupted through urban fabric. Rather than becoming differentiated at its intersections, the system replicated itself, generating products and morphologies of its own structure within more complex urban environments. Although initial speculations about the highway considered terminals and exchange points to be of the highest importance, eventually, with interchanges such as the cloverleaf, the chief intent was not interchange, but elimination of change and the creation of a smooth, homogeneous experience. Interchanges designed as switches or transformers from one kind of traffic to another would represent obstacles to continuous speed, and so in the organizational logic of highway building other forms of transportation should be segregated. The interstate highway system was designed as a frozen shape—a dumb network with dumb switches.

Since Bel Geddes' Futurama exhibit of 1939, the possibility of building intelligence and differentiation into the highway network by automating it has been a persistent dream. In fact, highways and electronic networks have often been paired in the public consciousness, sharing similar predictions and contradictions surrounding freedom versus control. For instance, the highway's promise of greater "elbow room" was not unlike the Web's promise of a new frontier. The promotions or coercions of automobile highway associations at midcentury resembled the insider's swagger of today's network aficionados like George Gilders and Nicholas Negroponte, as they advise the businessmen of America about power centers on the new information highway. Cars, like electronic keyboards, appeared to be at the individual's control while also providing access to a vast, expansive territory. Both networks have sponsored popular jargon and promotional imagery in lieu of an understanding of the real operatives of network space.

Communication systems inform the highway system, however, not only as an applied technology, but as technology that might loan its active repertoire or network protocols to the highway's own species of site. For instance, in communication networks, network intelligence relies on smart and flexible patterns of switching between heterogeneous components and multiple scales of activity. Multiplicity, differentiation, and diversity are understood to strengthen a network, and the smarter the system the more its operation runs counter to conventional notions of efficiency. Network redundancies serve this parallelism by providing a surplus of options and pathways in a network that are the key to its precision. The opportunity for switching within the system is one measure of this parallelism and depth. Much of the speculation about electronic networks concerns the central or individual control of these switches. Internet legislation differs significantly from that of the interstate highway since the utilities involved will develop greater by using each other's infrastructures to carry the various TV, video, and internet transmissions.

Ironically, both the history of cross-purposes and the multiple segregated transportation networks in cities and outlying landscapes potentially provide very fertile ground for a more intelligent network architecture in the highway system. Many of the redundancies among the various transportation networks have developed through cycles of replacement and supposed obsolescence, unaccompanied by a process of selection and recombination that would build parallelism in the network and better match carriers to transportation needs. Both the highway and the rail fought for exclusivity and dominance. This same fight for exclusive formats has not only been part of the history of highways and railroads but other kinds of utility networks as well. Even software-hardware platforms have been in dispute for this reason, despite the fact that the real intelligence behind their operation often involves the knowledge of how to patch between them. Redundancies among transportation systems, like highway, rail, and air, however, increase the possibility of switching between systems to produce a better fit between task and carrier. The system is rich with these potential switch sites for interchanges and urban terminals. Similarly, networks of land as well as the networks of other carriers, though often segregated, are positioned to operate in parallel with the highway. The highway right-of-way and its adjacent lands are critical sites in adjusting this kind of parallelism. These new sites might borrow a repertoire from not only our most recent telematic networks but also from the earliest experiments with the highway.

Before the system became so highly codified, some proposals for the highway treated it not as a single hermetic corridor of space containing roadway and right-of-way but rather as a set of separate, interdependent sites. Highway intersections, terminals, and rights-of-way, for instance, were among the sites that drew speculation from several independent practitioners who regarded the network as an active and variable organization that could be affected by several species of different programs. Just as various electrical and electronic networks often mimic each other or share a repertoire of organizational operatives, so the highway borrowed from, for instance, the railroad. Like the railroad, the highway was a long-distance insulated corridor with controlled exchange points for potential interplay between landscape and other transportation networks. Schemes for urban automobile terminals and urban or interregional interchanges also proposed to mix and exchange cargo and passengers between different kinds of vehicles and different kinds of transportation modalities. Some specialized highways also evolved from urban boulevards or interstate parks. While the highway may have become a tool of land exploitation, the origins of the long-distance highway were linked to the development of interurban or continental terrestrial networks. Some practitioners proposed a kind of parallelism among independent networks of railway, waterway, or roadway not only at the intersections but along the linear segments of each network, thus loading intelligence into the switches or surfaces of the highway corridor.

The episodes in part II look at various schemes for highway organizations both when the idea of an interstate system was relatively new as well as when it began to grow to completion in the ensuing decades. Although highways were almost exclusively controlled by federal traffic engineers, some designers considered the highway to be within their purview. Federal highway agencies and a broader cast of practitioners, including Warren Manning, Benton MacKaye, Norman Bel Geddes, Egmont Arens, Lady Bird Johnson, Lawrence Halprin, William Whyte, and the automated highway research teams of the 1960s and 1970s, are among the players included in the discussion.

Interstate Highway

Barraged with road-building proposals during the first-quarter of the twentieth century, the federal government, in association with state governments, assumed new responsibilities for highway planning. Federal involvement in road-building efforts at the turn of the century primarily addressed road improvement in areas beyond the paved streets of the city. Early government agencies cooperated with states and organizations like the American Automobile Association and the American Association of State Highway Officials (AASHO). In 1914, they even deputized the AASHO as an official consultant to federal road agencies.[2] In fact, the AASHO established a practice of writing the legislation to be presented in Congress and years later would be among the most influential groups in legislating the interstate network.[3]

By the 1910s, as automobile registration continued to rise, many of these private groups, who together formed the "good roads movement," assembled at various congresses to organize themselves and the state officials who represented them. This partnership among federal

Ask Vice-President Al Gore about telecommunication and he thinks of highways. During a recent interview at his office in the West Wing of the White House, Gore recalled that when he was a boy in Carthage, Tennessee, his family couldn't get into their new car and drive to Nashville—a fifty-mile trip—with any speed, because the road was just two lanes all the way. He also recalled a scene from the 1950s: "I watched my father preside over the creation of the interstate highway system as the chairman of a subcommittee of the Senate Public Works

Committee. I remember sitting in the room when they voted to make the signs green on the interstate system." He recalls, in sum, that an assertive government helped open the country to travel and commerce.[1]

and state officials as well as automobile interests would be critical to highway development in the coming years.[4]

Two highway acts, the Federal Aid Highway Acts of 1916 and 1921 marked the beginning of a recurring pattern in which neutral, apolitical technical expertise was the galvanizing force for highway legislation.[5] The acts also established protocols for financing and cooperation among federal and state governments in planning a national highway system.

In 1919, after two earlier reorganizations, the Bureau of Public Roads (BPR) took over from the Department of Agriculture and administered federal highway efforts during the critical planning stages of the interstate system. Thomas H. MacDonald served as bureau chief for the whole of this important period. The BPR became a clearing house for technical information, allowing the government to maintain authority with limited financial responsibility. Still, the roadways were often built according to conflicting standards and were often neither internally coherent or coordinated between counties and states. For instance, roads often did not meet across state lines. In addition, because there were no standards concerning access to frontage, these roads were already becoming lined with commerce.[6]

Meanwhile, in the 1920s, automobile manufacture had grown to be a major United States industry, and the National Highway Users Conference representing truckers, farmers, fuel companies, and automobile manufacturers had become a powerful lobby.[7] Still, even after another Federal Highway Act in 1921, the government did not legislate any of the many proposals for a national highway system.[8]

Toll Roads and Free Roads (1939) and *Interregional Highways* (1944) were landmark reports which provided the basic blueprint for Federal highway building in the next decades, and have often been referenced as a seminal documents in the development of the interstate system.[9]

The Federal Aid Highway Act of 1944 did not result in any interstate highway construction, however, it did initiate the process of negotiating routes for the system. By 1947, the federal-state partnership had designated the routes for 37,000 miles of the possible 40,000-mile network, and though that network included 2,900 miles of urban routes, congressional studies related to defense recommended additional urban mileage. In the late 1940s and early 1950s, more and more urban mileage was added to the proposed designs for an inter-state system, and with each new version of the highway legislation, the federal government took responsibility for a larger and larger percent-age of the total costs, until it was virtually paying for the entire proj-ect.[10] The BPR made yet another study, *Needs of the Highway systems, 1955–84*, in which they recommended a 37,700 mile system, costing $23.2 billion. Of this estimate, 46 percent would be spent on urban routes. The subsidies were attractive to those urban planners who were anxious for coordination between highway plans and existing ur-ban planning schemes, and many believed that highways would rejuve-nate urban areas.[11]

The Clay hearings (October 1954) and the Gore hearings (1955) were pivotal in legislating the interstate. Both heard testimony from private lobbying groups, planners, manufacturers, highway planners like Robert Moses, conservationists, and representatives of other transportation systems. The Clay Committee was composed not of planners or urbanists but rather of representatives from construction companies, teamsters, banking, and manufacturing. Most of the dis-cussion avoided any issues that involved rethinking the prevailing con-cept of the interstate as an urban connector. In fact, the hearing began with a report that indicated a doubling of the estimated cost of the highway from approximately $50 billion to $100 billion largely due to urban mileage. Helen Leavitt wrote in *Superhighway-Superhoax*, "They knew even then that the local traffic would provide the revenue to pay for an interstate system designed for long-haul and rural traffic. The hurdle was how to get the heavy traffic onto the system when the heavy traffic was urban and mostly short trips."[12]

The Gore hearings addressed the obvious problems of entering urban fabric with rather short-sighted concerns. The urban highway mileage was discussed as if it applied to circumferential routes, yet testimony reflected an awareness that the highway would generate more urban traffic. The assessment of this increased urban congestion became doubly perverse when regarded positively for the extra reve-nue it would generate. Some who testified were alert to defense and safety issues, while others were only concerned that municipalities might misuse government funds. There was little discussion of urban transit, or of the successes of long-distance railroad in World War II defense efforts. Interestingly, Howard Zahnister, chosen by Benton MacKaye to be director of the Wilderness Society, also received no response to his testimony. Without reference to any alternative intelligence about highway planning, Zahnister testified in the defensive posture of a conservationist and preservationist, pleading with the powers that be to protect wilderness landscapes. The days when a forester-technician would provide one of the most interesting speculations about the economies of automobile infrastructure and even propose a possible physical arrangement for that infrastructure were over.[13] Three bills, including an administration bill, were considered in the House of Representatives in 1955, but neither House nor Senate enacted legislation. Whatever variance in the legislation, each successive bill steadily increased both the urban mileage and the federal percentage of funding.[14]

Highway lobbies and legislators expected 1955 to be the year of highway legislation. The National Highway Users Conference stepped up its highway campaign.[15] The group's newsletter, *Highway Highlights,* had become a glossy magazine, featuring inspiring articles from the so-called "highwaymen," the planners or powerful businesses with interests in highway-related industries like automobiles, gasoline, rubber, and concrete. Other publications supported by these lobbying groups included the *American Road Builder Magazine, Roads and Streets Magazine,* and *Engineering News-Record.*[16] The National Highway Users Conference, among other groups, published pamphlets and articles emphasizing the importance of the new system to manufacturing, farming, defense, and industry. Automobile manufacturers like General Motors (GM) could also claim to have done a patriotic duty that should be rewarded in peacetime. C. F. Kettering of GM addressed the country on a regular radio show, "As 'Ket' Sees It," in which he described the ways that the automobile industry had unified America. It had trained the technicians who were critical in wartime production and returned to the job to meet the postwar demand for automobiles. Typical of the promotion efforts was a 1954 GM film, entitled "Give Yourself the Green Light," that told the familiar saga of the inevitability of the highway and claimed that the country "didn't dream big enough." Given the massive proliferation of vehicles, it was the responsibility of every American to make highways for themselves and for "those in the back seat."[17]

When Congress returned in 1956, the highway lobbyists and promoters had done a thorough job of arousing the public. A joint House committee developed a bill that was revised by the Senate to incorporate some points of an earlier Gore bill. With additional compromises between the two houses, the bill was passed on June 26, 1956, and signed by President Eisenhower on June 29, 1956. The 42,000 miles of four-lane highways would be called the National System of Interstate and Defense Highways. The federal government would pay 90 percent of the costs, an even larger proportion than it did for defense highways in 1941. The bill had two titles, one controlling physical standards and the other controlling revenues. The physical standards were consistent with those reports of the BPR that had been published since 1939. Previously, federal highway funds had been allocated from the General Fund of the Treasury, but now revenues collected from state motor-vehicle user taxes would be held in a Highway Trust Fund and used on a pay-as-you-go basis for highway construction.[18]

Not only did interstate legislation describe a dumb network in terms of urban intermodality, but it would also control a fixed plan for a period of over twenty years. If anything, the highway system excluded information other than that which reinforced its own rules, funding mechanisms, and commercial interests. Highway critiques, like *Road to Ruin* (1968) by A. Q. Mowbray, specifically targeted the trust fund as a self-perpetuating institution that could direct tax monies to highways despite other transportation needs, and Helen Leavitt's *Superhighway-Superhoax* (1970) even included a family tree showing personnel linkages among highway-related business organizations and official state and federal highway departments. As evidenced by repeated articles on such things as materials, maintenance costs, trip length, traffic volume, and tire longevity in the BPR's journal, *Public Roads*, not only the market field associated with vehicle ownership but the statistical data regarding highway bankability and durability began to shape the traffic-engineered highway. As a federal project the highway system was also seen in terms of jobs and other conditions that could be quantified statistically or mathematically. The highway-building process was the most extended public works project in American history, and yet there were no mechanisms for learning and adaptation in the process but rather a process of monitoring greater return on the federal investment.

Notes

1. Ken Auletta, "Annals of Communication: Under the Wire," *The New Yorker* (17 January 1994):49.
2. The first official agency was the Office of Road Inquiry (ORI) established in 1893. Its next incarnations were the Office of Public Road Inquiry (OPRI) 1899 and the Office of Public Roads (OPR) in 1905. U.S. Federal Highway Administration, *America's Highways, 1776–1976*, 46, 52, 54, 60, 79.
3. Mark H. Rose, *Interstate: Express Highway Politics 1941–1956* (Lawrence: Regents Press of Kansas, 1979), 23.
4. U.S. Federal Highway Administration, *America's Highways, 1776–1976*, (Washington: Department of Transportation, U.S. Government Printing Office, 1977). Even before the turn of the century, an official of the Federal Office of Public Inquiry (OPI) proposed a transcontinental highway connecting two north-south highways, one on the east coast and one on the west coast.
5. Seely, *Building the American Highway System: Engineers as Policy Makers* (Philadelphia: Temple University Press, 1987), 38, 68, 225.
6. *America's Highways, 1776–1976*, 87; and Helen Leavitt, *Superhighway-Superhoax* (Garden City: New York: Doubleday and Co., 1970), 28.
7. Rose, 9, 2, 3, 10. In 1905, 78,000 automobiles were registered; in 1910, 458,500 automobiles were registered and by the 1920s automobile manufacturing was a major American industry.
8. Leavitt, *Superhighway-Superhoax*, 23–24; and U.S. FHA, *America's Highways, 1776–1976*, 108.
9. *America's Highways, 1776–1976*, 466.
10. Leavitt, 29, cites an issue of *Roads and Streets*, August 1954; and U.S. FHA, *America's Highways, 1776–1976*, 468.
11. Mel Scott, *American City Planning Since 1890* (Berkeley: University of California Press, 1969), 539–41.
12. Leavitt, 30, 30–51, 29–36, 32.
13. Ibid., 37–51.
14. *America's Highways, 1776–1976*, 468.
15. Ibid., 470.
16. Leavitt, 28–29, 115; and A Q. Mowbray, *The Road to Ruin* (New York: J. B. Lippincott Company, 1968), 22.
17. Charles F. Kettering, *As "Ket" Sees It: A Series of Radio Talks by C. F. Kettering of General Motors* (Detroit: General Motors Corporation), Undated; and *Give Yourself the Green Light*, Produced by the Jam Handy Organization for General Motors public relations, March 19, 1954.
18. *America's Highways, 1776–1976*, 471–72, 467–471.

2.1 REDUNDANCY AND INTERSTICE: TRANSCONTINENTAL AND INTERCITY NETWORKS

Although the interstate highway system was designed as an intercity network, some earlier experiments and proposals treated the highway as a long-distance transcontinental route that bypassed cities and interfaced terrestrial networks as well as other forms of conveyance like the railroad. Some even replicated the terminal and switching operatives of the railroad, while others proposed to place the highway in the service of national parks. In these proposals the highway not only mimicked the organizational repertoire of adjacent networks but also generated some interdependence or parallelism among them. Redundant or coincident organizations potentially facilitated interface among rail, water, and highway for not only intermodal exchange but network specialization.

Transcontinentals

Even the earliest transcontinental automobile crossings linked road building to the growing population of vehicles and to the vehicle as a product. Many of the turn-of-the-century crossings were promotional stunts where motorists set out across the country until they passed the edges of the last field and began to follow the ruts of the wagon trails that had settled the West. The first true cross-country highway was the Lincoln Highway (1913–1927). It was sponsored by the Lincoln Highway Association through donations and subscriptions from cement companies and automobile industries, and it was built, ostensibly, to promote a relatively insignificant invention—the Prest-O-Lite automobile lighting system.[1] Other booster groups who sponsored "themed" highways like the Lincoln Highway maintained private control over their projects but associated with the government to avail themselves of highway design expertise.

Perhaps the most unusual transcontinental highway networks were planned in conjunction with interstate parks. Some were privately funded by tourism while others were proposed as part of the national park system. For instance, in 1930, Congress entertained a proposal for an Eastern Park-to-Park Highway connecting Washington, Shenandoah National Park, the Great Smoky Mountains, and Mammoth Cave, near Louisville, Kentucky.[2] Another park-to-park highway bill, proposed in the House of Representatives in 1934 described four parkways that would link national parks across the entire continental United States. The interstices of these networks were not major U.S. cities, as they would later be in the interstate network, but were rather locations like Grand Canyon National Park, Boulder Dam, Yosemite, or Niagra Falls.[3] Yet another transcontinental park-to-park highway plan proposed to connect Acadia National Park in Maine with Everglades National Park in Florida, providing along the way an intercity route between Boston and Washington.[4] Skyline drives were another popular park-highway hybrid that routed a limited access roadway along the crest of a mountain range. In 1934, skyline drives were proposed for the Presidential Range, the Green Mountains, the Blue Ridge, and the Great Smoky Mountains.[5] The Blue Ridge Parkway, and another similar interstate parkway, the Natchez Trace, did not link national parks but rather merged the protocols of park and highway into giant linear interstate organizations of public land.

By the late 1930s and early 1940s, transcontinental roads were generally proposed in conjunction with national highway systems. The 1938 Bulkley Bill proposed a system of ten transcontinental highways. Three would run east-west and seven would run north-south. The highways would have from four to twelve lanes arranged within a 300 foot right-of-way, and like a railroad, they would be as straight as possible to efficiently connect two points, in most cases two cities (figure 2.1.1). In 1939 the Synder Bill proposed a similar system of nine transcontinentals each with 100 foot roadways and 500 foot-wide rights-of-way. By 1940 there were several different working models of the limited-access highway or parkway in America and four major transcontinental routes, the Lincoln Highway, the Santa Fe Trail, the Broadway of America, and the Yellowstone Route. Cross-country motorists could also weave through the many federal-state sponsored roads some of which operated across state boundaries and even within subnational regional systems.[6]

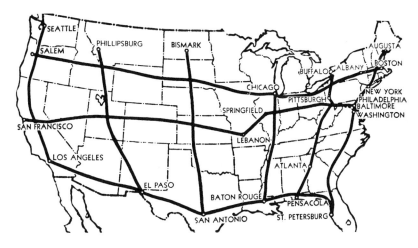

2.1.1 Bulkley plan for superhighways (1938). Norman Bel Geddes, *Magic Motorways* (New York: Random House, 1940), 257.

"Trunk-Line Traffic Tracks"

One of the first highway proposals that looked opportunistically at redundancy and possible intermodality among various transportation networks was made not by a traffic engineer but by a landscape architect. In 1923 Warren H. Manning (1860–1938) published what he called "A National Plan Study Brief" that, similar to the proposed studies of the technocracy movement, surveyed water power, mineral resources, soils, factory centers, rainfall, forested areas, and infrastructure within the United States and proposed a new plan for their management. Manning also called for a national planning committee that would, after a similar survey, establish regional designations across the country. Saying that "The great world nations are now interdependent units," Manning imagined that these regions would be the main units in a national and international system of production and distribution. He also assumed that production quotients and regional designations could be determined and quantified and that the transportation routes could be sized and routed accordingly. Manning inventoried the country's main geological formations and identified the well-worn paths of travel through its valleys and basins. Acknowledging federal and private efforts to build transcontinental highways and noting that the federal government was "opening the way for great national trunk-line thoroughfares," Manning proposed a system of "trunk-line traffic tracks." The tracks would be composed of 220 foot-wide trunk lines with eight roadways, four in each direction, and the roadways would be specialized for freight vehicles, express trucks, passenger buses, and automobiles. They would be located outside the city and Manning proposed, "Where practicable such great trunk-lines should lie next to railways and waterways, and be provided with facilities for freight interchange." He also proposed adjustments to reorganize the railroad system so that highways might serve the railroads "as feeders rather than competitors." When framing the main issues of a national transportation system, Manning predicted that the greatest challenges would be related to "adequate terminals, traffic classification, and exchange points for the highway, railway, waterway, and airway routes." Traffic from the city and from other kinds of state roads would access the trunk line through interchanges where "directors of traffic" would "classify" the vehicles and dispatch them onto the appropriate and least trafficked roadway (figure 2.1.2).[7]

In its organizational architecture, the most significant aspect of Manning's proposal was the way in which he increased the complexity and capacity of the network by simply doubling it. Manning mapped two sets of thoroughfares, one for commercial routes and another for recreational routes. These two networks of roadways and landways were to cross and run in parallel. The recreational routes were given names like "Niagra way," "Grazing way" or "Ozark way," while the commercial routes were called "great north tracks" or "great south tracks." The recreational routes would accommodate the changing character of the land and deliver the motorist to diverse regions, while commercial routes would accommodate changing patterns of distribution for agricultural and industrial products. The apparent redundancies and inefficiencies of the system would help to make it more specialized and intelligent since, though limited, the network would have some internal means of flexibility and adaptation. These networks were determined by existing conditions in the land but they would also begin to provide a framework for the acquisition of additional urban or recreational land.[8]

Cement Railroads

Like Manning's network, MacKaye's "cement railroads" also merged highways with railroads to achieve several different kinds of intermodal exchange. MacKaye called the highway a "new kind of railway" and likened the automobile to an individually operated locomotive or a "cross between a carriage and

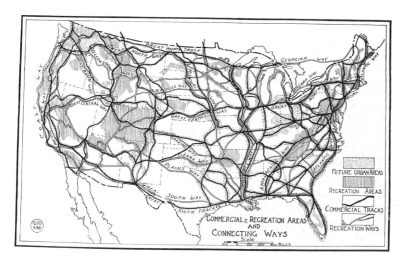

2.1.2 Warren Manning's 1923 mapping of transcontinental highways, titled "Commercial and Recreation Areas and Connecting Ways." Warren H. Manning, "A National Plan Study Brief," special supplement to *Landscape Architecture* (July 1923) vol. 13, no. 4:17.

a railroad car." He would later even describe the automobile as an amphibious vehicle because it potentially reduced the number of exchanges between car, water, railroad, and automobile, saying, "Our motorcar jumps in and out from one medium of transport to another, just like a frog jumping from dry land into the water and out again."[9] Cement railroads would be designed with double tracks, junctions, and separations between freight, passenger, express, and local traffic. They would be insulated from commercial buildings and residences, and the junction points or "station stops" would be operated as they were for the railroad by "switch and signal."[10]

Most significantly, the cement railroad proposed to build the automobile tracks along the abandoned rights-of-way of other infrastructure networks so that they might be better positioned "to serve as links in an allied system." MacKaye claimed that half of a highway between Boston and New York already existed in the form of approximately 100 miles of abandoned railroad tracks between the two cities, and he mapped possible routes for converted railroads in Connecticut and Massachusetts as well (figure 2.1.3). Abandoned, short-distance rail rights-of-way could be converted from steel to concrete, thus making highways and railways part of an economy of land use and

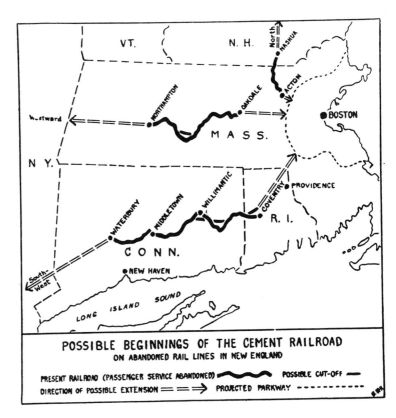

2.1.3 Map showing reuse of railroad rights-of-way for limited access motorways. Benton MacKaye, "Cement Railroads," *The Survey,* LXVIII (November 1, 1932), 541–542.

making both networks more viable in terms of construction costs and unrecovered revenues. The redundant networks would provide specialized services beyond the capacity of any one network.[11]

Regional-Metropolitan Highways

In the same way that early long-distance highways replicated railroad operatives or responded to landscape activities, regional parkways were influenced not only by the activities of the landscape but also by the complexities of the urban core. Just as the Lincoln Highway reached the west coast, the Westchester parkways joined the Bronx River Parkway to form a metropolitan highway network north of New York City. Parkway designers used the expanded street section to address a number of civic and landscape agendas related not only to aesthetics but also to the manipulation of land value and the control of the metropolitan regional environs. City Beautiful planners, designed the spatial relationships as well as the financial protocols and the logistics of collaboration between different planning jurisdictions, projecting parkway networks as a new framework for transportation between city and country. The Bronx River Parkway, outside the New York City limits, for instance, was designed to organize utilities and transportation while also addressing issues of conservation and pollution. The Bronx River was cleaned and dredged to build the parkway, and the wide right-of-way purchased for the parkway would be an obstacle to further pollution. New York City and Westchester County shared the costs and Westchester County provided a new sewer line along the length of the parkway. From 1910 to 1932 land values increased along the parkway by almost 1,200 percent.[12] Regional-scale, intercity parkways also served as the federal government's rehearsals for the long-distance interstate highways. The first federal parkway, legislated in 1928, was the Mount Vernon Memorial Highway, and it was followed in 1930 by the George Washington Memorial Parkway and the Colonial National Parkway that traveled from Jamestown through Williamstown to Yorktown. Meanwhile state and federal partnerships or metropolitan agencies like those headed by Robert Moses in New York City continued to develop parkways turnpikes and other intercity highway networks that would also serve as models for the Interstate.[13]

Toll Roads and Free Roads and Interregional Highways

Two federal reports that would provide the blueprints for interstate highway design were ostensibly initiated in the context of plans for a transcontinental network. In 1938, Congress charged the Bureau of Public Roads (BPR) to study the feasibility of three east-west and three north-south transcontinental superhighways to be operated as toll roads. The BPR's report, *Toll Roads and Free Roads,* however, was a trial balloon for the bureau's new science of traffic engineering. Another pivotal federal report entitled *Interregional Highways* (1944), inherited conclusions and data generated by *Toll Roads and Free Roads.* Taken together, the two reports recorded the prevailing intelligence associated with traffic engineering as well as some of the last alternative proposals to the midcentury interstate highway. The dry bureaucratic tone of the reports was essential to their persuasive power, and even when leading to illogical conclusions the sober, stepwise presentation of engineering expertise was rarely questioned. Using statistical models, the active organization of automobile movement would gradually begin to reflect the shape of a population of vehicle owners.

The BPR's initial charge to determine the feasibility of long-distance highways as toll roads proved to be pivotal in the determination of the interstate highway as an intercity rather than transcontinental system. As proposed, the 14,300 mile system would bypass most cities. Through data collections, however, the bureau determined that neither transcontinental or semicontinental travel was insufficient to warrant construction of these highways as toll roads. Most trips were relatively short and they originated in cities. There was also a greater likelihood that long-distance travel would originate in cities. If the highways were to be operated as toll roads, only the areas surrounding the largest cities would provide the necessary traffic to make the proposal feasible.[14] Consequently, the bureau recommended a network of free highways arranged as an intercity matrix. The BPR had already aligned itself with the policies of the War Department and the state highway departments in support of a comprehensive nationwide system of interregional highways. The recommended plan proposed, not six transcontinentals (14,300 miles), but a 26,700 mile system with the federal government supporting more than half the costs. Highway taxes on gasoline would be one source of funding. This funding scheme was in effect until the legislation of the interstate highway in 1956, when the government virtually funded the highway building project in its entirety.[15] The various mappings of the network showed the highways entering the center of large cities, and while there was a some indication that specialized infrastructure would be necessary for urban areas, apart from the mention of terminal and beltlines, there was no discussion of what would constitute "adequate facilities" for handling increased traffic. In fact, there was some evidence that the BPR believed these highways would address urban congestion.[16]

Another significant highway report, *Interregional Highways* (1944) was requested by FDR to investigate the possibilities of a national interregional highway system. Not surprisingly, after studying data from BPR and Defense Department deliberations, the report reached the same conclusion that a nationwide system relying on taxation for its funding must serve the urban

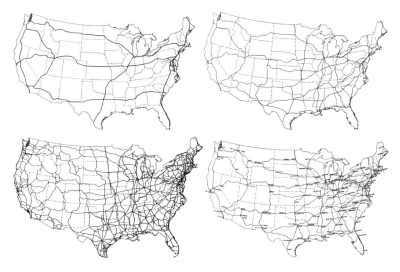

2.1.4 Interstate highway networks projected by the Interregional Highways Committee (1944) and based on similar mappings from the Bureau of Public Roads publication *Toll Roads and Free Roads* (1939): the 14,300 mile, 26,700 mile, 78,800 mile network and the recommended 33,920 mile network. President of the United States, *Interregional Highways*, 78th Congress, 2d session, House document No. 379 (Washington, D.C.: Government Printing Office, 1944), 138, 139, 142, 7.

areas where traffic was greatest. A staff from the BPR served the committee in analyzing 14,300, 29,300, 48,300, and 78,800 mile networks, and it finally endorsed a 39,000 mile interstate scheme with 33,900 miles of rural highways and 5,000 miles of urban routes. The committee was aware that the network would both "attract" and "serve" a greater traffic volume, and that it would not solve urban congestion problems.[17] Highways were portrayed, however, as urban planning tools for redistributing population to the suburbs and paving over urban blight, and though urban routes would be responsible for two-thirds of the total cost of the network, the report treated even the 78,800 mile network as another iteration of a similar organization (figure 2.1.4).[18]

The transcity connectors and the long-haul routes had entirely different requirements in relation to congestion, finance, and intermodality. Yet surprisingly, apart from showing urban sections of the highway as elevated or stacked structures, both reports indicated that the physical specifications for intercity highways should be essentially the same as for transcontinentals.[19]

Norman Bel Geddes

For Norman Bel Geddes, architect of General Motors' Futurama exhibit, highways were the work of designers as well as traffic engineers. Bel Geddes' book *Magic Motorways* (1940) published many of his own ideas for, among other things, intersections, lighting systems control towers, and a national system of highways. Bel Geddes designed his national scheme as an overlay on the BPR's 26,700 mile proposal that he considered to be a "palliative for present traffic ills rather than as a preventive for the future." In determining the interstices of the network, he first attempted to connect all the urban areas. When the result was a very dense web of highways concentrated on the east coast, he devised another triangulated grid of straight highways evenly distributed across the entire country. The grid would pass very close to but not enter the largest cities. Intersections in the resulting grid were subcenters that served smaller metropolitan areas.[20] Bel Geddes recognized the importance of traffic loads coming from cities, but he did not necessarily wish to reinforce that pattern. If anything, his national motorway plan favored the idea of building highways on land that was less expensive and that would transport a population away from the city into more open country. Bel Geddes' prophesies often aligned with Frank Lloyd Wright's concerns about the use of open land for new development patterns. Farms and towns like those in the Futurama model would develop along transportation routes rather than in direct dependence on the metropolis. The difference between Bel Geddes proposal and the BPR's transcity proposal was enormous, since Geddes' grid would have established an entirely new network of urbanism and exchange, operating independent of urban areas (figure 2.1.5).

What is inexcusable, it seems to me, is that highway engineers have, with magnificent fidelity repeated all the worst errors of the railroad era and, because of their public support, have widened their scope. Instead of adding a new element of flexibility and breadth to a railroad system that had become rigid in its concentration on intercontinental traffic and had produced a linear distribution of population, the highway engineers have largely been duplicating the railroad system and—as in the New

Though the highway was designed specifically for a single carrier and a limited range of speeds, it would eventually be routed in a way that maximized its contact with the most intricate and complex networks in dense urban areas. The chief parameters for design of the interstate system would be vehicle populations and numbers of trips between cities. These statistical studies reinforced easy, sure equations about the size and morphology of highways as well as their financing. There would be no diverse set of urban exchange points offering specialized or adaptable service and, while the highway would actually follow the railroad into the city, it would remain segregated from it (figure 2.1.6).

Helen Leavitt's exposé of highway legislation, *Superhighway-Superhoax* (1970) concludes with a story about President Eisenhower in a meeting with

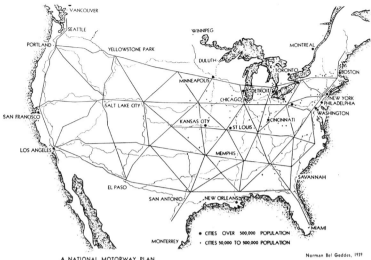

A NATIONAL MOTORWAY PLAN

Norman Bel Geddes, 1939

● CITIES OVER 500,000 POPULATION
· CITIES 50,000 TO 500,000 POPULATION

2.1.5 1939 national motorway plan. Norman Bel Geddes, *Magic Motorways* (New York: Random House, 1940), 278.

2.1.6 Cartoon with caption—"Nature's Carpet" [city parkways] by John W. Morley. National Committee on the Housing Emergency, Inc., *Tomorrow's Town,* June 1944, 1.

York and the Connecticut throughways—have been supplanting it. Rejecting the opportunity of enlarging the scope of our public transportation system, our public authorities have been dismantling it; and in the very act of doing this, they are both undermining the city and degrading the country side, and, not least, reducing our transportation facilities.[22]
—Lewis Mumford

highway engineers in 1959, three years after he had signed the interstate highway legislation. As he viewed plans for the local network in Washington, D.C., he was surprise to learn that interstate highways would go through urban areas, since he had understood that they would go around urban centers. He was distressed by the amount of automobile traffic entering the city as well as the highway traffic he encountered when going outside of the city to play golf. Just a few years earlier in 1954, Eisenhower had proposed two transcontinental highways, one going east-west from New York to Portland, Oregon, and another traveling north-south from the upper Mississippi to the Gulf. Ironically, Eisenhower's proposal, though fairly late in the history of highway developments, resembled in intent and character some of the earliest efforts at building transcontinental highways and parkways.[21]

Notes

1. Lincoln Highway Association, *The Lincoln Highway: The Story of a Crusade that Made History* (New York, Dodd, Mead and Company: 1935), 9; and Norman Bel Geddes, *Magic Motorways* (New York: Random House, 1940), 144.
2. Harley E. Jolley, *The Blue Ridge Parkway* (Knoxville: The University of Tennessee Press, 1969), 15–18.
3. U.S. Congress, House of Representatives, "A Bill: For the utilization of the recreational areas of the United States by a national parkway on a 200 foot right-of-way connecting the national parks." H. R. 9896. 73rd Congress, 2nd Session. Washington: U.S. Government Printing Office, 9 June 1934. The bill proposed that in the East, a parkway would run from Bar Harbor, Maine, to Miami, Florida. In the West, the parkway would connect Grand Canyon National Park, Boulder Dam, Yosemite, and finally Mount Rainier National Park in Washington. In the North, the parkway would connect Mount Rainier, Yellowstone, Grand Teton, Wind Cave National Parks, the Great Lakes, Niagara Falls, the Mohawk Valley, and finally the Eastern National Parkway. In the South, the Great Smoky Mountains would be linked to the Grand Canyon National Park.
4. U.S. National Resources Board: District No. 1, New England Regional Planning Commission. Boston to Washington Limited Motorway, preliminary report. Boston: New England Regional Planning Commission, 22 May 1935.
5. Benton MacKaye, "Flankline vs. Skyline," *Appalachia*, 20 (1934): 104. MacKaye was opposed to skyline drives, proposing instead that the highway occupy the "flankline" and leave the crestline for exploring on foot.
6. Bel Geddes, 255–56, 145.
7. Warren H. Manning, "A National Plan Study Brief," special supplement to *Landscape Architecture*, vol. 13, no. 4, (July 1923): 3, 4, 16–18. Manning included an alarming remark in the article, saying, ". . . the United States is especially favored as a home for the white race and for the development of its highest civilization."
8. Ibid., 18, 17, plate after 16.
9. Benton MacKaye, "Motorway Legislation: Dual Transport vs. Monotransport," of-

fice memorandum to Tracy Augur, head planner, from Benton MacKaye, regional planner, 19 February 1936, 9.

10. Benton MacKaye, "Cement Railroads," *The Survey* 68 (1 November 1932): 541–542. MacKaye was familiar with Manning's proposals.

11. Ibid.

12. John Nolen and Henry V. Hubbard, *Harvard City Planning Studies, Volume XI: Parkways and Land Values* (London: Oxford University Press, 1937), xii, xi; U.S. Federal Highway Administration, *America's Highways, 1776–1976* (Washington: Department of Transportation, U.S. Government Printing Office, 1977), 133; and *Parkways and Land Values*, 93, 72–100.

13. *America's Highways, 1776–1976*, Rae, 79–81. The Saw Mill River Parkway (completed in 1930), the Hutchinson River (completed in 1928), and the Cross County were characterized as recreational throughways and park connectors. They were based on the Bronx River Parkway idea but were largely used by commuters. The parkways were tied to several urban programs, but the parkways of Westchester Boston and Kansas City all followed natural features of the land. At the time in Westchester, following the rivers generally also meant following existing lines of traffic flow into and around the city.

14. U.S. Bureau of Public Roads, *Tolls Roads and Free Roads*, 76th Congress, 1st session, H. doc. no. 272, v. 20, 1939, 13, 44, 41, 33, 50–52.

15. Ibid., 121–22. In 1941, The Defense Highway Act increased state subsides for roads connecting to wartime defense plants. The federal government stepped up its contribution from 50 percent to 75 percent for this effort. Since defense justified increased federal expenditures, this act set an important precedent. All ensuing legislation and arguments for highways emphasized the highway as a defense asset. The interstate was even discussed as a method of evacuating cities, though the common wisdom was that it was not a network designed for heavy or variable urban traffic volume. *America's Highways, 1776–1976*, 467.

16. U.S. Bureau of Public Roads, *Tolls Roads and Free Roads*, 90, 110, 111. Not only did the report assert the need for this intercity network but it also proposed that this kind of limited-access highway addressed central urban congestion. The report praised the "bold" deployment of the idea in the New York City region with the Henry Hudson Parkway and Merrit Parkways, and it called for new transcity arteries as a means of replacing aging inner-city infrastructure.

17. President of the United States, *Interregional Highways*, 78th Congress, 2d session, H. doc. no. 379. Washington, D.C.: Government Printing Office, 1944, 4.

18. Ibid., passim.

19. U.S. Bureau of Public Roads, *Tolls Roads and Free Roads*, 121–22; and President of the United States, *Interregional Highways*, 64 and plates VII, X.

20. Bel Geddes, 257, 278, 81, 275–78.

21. Leavitt, *Superhighway-Superhoax*, 298–99, 29.

22. Lewis Mumford, "On Freedom, Freeways and Flexibility: The Private Correspondence of Messrs Wolfe and Mumford," *JAIA*, 1959, 74–77.

2.2 SWITCH: TERMINAL, INTERCHANGE, VEHICLE

During the interstate's many design deliberations, federal traffic engineers and other transportation experts continually emphasized the importance of terminals and points of interchange between air, rail, surface, and water routes as among the most critical sites in the new limited-access highway network. Despite all the careful and controversial planning of the highway, however, federal agencies did not conduct sustained research concerning the effects of this long-distance system on the urban fabric before the interstate was built. Outside of the federal bureaucracy, however, municipal authorities, railroads, electronics companies, independent designers, and even automobile companies proposed intermodal inventions for interchanges, terminals, and specialized vehicles that would act as switching mechanisms for exchange between carriers and networks. Some were mechanical, and some were electronic. Unlike a binary switch with two positions, however, most of these transportation switches were like a differential, designed to perform a more continuous operation of translation to regulate or modulate the organization over a period of time. Some were located at the intersections of various networks and others operated as distributed agents or vehicles within the network.

Terminals

When federal agencies or Washington think tanks recommended urban highway terminals, which—like railroad terminals—would store vehicles and transfer freight or passengers to other carriers, there were few precedents to which they could refer. Throughout his career, in and out of government, Wilfred Owen was among those who wrote, in the voice of the Washington-trained policy technician, about the need for consolidated urban and regional transportation authorities as well as bus, truck, and automobile terminals.[1] In writings for the NRPB or the Brookings Institution, Owen studied a range of intermodal issues from terminal logistics and economics to new transportation gadgetry like carveyors, moving sidewalks, and convertiplanes.[2] He applauded New York's Port Authority Bus Terminal that integrated expressway, bus, and parking facilities. The Port Authority's Union Motor Terminal, between the Holland Tunnel and Hudson River, piers was also a complete facility for freight transfer from large to small carriers with specialized equipment, mechanical conveyance, truck repair, and parking as well as areas to accommodate business functions and traveling truckers. Another Port Authority terminal, the Union Inland Terminal, was essentially a vertical loading dock inside a block-sized commercial loft building. With giant truck elevators, it collapsed storage, business, and delivery functions into a single intermodal structure. Entrepreneurs and municipal authorities in other large cities also attempted individual experiments like those in the New York metropolitan area.[3] *Interregional Highways* has sometimes been considered one of the better federal highway planning documents because it discussed, even if in a limited way, the need for terminals, parking structures, and circumferential transfer points.[4] The committee recommended consolidating infrastructure networks, specifically rail and highway lines, and it cited two examples of infrastructure stacking in New York City—the Henry Hudson Parkway and the East River Drive.[5]

In 1946 industrial designer, Egmont Arens, designed a series of terminal facilities that he called the "Manhattan Inner-Loop Skyway." Arens was among a generation of industrial designers that included Norman Bel Geddes, Raymond Loewy, and Donald Desky who would be fascinated with vehicles, from automobiles to space capsules. Though futuristic vehicle designs often satisfied the desire for transportation innovations. Arens project proposed to reorganize the city's highway networks, and with typical planning brarado, it also claimed to both traffic congestion and housing shortages. An elevated arterial roadway would provide a continuous loop of terminal facilities "for every type of vehicle, including several decks of parking space, bus terminals, mail freight, and package sorting stations" as well as interurban bus connections, airport links, and helicopter transportation. Towers rising above the arterial would maximize "housing cubage." The loop would simply subtract existing urban fabric in its path. Only modern buildings would be "left standing." On-street parking would be replaced by parking garages. The entire system would link up to Moses plans for elevated crosstown arterials, like the proposed Mid-Manhattan Expressway. Arens also optimistically predicted that the entire loop could be traveled in sixteen minutes.[6]

Interstate legislation sanctioned the use of not only air rights but also the area below the highway for parking or other public programs. This feature might have been used to pursue peripheral parking facilities, stacking of various transportation modalities, or specialized switch buildings for exchange of passengers and freight, but in most official planning reports, air rights were treated as stand-ins for real considerations regarding the highway in urban fabric. When faced with the argument that highway funds robbed money from other urgently needed urban programs like housing, public administrators often offered air rights as a possible consolation site for housing or as a bargaining chip in relocating housing that was to be pulled down for highway building.[7]

Just as the interstate was being legislated in the 1950s, reinforcing the dominance of wheeled vehicles among all carriers, railroads and automobile companies were beginning to experiment in earnest with intermodality. The federal government freely subsidized the automobile and trucking industries while curbing the power of the railroad through regulation of its sometimes corruptible practices. This combination of policies exacerbated the segregation between highway and rail companies. Railroads and truckers were often wary of each other and not always enthusiastic about adopting intermodal plans. Many carriers continued to experiment within existing ports, warehouses, and terminals, however, to facilitate freight exchanges between trucks and railroad cars since often a mixture of train, truck, and ship travel was the most efficient means of conveying freight. Even automobile companies understood the power of controlling the switches in transportation systems.[8]

Like contemporary battles over software platforms, from the 1920s on, a number of competing intermodal inventions were introduced, each vying to be the dominant platform. Most were inspired by eccentric situations that invited some cross-reference between different transportation protocols. For instance, some railroads provided a "piggyback" service where truck trailers could be transported on flat cars, and the piggyback idea was often called "circus loading" because it borrowed a technique that had been used in loading circus wagons onto flatcars. A few railroad executives also had experience

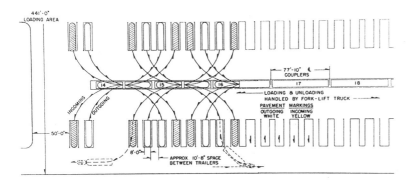

2.2.1 Intermodal arrangement designed by General Motors in 1953. David DeBoer, *Piggyback and Containers* (San Marino, California: Golden West Books, 1992), 30. Illustration from GM Rail-Highway Coordination booklet.

in both the automobile and railroad business, and to them the intermodal puzzle was particularly compelling since trucking was taking over a growing percentage of their business. In 1953, even General Motors Electro-Motive Division engineered equipment and designed a loading protocol for piggy-back trailers that would allow them to be driven onto the flatcar by truck, unleashed and secured for travel (figure 2.2.1). Each gadget, machine, or coupling entered the market place with optimistic claims of fitness and usually an enthusiastic name, such as Adapto, Minipiggi, Flexi-van or Trailer Train. There were also several ways in which either the truckers or the railroad could legally provide the service of truck-trailer transport. Either company could broker the shipment and provide the equipment, or a third party, based in the terminal, could handle any portion of the shipping transfer. As inventions and protocols proliferated however, and no standard emerged from the lengthy trial-and-error process terminals were often outfitted with incompatible couplings and equipment for piggyback service.[9]

As early as the 1920s and 1930s, railroads provided a container service for freight that occupied less than a train-car load and even developed mechanized terminals to hoist the containers onto trucks. In the mid 1950s, the container idea resurfaced not as the small stackable box of previous years but as a truck trailer without wheels. Container handling required terminal mechanization of some kind, however, and the closest thing to a standard in most ports or terminals was still the truck trailer with its wheels in place. As terminals began to mechanize in the 1960s and 1970s, several different types of cranes and hoists were used for fitting either trailers or containers onto flatcars. With some guidance from the federal government, many of the competing formats gave way to con-tainer shipment during the 1970s. Mechanized terminals handling double-stacked containers provided a truly competitive alternative to long-haul trucking. In the 1980s various carriers not only consolidated within their own ranks but also merged with other carriers. In the same way that computer companies have merged with compa-nies providing television and internet services, rail, truck, and steamship merged and created their own intermodal terminals and cross-formats.[10]

One idea for terminal switching, which—like Aren's proposal—included not only freight but passenger exchange, came from Lawrence Halprin, an architect, planner and Washington consultant during the 1960s and 1970s. Halprin called for "multiple use of the highway corridor both vertically and horizontally. . . ." His "traffic architecture," as he called it, proposed new sec-tions for stacking and condensing highways, transit, and other programs in the urban fabric. Outside the city, Halprin proposed selective land acquisition of parcels adjacent to the highway as a means of gaining additional revenues and thus leveraging renovations to the system.[11] In *Freeways*, one of Halprin's several books about highways, he featured a photomontage design by Geof-frey Jellicoe for the Ponte Vecchio in Florence that proposed to condense traffic, hotels, entertainment, and sports facilities in one building envelope. Halprin's traffic architecture also appeared to reference Jellicoe's *Motopia*, a projected city that merged automobile circulation with other conglomerate programs into a giant grid of richly sectioned megastructures and rooftop roadways.[12]

Interchanges

Prior to the design of the interstate, several designers of the period consid-ered traffic engineering to be within their purview and developed new types of highway interchanges for exurban highway junctions. Most highway inter-changes systems, like the "T" crossing and the cloverleaf, were designed to provide uninterrupted speed and increased safety through simple grade sepa-rations and entry ramps. In 1935, landscape architect Charles Downing Lay proposed an unusual merger of highway interchange and community. In Lay's formulations, the limited-access highway was a protocol for recombining new and old roadways as well as a means of appropriating land for different kinds of development. Given several separated lanes of traffic, directions could be assigned to each lane on an alternating basis according to traffic flow. Through independent alignments and the possible divergence of the two roadways, Lay also proposed to incorporate existing roadways and create parks within the irregular spaces between them. Exurban communities might also be sited between separated roadways that were approximately a mile apart. The roadways would meet again for important bridges or intersections. The several hundred feet insulating the roadway would provide a kind of greenbelt around the small community, and routing the highway away from urban areas thus reduced land acquisition costs.[13] Frank Lloyd Wright also designed interchanges within the context of Broadacre City designs, and like most interchanges, his designs provided continuous movement through grade separations. Wright's interchange was a monolithic landscaped structure, however, bermed into the ground by its underpass and designed to include a partially covered walkway so that it provided its own spatial enclosures rather than merely a crossing between two highways.[14] Though the typical cloverleaf radius was 75 feet, the Bel Geddes interchange featured in the 1939 Futurama exhibit allowed each lane to thread its way through the crossing around a 1,000 foot radius without reducing speeds. Multidecking at large intersections would further relieve congestion. Borrowing operatives from both the railroad and the airport, Bel Geddes also proposed that overpass bridges broadcast electronic radio controls to dispatch cars and monitor speeds. The roadway would also be redesigned so that the control strip and lighting source would run under the center-line of the automobile. While in the 1960s there was interest in America in buildings accommodating highways, vehicles, and conglomerate programs, there was perhaps nothing that displayed an overt interest in exurban interchange design, and very little work addressed urban interchanges as directly as did the proposals of, for instance Brian Richards and Warren Chalk in Britain with their 1966 design of a superstructure to handle exchanges between four transportation systems. Switching intelligence became less important than optimizing larger networks of movement (figures 2.2.2 and 2.2.3).[15]

Convertible Vehicles and Automatic Systems

Many speculations about intermodality would eventually reside in the car itself as a convertible object. Wright was one of the few architects to make spatial relationships of community at least somewhat dependent on the

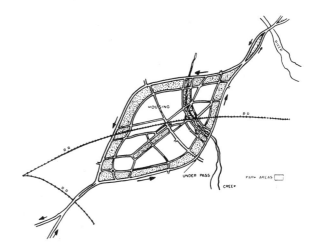

2.2.2 Scheme for housing communities built between roadways of a limited access highway. Charles Dowing Lay, "New Town for High Speed Road," *Landscape Architect* (November 1935):353.

2.2.3 Control bridge: Future motorway style. Norman Bel Geddes, *Magic Motorways* (New York: Random House, 1940), 81.

convertibility of the vehicle. With the autogyro, the vehicle itself provided an intermodal switch by adapting to short and long-distance travel. By the late 1930s and early 1940s, science fiction designs for futuristic vehicles crossed the car with airplanes, trains, and rockets. In 1944, in his regular radio address, "As 'Ket' Sees It," General Motors President C. F. Kettering, assessing the many magazine illustrations of "your car of tomorrow" that appeared during the war years, said, "Some of the cars they show have transparent, plastic tops, and bodies shaped like an egg. Others have detachable helicopter blades or wings so that you can drive through Main Street traffic like an ordinary car. When you get home you simply snap on the wings or blades. Then you travel through the air to lake or seashore for the weekend. These 'dream cars' or 'magic carpets' capture the fancy of everyone."[16] When individual vehicle production could not support these more extreme forms of convertibility, rocketship and airplane hybrids would only be evidenced in the car's aerodynamic styling, thus substituting futuristic imagery and vestigial details for intelligence and complexity in the system.

In the end, the typical car was not very convertible or amphibious. It did not fly, swim, or attach itself to radio controlled tracks. Bel Geddes' vision of an automated highway, however, remained an ongoing quest among transportation researchers. Radio, radar, and other electronic devices were primarily used in piecemeal ways by law enforcement and for traffic engineering studies. Publications like Science Digest projected the expanded use of these devices to create the "car that drives itself," and in the 1950s General Motors developed the "Autoline" prototype for electronically controlled vehicles and tracks not unlike those of the Futurama exhibit. Communications companies like RCA and Philco also researched the concept.[17]

Although early twentieth-century transportation research focused on replacing mass transit with individually controlled vehicles, from the 1950s through the 1970s, both public and private research often focused on either new forms of mass transit or dual-mode, personal transit vehicles that hybridized automobile and mass-transit vehicles, thus providing not only fixed stops within the city but also individual destinations outside the city. For instance, an automatic skybus or monorail might follow standard routes through the city and then enter a more finely grained network of roadways. Some of these proposals involved an entirely new physical infrastructure while others devised some kind of adaptive mechanism for the car, allowing it to attach to a roadway control track. Most of the control tracks involved some kind of guideway to propel the car's wheels or lock into its chassis while others proposed undercarriage pallets or roof-mounted systems. Among these prototypes were the Commucar, the Glideway, the StaRRcar, the Urmobile (Cornell Aeronautical Laboratories), the PAT or Palletted Automated Transport System, and the Mustang (Ford Motor Company).[18] Other dual-mode systems proposed that the individual car might be conveyed by mass-transit tracks. For instance, one project for a pneumatic system provided automobile adapters onto which one's vehicle could ride piggyback. This assemblage would be propelled on a cushion of air over a double-track system and switched at particular stops.[19]

Though the automatic vehicle might only be desirable for long trips, it was only financially feasible in congested areas. In America in the 1970s, research continued on a dual-mode transport system for repetitive commuter trips in large cities. Congress also heard testimony about the Aramis project in France. For twenty years, this project attempted to develop a mass-transit system of autolike vehicles that would follow tracks but split off to deliver individual passengers to their destinations. Though most of these proposals ran into insurmountable problems, the idea appeared to present such a tantalizing possibility to academic researchers, automobile companies, aeronautical companies, and governments both in America and abroad that all of them continued to fund projects for dual-mode vehicles (figure 2.2.4).[20]

Systems Analysis

Highway planners of the 1960s and 1970s used computers to study as well as to automate transportation systems. They were also using systems analysis and abstract biological metaphors similar to those of the cyberneticists to make projections about the future organization of the city and its infrastructure.[21]

For instance, in 1966, *Scientific American* featured an article on systems analysis of urban transportation published by a research group working from a federally funded Housing and Urban Development study contract. The group built mathematical computer models for several cities and used them to study different approaches to renovating urban transportation problems. As the quintessential planning committee, the research group was composed of a "large team of specialists: engineers, city planners, mathematicians, sociologists, economists, and computer programmers." They set out to test the effectiveness of either making piecemeal adjustments to the transportation system or replacing it with new personal transit systems. Perhaps not surpris-

2.2.4 Dual-mode tracked air cushion vehicles Francois Giraud, "Tracked Air Cushion Vehicles," *High-Speed Ground Transportation; Proceedings* (Pittsburgh: Transportation Research Institute, Carnegie-Mellon University, 1969), 26.

ingly, when the eager scientists and planners loaded in the data for a new transit system with all-new personal transportation "capsules," it performed significantly better than the piecemeal approach. The report also concluded that replacing all the infrastructure of the various cities modeled would even be cheaper than attempting to gradually improve existing ones. No personal transportation systems had been successfully built, but the group saw no reason to think that the technology would not soon be perfected.

Whereas dual-mode mass transit systems usually encountered difficulty in accommodating a large volume of destinations, more recent pilot projects have targeted commuters as a traffic population that not only travels a clear and repetitive route but is also responsible for a great deal of urban congestion. Several new plans have suggested that a commuter lane, not unlike the carpool lane, be devoted to automated systems if either the vehicle or the lane was equipped with special infrastructure. A "free-agent" computerized vehicle could presumably sense obstacles, regulate the speed and route, and even mix with other kinds of traffic. Gathering the cars in groups or platoons would offer the added advantage of increasing the capacity of the highway. Options for these infrastructure additions might include magnetized roadways, transition ramps, barriers, control towers, and holding areas for cars whose drivers have exited the automated portion but have either fallen asleep or are not prepared to regain control of the vehicle. Highway interests have always been good at organizing themselves and sponsoring research efforts. The National Automated Highway System Consortium (NAHSC) has already tested demonstration projects in the field. Many ideas about automated controls are already being rehearsed not only in pilot projects but in new automobile gadgetry involving both digital and radar equipment, such as cruise control, global positioning systems (GPS), and collision alerting systems, all of which relinquish some control over the vehicle while also enhancing its performance.[22] Some navigational systems, like the ADVANCE system tested in the Chicago area, simply provide information about traffic patterns and congestion along commuter routes so that drivers may respond more intelligently.[23]

Supported by increased computing power, late twentieth-century complexity theorists have continued the work of midcentury systems analysts, and both groups have demonstrated the inadequacy of the BPR's statistical method of traffic analysis. Most of these efforts have involved simulation models that with some accuracy replay traffic patterns in major urban areas and potentially uncover relationships useful to highway planning as well as efforts to program automated vehicles. The experiments have often positioned the vehicle as itself a switch multiplied within a population of switches, and the enthusiastic promotion of these studies has often appeared to be motivated by the desire for the discovery of some kind of recursive or comprehensive structure in complex traffic organizations.[24]

Meanwhile, planners like Lawrence Halprin were alienated from the giant bureaucratic processes that continued to produce traffic-engineered highways. Halprin regarded himself as an enlightened, artistic planner who worked within the complexities of many social and cultural patterns, unlike the traffic engineers, who he called "boors." Traffic engineers were not familiar with sophisticated sociological and anthropological studies as he was, and they could not describe the city as a matrix of organic or holistic growth patterns. Halprin too indulged in the prevailing sentiments surrounding the "systems approach." He used systems' jargon to discuss "technological forecasting" or the probable propagation and diffusion of technological advances in highway design, and he was interested in the power of computers to perform various highway computations.[25] Countering the tendency to eliminate or replace transportation networks in favor of the dominance of either railroad or automobile traffic, Halprin was interested in multiplying transportation modes and wrote about hydrofoils, electric cabs, monorails, and even funiculars not simply with a futuristic enthusiasm for motion and gadgetry but a sense of the need to diversify transportation modes to achieve a better fit.[26] He also called for electronically controlled roadways and long-distance vehicles that would move by jet tube or jet rail. He projected that "individual auto units" might be "fitted together for express transportation or for long-distance move-ment within a larger transportation shell or wheeled carrier." "Mandatory force fields" preventing impacts between cars as well as the re-routing and separation of freight and urban traffic were among his other recommendations for automated highways.[27]

Even though Halprin may have been alienated from the traffic engineers, his planning methods resembled those of the technical planners in their reliance on data collection and direction from Washington. To some extent, his writings blended with the large volume of planning documents from this period that attempted holistic reorganization of transportation networks and were often illustrated with fountains, "participatory plazas," sunny parks on top of urban garages, and stacked roadways running within the sections of skyscrapers, all surrounded by rapidograph vegetation and lit by a rapidograph *soleil*.[28]

The field of electromagnetic emanations, which cover a very wide field of electric-wave impulses, is probably the best adapted to the control of traffic. It is conceivable that a control operating directly—as a radio beam, broadcast from stations located along the highway—could provide the control desired. . . . At regular intervals along the motorway there are traffic control stations. These may be located about five miles apart. The officers in each tower have complete authority over the section of road two and a half miles on either side of the. From their vantage point they can see the traffic flowing past them, and with their instruments they can communicate with any car in the territory under their jurisdiction.[29]

—*Norman Bel Geddes*

Notes

1. Wilfred Owen in U.S. National Resources Planning Board, *Transportation and National Policy* (Washington, D.C.: Government Printing Office, May 1942), 384, 399; Mark H. Rose, *Interstate: Express Highway Politics 1941–1956* (Lawrence: Regents Press of Kansas, 1979), 18.

2. Charles L. Dearing and Wilfred Owen, *National Transportation Policy* (Washington, D.C.: Brookings Institution, 1949), 351–378, 305–315; and Wilfred Owen, *The Metropolitan Transportation Problem* (Washington: Brookings Institution, 1956), 134, 116, 156–164, 247, 22.

3. The Port of New York Authority, *New York Union Motor Truck Terminal: A Complete Service for the Handling of Over-the-Road Common Carrier Freight* (New York: The Port of New York Authority, 1949).

4. President of the United States, *Interregional Highways*, 78th Congress, 2d session House document no. 379 (Washington, D.C.: Government Printing Office, 1944), 64 and plates VII, X.

5. Ibid., 66, 67–69, 76–77. The 1944 Federal-Aid Highway Act called for the design of

an interstate highway system of 40,000 miles. The recommendations of the Interregional Highway Committee would not be part of this legislation. Parking lots and wide rights-of-way were less important than the simple promise of roads and the jobs that accompanied their construction. Mark H. Rose, *Interstate: Express Highway Politics 1941–1956* (Lawrence: Regents Press of Kansas, 1979), 27; Leavitt, 26.

6. Egmont Arens, "Design for a New Skyway," *New York Times Magazine* (13 January 1946), 18–19.

7. Helen Leavitt, *Superhighway-Superhoax* (New York: Doubleday and Co., 1970), 59–60, 106.

8. David DeBoer, *Piggyback and Containers* (San Marino, California: Golden West Books, 1992), passim.

9. Ibid., 11, 28, 33–41.

10. Ibid., 56, 64, 72, 177.

11. U.S. Urban Advisors to the Federal Highway Administrator, *The Freeway in the City: Principles of Planning and Design*, A report to the secretary, Department of Transportation (Washington: U.S. Government Printing Office, 1968), 81; and Lawrence Halprin, *Freeways* (New York: Reinhold Publishing Corp., 1966), 113–148, 95, 101, 202–203.

12. Geoffrey Jellicoe, *Motopia: A Study in the Evolution of Urban Landscape* (New York: Praeger, 1961). Both federally and privately funded research teams worked on similar sectional stacking systems. The Romulus project, for instance, conducted by an MIT research team worked on a variety of networks and sectional building structures to accommodate multiple carriers and programs. MIT research team, "Project Romulus, team concepts for urban highways and urban design; 6 reports," Washington: Highway Research Board, National Research Council, 1968, 29–47.

13. Charles Downing Lay, "New Town for High Speed Road," *Landscape Architect* (November 1935), 351–353.

14. Frank Lloyd Wright, *The Living City* (New York: Horizon Press, 1958), 126–129.

15. Norman Bel Geddes, *Magic Motorways* (New York: Random House, 1940), 96–99, 121; and Charles Jencks, *Modern Movements in Architecture*, (Garden City: Anchor Press), 1973, 336.

16. Charles F. Kettering, *As "Ket" Sees It: A Series of Radio Talks by C. F. Kettering of General Motors* (Detroit: General Motors Corporation, January 16, 1944), New York Public Library.

17. "Electronic Highway of the Future," Science *Digest*, 46 (October 1959):32–5; "Automobiles that Drive Themselves," Dwight Baumann, "Dual-Mode Systems," Carnegie-Mellon Conference on Advanced Urban Transportation Systems, Pittsburgh National Technical Information Service 1970, 23–31.

18. Dwight Baumann, "Dual-Mode Systems," Carnegie-Mellon Conference, 23–31.

19. Francois Giraud, "Tracked Air Cushion Vehicles," Carnegie-Mellon Conference on High Speed Ground Transportation (Pittsburgh: Transportation Research Institute, Carnegie-Mellon University, 1969).

20. Bruno Latour, *Aramis of the Love of Technology* (Cambridge, Mass.: Harvard University Press, 1996). Latour's book is a "science fiction" novel about the desire for an impossible emblem of modernity.

21. Even Lewis Mumford used systems jargon when speaking to the Senate Subcommittee on Executive Reorganization in 1967, he said "Unfortunately, your predecessors in the Congress developed an almost pathological fear of planning, and hated the very word; though no great enterprise of any kind, as A. T. and T. or General Electric or Dupont would tell you, can be carried on without long-term planning of the most detailed sort, carefully coordinated, and constantly corrected in the light of

new conditions and fresh appraisals—what is now, in the jargon of the computer specialists, called 'feedback'." April 21, 1967, 1, 8. MacKaye papers, Dartmouth College Library, manuscript copy.

22. James H. Rillings, "Automated Highways," *Scientific American* (October 1997), 81–85.

23. "Let Your Car Do the Driving," *Edge City News* (April, 1994), 1.

24. Kenneth R. Howard, "Unjamming Traffic with Computers," *Scientific American* (October, 1997), 86–88.

25. Lawrence Halprin, *Notebooks 1959–1971* (Cambridge, Mass.: MIT Press, 1972) 265, 157, 155. U.S. Urban Advisors to the Federal Highway Administrator. *The Freeway in the City*, 124, 126.

26. Halprin, *Freeways*, 149–154.

27. U.S. urban advisors to the federal highway administrator, 125, 126.

28. Halprin also dealt with what he called "microinfrastructure" which he identified as the spaces of public amenities, or the "spaces between buildings." But he often discussed the adjustment of these spaces in cosmetic terms, speaking of, for instance, "revitalized" or "participatory plazas and fountains linked by pedestrian malls." Lawrence Halprin, "Landscape as Matrix," *Ekistics* 191 (October 1971):290, 291.

29. Norman Bel Geddes, *Magic Motorways* (New York: Random House, 1940), 74–76.

2.3 PARALLEL NETWORKS: ROADSIDES

By the 1960s, segments of the interstate highway had been completed all across America through many different regions and terrains. Eventually, the over 40,000 miles of four-lane highways would be approximately 150 feet wide including shoulders. They would consume forty-two acres for every mile they traversed and cover 1.5 million acres of land.[1] The highways were unfamiliar as a public utility. The right-of-way was a neutralized version of the more varied surrounding landscapes. It was not property, and it was neither cultivated nor preserved. Consequently it was perceived as a kind of nonsite or a site that was fused to the roadway as a consequence of traffic engineering. Not only were the intersections of the highway network determined by vehicle populations, but the actual contours of the highway were also shaped by a cone of vision originating inside a moving vehicle. By altering the legal-mathematical topography, however, some proposals intended to create from this right-of-way a parallel network that would add diversity and intelligence to the entire organization.

Highway Beautiful

When critics, practitioners, and the photographers ventured out to the highway landscape in the 1960s, they returned with uneasy images of this new form, which now no longer part of a model or a rendering, was standing in the naked sun. Commentary and photography usually focused on the visual attributes of the scene, either declaring it "ugly" or aestheticizing its as an engineered object.

In a sense, God's *Own Junkyard: The Planned Deterioration of America's Landscape* (1963) by Peter Blake was a late entry in a series of midcentury critiques, including John Keats' *Crack in the Picture Window,* (1957), William

Whyte's *Organization Man* (1952), and other sociological and/or journalistic exposés of the horrors of the growing suburban landscape. Typically, the critic, somewhat restrained by good breeding and a prestigious position in the New York publishing world, took a soul-searching look at group behavior in the postwar period and raised a hue and cry about a cultural conspiracy of bad taste played out in the landscape of houses and highways outside the city. The photography in *God's Own Junkyard* appeared almost to stare at the highway as an abstracted and not entirely comprehensible organization. The car and the house, which shared a similar means of production, were compared in low aerial photography as repeatable, identical units lined up in parking lots or subdivision streets. The sites were portrayed as vacant, in a way that inspired angst rather than invention. The right-of-way, perceived as an unidentifiable nonplace or negative space, was a place to dispose of litter or even entire cars. In fact, the metallic buildup of junk cars and car scraps was perhaps the single-most horrifying detail to the esthetes who visited this landscape during the 1960s, and their prescription usually involved the screening of this ugliness through beautification efforts.[2]

Man-Made America: Chaos or Control? (1963) by Christopher Tunnard and Boris Pushkarev or *A View from the Road* (1964) by Donald Appleyard pursued a somewhat more detailed analysis of the changing visual perspective from a moving automobile by identifying a new spatial order and formalism to accompany this visual experience. *Man-Made America* celebrated the new engineered forms and design parameters that shaped these landscapes. Tunnard and Pushkarev examined the visual experience of driving on a straight versus a curving road for attention span and safety, and they speculated about the composition of building in relation to movement along the highway. The book even included a supposedly serious analysis of how the identical rows of suburban houses might be relieved of monotony by varying the setback of the houses. Since the roadside was understood visually from a viewpoint inside a car, cosmetic ideas of planting vegetation along the roadside or punctuating a visual experience with carefully placed stands of trees or shrubs continued to be an acceptable response.[3]

When President Lyndon Johnson took office in Washington in 1963, the interstate was growing, adding significantly to its projected 42,500 miles and billions of dollars to its original estimate of $27 billion. His wife, Lady Bird Johnson, had trained herself to be a powerful and amiable mascot for his administration, and her "women doer" luncheons entertained presentations about the national parks and interstate highways as well as urban theorists like Jane Jacobs. Highways became a major focus of the first lady's beautification program and the president's task force on natural beauty. She is often best remembered for her program to plant wildflowers by the roadside, an approach that would appear to be largely cosmetic. She was interested, however, in graphically depicting the roadside as a meaningful site, one that was neither vacant nor neutral but rather offered diverse soils and climates, as evidenced by wildflowers particular to each region.

Mrs. Johnson's position about beautification was somewhat contradictory since she expressed great pleasure over attractive visual arrangements, but she also felt strongly that the word "beauty" was inadequate to describe her interests and made the beautification program an easy target for detractors. Lyndon and Lady Bird Johnson joked about their use of the word "beauty" since it was often associated with garden clubs or treated as an anachronistic holdover from the turn-of-century days of civic beautification. Lady Bird described herself as a "born housekeeper," a comment that for many might confirm the weakness of her position, but which probably better reflected her understanding of interplay among different species of information. She had managed households, businesses, the White House, and even some of her husbands political chores. However naive in its specifics, her understanding of land management as a complex of problems addressed by a diverse and interdependent economy of solutions was what distinguished Mrs. Johnson's approach. She once said that she wanted to move from the "garden club to the hardware stage of the problem."[4] Still, the beautification movement was split between attempts to beautify with landscaping and plantings and attempts to deal with the real mechanisms of inner-city blight, or the larger organizations of national land holdings and parks. The beautification movement was perhaps better understood as a persuasion that gently aroused consciousness about issues ranging from land preservation and environment to urban decay and, in doing so, identified sites like the roadside right-of-way.

Scenic Roads

President Johnson's Highway Beautification Act called for the development of "scenic" roads and parkways, and one federal publication, *A Proposed Program for Scenic Roads and Parkways,* prepared in support of the legislation was a remarkable artifact of this science of scenic highway design—a hybrid of traffic engineering and landscape design. The report emphasized fictions about the psychological well-being associated with driving from sea to shining sea, and it expressed the ambient sentiment that Americans had a right to more "elbow room." To ensure that Congress would take up its responsibility to provide this increased freedom however, the report also advanced parallel motives associated with defense evacuations and increased revenues from tourism.[5]

Although the scenic highway would supposedly accept variety and circumstance from the terrain through which it passed, the recommendations were nevertheless born of the systemic science of highway engineering. As portrayed in the report, traffic engineering was itself a kind of new nature, a natural-mathematical topography composed of contours associated with speed and vision in motion.[6] And when the curvatures of traffic movement were coincident with the natural topography, (making dynamite unnecessary) "environmental highway engineering" congratulated itself for its appropriateness and even claimed to make scenery possible. Highways created "anticipation" and visually enhanced the natural beauty of the scenery. They offered "drama" by framing nature for the automobile viewing excursion. Highway designers could sculpt a "curvilinear alignment that harmoniously integrated the road into its environment without unsightly scars and relieved the driver of monotony and dullness so that he can enjoy a 'driving for pleasure' experience." If properly designed, the various views from scenic overlooks would present a series of boiled-down regional highlights and the report's illustrations supported a vision of this roadside landscape as one that was filled with photo opportunities (figure 2.3.1).[7]

Legal Topography
Although most discussions of the highway landscape treated the roadway and the right-of-way as a single site, some considered the right-of-way to be a separate site with a separate jurisdictional and legal framework. While the scenic roads were shaped by visual parameters and driving dynamics, their larger rights-of-way also allowed them to be a mechanism of land acquisition and land linkage. Private lands and recreational activities, golf courses, farms, ranches, wooded areas, and resorts could all be gathered along the length of a road.[8] William Whyte's The Last Landscape (1968) resembled both the midcentury aesthetic critiques of the suburban landscape as well those of

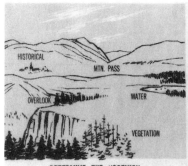

DETERMINE THE "SCENIC"   THEN LOCATE THE "ROAD"

2.3.1 Illustrations from *A proposed program for scenic roads and parkways.* (a) "Determine the 'Scenic', Then locate the road," (b) "Illustration showing how screens of vegetation block views of "objectionable landscape features." U.S. Department of Commerce, President's Council on Recreation and Natural Beauty, *A Proposed Program for Scenic Roads and Parkways* (Washington, D.C., U.S. Government Printing Office, June 1966), 56, 43.

the environmental movement and its growing sense of crisis. Whyte took an almost proprietary view of the roadside landscape, finding ways to claim perceptual and legal ownership of the land between and at the edges of developments in a way that blended public and private mechanisms and engaged the highway in other cultural activities. He studied the long-standing practice of acquiring highway easements for the parkways of metropolitan Boston or the national parkways like the Blue Ridge and the Natchez Trace, and he outlined a constellation of political, legal, financial, and aesthetic opportunities for doing so.[9] One of Whyte's ideas, one echoed by the government's proposal for scenic highways, involved the leasing of land to farmers and conversion of farm land for recreational use. He also proposed innovative ways to incorporate farm land and reforestation into this view corridor.

The two essential relationships in Whyte's writings were *linearity* and *linkage*. Given that linear land formations had an increased surface area, linear preserves had not only the greatest capacity for contacting a population but also the greatest capacity for linkage. "By linking open spaces . . . we can achieve a whole that is better than the sum of the parts."[10] These essential relationships of linearity and linkage led Whyte to envision the potential for land conservation along linear formations like transportation corridors. He outlined contemporary efforts to establish corridors of preserved space along existing lines within the landscape. With a kind of ecostyle appreciation of trails, cycling, and horse-back riding, Whyte also reviewed the contemporary efforts to form networks of greenways along various kinds of existing linear formations such as transportation and utility easements. Perhaps most fundamental was his identification of a line of action within the land, like a linear path of water, as the defining factor of such a network.[11]

Though Whyte identified a variety of highway sites with physical, legal, and virtual components, the ideas that survive from his recommendations have largely supported the goals of environmentalists and preservationists as cautions against wasting or abusing land.[12] Throughout most of these highway proposals, the perception of the roadside as a visual and commercial site or as a site that was fused to the highway as right-of-way still appeared to obstruct the promise of a potentially more diversified designation of site within the easement and right-of-way. Whyte did not share MacKaye's outdoorsy enthusiasm for leaping from the car and trekking through roadside land preserves. He stayed inside the car and maintained a kind of preservationist attitude that kept the working landscape at arms length. Like his

Getting on the subject of beautification is like picking up a tangled skein of wool: all the threads are interwoven . . . recreation and pollution and mental health, and the crime rate, and rapid transit, and highway beautification, and the war on poverty and parks—national, state, and local. It is hard to hitch the conversation into one straight line, because everything leads to something else.[17]
—*Lady Bird Johnson*

Sheep can still help. Quite aside from the pastoral touch they add, they are very efficient groundskeepers and have done an excellent job in many parks. A government aided program to put them to work on landscapes could

prove quite economic. On a rotation basis, one flock could graze a very considerable area, and as with mowing machinery the costs might be more than met by the fees paid by landowners in some cases, particularly where there are large public areas to be maintained, a municipal flock could be set up.[18]
—William Whyte

You may gather that I am not enthusiastic about the current beautification program. I am not. I recognize the goodwill and patriotism of its instigators, and I recognize the need for order and control in the American landscape. But I am convinced that the basic philosophy of this crusade is little more than a collection of tired out middle-class platitudes about the need for beauty, greenery, and the wickedness of bad taste.[19]
—J.B. Jackson

In the last two months I have ridden some 10,000 miles through the United States—from New Mexico to Vermont, from Georgia back to New Mexico by way of Texas.
If I were a foreigner this mileage and length of time would qualify me as an authority on the American scene, particularly if I had never been here before. And doubtless by now I would be writing a book for

contemporaries Tunnard and Pushkarev and other critics, Whyte was interested in relieving monotony. Curving roads, Tunnard and Pushkarev had reported, were not only more pleasant but also had lower fatality rates. Plantings could make a view corridor and even help to control traffic speeds. Billboards and other ugliness should be removed. But Whyte also wrote of the "overpowering monotony" of, for instance, tree farms or agricultural parcels, and he suggested that farmers should be paid to "make it look better" with ponds, recreational facilities and ornamental animals.[13]

Virtual Roadside

During the late 1950s, the vehicle, a sealed environment that contained the body in relative stillness, prompted speculations that were very similar to those associated with computer-generated virtual realities of the late twentieth century. As the differences between automobiles became largely a matter of style, most of their adjustability and convertibility involved finely tuning engine mechanisms and speeds, and the internal climates of air, temperature, and sound. Some argued that the car provided a kind of insulated chamber that neutralized physical experience and removed one from the physical pleasures of the outdoors. In addition, the design of the highway right-of-way and its wayside land was formatted according to protocols of use and vision originating from inside the car, making the highway corridor a strange kind of hermetic, mathematical baffle.

Though he joined those who found the interstate monotonous, J. B. Jackson, was also attracted to the "lively and lawless" highway landscape, and he articulated ideas about more subtle changes in car culture and roadsides sites. Though many thought that the automobile sponsored "contemplation without participation," Jackson saw it differently. He was perhaps already developing nostalgia for the new roadside culture. He wrote, "The highways leading out of our towns and cities are alive with cars, driving when work is over and before the evening meal to see how the new subdivision is getting on; out to the Dairy Queen five miles east to have a giant malt; to the drive-in movie still further away; cars with couples necking, souped-up cars racing down the measured mile; cars playing chicken, car pickups, motorcycles, scooters all driving merely for the sake of driving."[14] In "The Abstract World of the Hot-Rodder" Jackson associated the new culture of fast cars and physical sports with a desire to participate rather than spectate. Water skiing, climbing, motorcycling, or hot-rodding reflected an addiction to physical contact and motion, in reaction to "foolproof, sleep-inducing highways" that did not allow one to "sense the surface under the wheels or to feel the exhilaration of a steep climb, a sharp curve, or a sudden view. We are compelled to move at a uniform speed, and we no longer even have that earlier, model-T sense of participation in the functioning of the automobile."[15]

Since the car was attuned to more subtle atmospheric changes and ergonomic conditions, and since what lay outside the highway might also, by its abstraction, not only indulge virtual wandering but merge with any other available reality, it was easy for the car to be a kind of environmental capsule. The vehicle was a popular site for many kinds of speculations about mobile virtual environments not only in industry promotion but in information age projections about the uncertain future of "spaceship earth." For instance, in the 1960s, Archigram, a cadre of British architects and thinkers, developed parodic, apocalyptic designs for portable plug-in environments like the Cushicle, the Rokplug, or the Logplug. For the urban nomadic cowboy these vehicles were like second skins or robots designed to enhance or created a virtual reality. The group even speculated about whole cities becoming vehicles or walking cities. By appropriating the protocols of advertising, Archigram's brilliant synthesis was at once a cynical critique of cultural coercion and a clever use of market protocols to promote the paraphernalia of a new urban organization.[16]

Just as the vehicle became the primary mechanism for switching between carriers and networks, so it also became the chief lens through which to understand the surrounding landscape, and the highway, already a monovalent organization in its approach to roadway, would also treat the right-of-way as monovalent. Designers, traffic engineers, and even land management experts so often understood this landscape as one that was organized by vision. So many post interstate practitioners appear compelled by the same peculiar bias, one which did not necessarily rule the thinking of highway and landscape designers of the previous generation. The highway planner, miscast as the landscape painter, would better nature with visual contours that, by some fabulous coincidence, reinforced the main rules of traffic engineering. Even those who worked with the right-of-way as a mathematical and legal topography were often working toward goals that associated the idea of landscape with greenery. They worked to acquire land like farms and golf courses that could pass as green preserve. The right-of-way was, however, potentially a parallel network, one perhaps more diverse because of the

the Christmas trade. I would have illustrations in it of neon signs and dump heaps and monotonous subdivisions, alternating (for I should want to be fair, of course) with bucolic scenes of Colonial New England and the Grand Canyon and the Redwood groves of California. And I know the title I would give the book: "The Challenge of Ugliness." That in itself would guarantee a sale of at least 10,000 among garden club members.[20]
—J.B. Jackson

We all know that a car is a self-powered mobile room, with limited support systems (air-conditioning, communications). We also know that a traffic jam is a collection of rooms, so is a car-park—they are really instantly formed and constantly changing communities. A drive-in restaurant ceases to exist when the cars are gone (except for cooking hardware). A motorized environment is a collection of service points.[21]
—David Greene, Archigram

Cowboy international nomadhero. It used to seem a nice idea to carry your environment around with you . . . But it can be as much of a drag as having it stuck in one place. Cowboy was probably one of the most successful carriers of

his own environment because his hardware needs were low (mug, saddle, bedroll, matches) and because his prime mover, horse, selected its own fuel and was a fairly efficient animal robot.[22]
—*David Greene, Archigram*

neutral presence of the highway. These ribbons of land whose existence depended on potentially pliable design rules were sites that became all the more powerful because of their peculiar linear geometry and increased surface area. This surface potentially defined a network unto itself one not entirely dependent on the highway's commercial or military goals but rather one that compounded the intelligence of the organization through its diversity and parallelism.

Notes

1. Peter Wolf, *Land in America: Its Value, Use, and Control* (New York: Pantheon Books, 1981).
2. Peter Blake, *God's Own Junkyard: The Planned Deterioration of America's Landscape* (New York: Holt, Rinehart and Winston, 1963), passim.
3. Christopher Tunnard and Boris Pushkarev, *Man Made America: Chaos or Control* (New Haven: Yale University Press, 1963) and Donald Appleyard, Kevin Lynch, and John R. Myer. *The View from the Road* (Cambridge: Published for the Joint Center for Urban Studies of the Massachusetts Institute of Technology and Harvard University by MIT Press, Massachusetts Institute of Technology, 1964).
4. Lewis Gould, *Lady Bird Johnson and the Environment* (Lawrence: University Press of Kansas, 1988), 63.
5. U.S. Department of Commerce for the President's Council on Recreation and Natural Beauty, *A Proposed Program for Scenic Roads and Parkways* (Washington, D.C.: U.S. Government Printing Office, June 1966), 1, 6, 3–4. The proposal called for over twenty-nine projects covering 54,411 miles of primarily existing roads and highways.
6. Ibid., 4, 185–196, 105–129, 6, 33–39. The report referenced the Westchester County parkways, California's Route. One, the Scenic Corridors in Wisconsin, the Van Duzer Corridor in Oregon, the Mount Vernon Memorial Highway, the Blue Ridge Parkway and the Natchez Trace, the George Washington Memorial Parkway, the Kancamagus Scenic Road, the White Mountain National Forest, and the Gunflint Trail, Minnesota.
7. Ibid., 73.
8. Ibid., 2, 51–52. The *Scenic Highways* report cited one interesting case in Wisconsin, which in the 1960s began a program whereby the highway rights-of-way provided the opportunity for accretional growth of public lands for conservation and cultivation. The project began with the Great River Road that runs through the state, and it established a legal architecture involving the purchase of scenic easements. As each county in the state began a similar practice, the possibilities for a network of not only roadway but land began to emerge. Some of the properties were acquired through condemnation, while zoning in combination with tax incentives facilitated agreements with other landowners.
9. Ibid., 84; William H. Whyte, Jr., *Securing Open Space for Urban America: Conservation Easements*, Urban Land Institute, Technical Bulletin no. 36.
10. William H. Whyte, Jr., *The Last Landscape* (New York: Doubleday and Company, 1968), 179.
11. Ibid., 182–195, 181. Whyte reviewed the work of Ian McHarg in proposing routes for an interstate highway in New Jersey and the work of Philip Lewis in surveying a potential network of preservation corridors for the State of Wisconsin.
12. Ibid., 212–223, 136.

13. Ibid., 289.

14. J.B. Jackson, "Various Aspects of Landscape Analysis," Texas Conference on Environmental Crisis, University of Texas at Austin: School of Architecture, 1966, 155, 157; and J. B. Jackson, "Other-Directed Houses," *Landscape*, vol. 6, no. 2 (1956–57): 60.

15. J.B. Jackson, "The Abstract World of the Hot-Rodder," *Landscape*, vol. 7, no. 2 (1957–58), 22–27, 26.

16. David Greene, Peter Cooke et al. in *Archigram* (New York: Praeger Publishers, 1973) No. 12 "Gardner's Notebook," 110–115.

17. Lady Bird Johnson, *A White House Diary* (New York: Holt, Rinehart and Winston, 1970), 234.

18. William Whyte, *The Last Landscape*, 310.

19. J.B. Jackson, "Various Aspects of Landscape Analysis," 157.

20. Ibid., 150.

21. David Greene, Peter Cooke et al. in *Archigram*, 110–115.

22. Ibid.

2.4 SITES

By excluding information that did not fit into its own internally consistent equations, traffic engineering neutralized the organizational architecture of the highway network. Those proposals that treated the highway as a set of distinct sites, however, rather than a single homogeneous channel of space, compounded the network's intelligence. Like a game that exponentially increases in complexity as it introduces wild cards or increases the number of players, the highway potentially gained intelligence by allowing vehicles, intersections, and roadsides to operate in ways that were eccentric to the rigid rules of traffic engineering.

Vehicles

With the help of federal endorsements and funding, the vehicle whether in a population or on its own became the primary site for transportation innovations and a chief source of switching, convertibility, and translation between different modalities. Even in the face of many failures and obstacles, vehicles, through industry support, have continued to be primary sites of research concerning differential or adaptable highways. Statistical models of traffic patterns turned out to be the wrong models to respond to a population of vehicles. Recently, more sophisticated computer models of traffic patterns have effectively distributed the power of switching to each individual vehicle. While perhaps lured into similar traps regarding predictability and optimization, these models are at least not intent on organizing the entire population of vehicles into a single protocol and a single physical arrangement. Similarly, dual-mode vehicles have found specific repetitive tasks for which they are, at least for now, best suited.

Though a great deal of cultural intelligence has focused on slight personalizations and modulations of the vehicle, the idea of vehicle as prosthesis, second skin, or virtual reality capsule fits easily, perhaps too easily, into our late twentieth-century revivals of sci-fi techno-prophesies. The vehicle dramatizes some of our favorite crises and fetishes; the vehicle as product, however, offers other opportunities. Both traffic engineering and merchandising use statistical studies and population models to derive techniques for managing consumption and relating it to investment. It is not surprising that most of the transportation inventions also follow a product model as some kind of vehicular fitting or enhancement. Even railroad-truck intermodal systems are designed to make the vehicle part of a telescoping order of packaging that ends with the truck-sized container. The container is a vehicle that, like the suburban home, has become a generic box with the power to format many different products and spaces. However over-determined the network architecture of the highway system, the distributive organization of vehicles offers other wild cards or tactical sites as well. The vehicle population migrates, for instance, often rapidly changing its course in response to other volatile formats in culture. Malls, for instance, just completing a half-century wave of growth that altered millions of acres of territory, are now being replaced by giant new retail formats. These new formats, which often colonize an outer ring around the mall parking lot, have essentially begun to invert the centralized format, bringing thousands of acres of automobile infrastructure with them. In some ways, they respond to shifting parking populations during the course of the day since the outer ring of stores feeds on afternoon and evening vacancies at the edges of the lot. The individual vehicle is sited at the center of these and other larger ambient shifts. So many diverse organizations have been trained to interface with the vehicle that it is potentially a useful site for distributing another set of circumstances into the field, a field that travels outside of any one frame of reference.

Projects for mammoth new rail and airport terminals with hotels, convention centers, entertainment complexes, and other programs have been recurrent design programs in the last half of this century, and they have often generated an organization or an urbanism that overwhelms conventional architectural controls and orders.[1] These are the switches in new global patterns of distribution and transportation. While these projects, from those of Lawrence Halprin and Geoffrey Jellicoe to those of Rem Koolhaas, address interplay between different transportation systems, consistent with the customary desires of architects and planners, they often address with building envelope problems related to a distributed condition. These new hubs, however, are not the only new sites of infrastructure intelligence. The same network under-standing is also found in smaller distributed switch sites within the existing infrastructure fabric—in those areas of easement and right-of-way where segregated and redundant networks overlap or communicate.

Referencing these sites one could reinterpret an illogical sequence of infrastructure building as a series of happy accidents. The highway's history of cross purposes includes a lack of coordination among modalities, cycles of obsolescence and abandonment, redundancies and fights for dominance among the various formats, and finally the segregation of various networks coexisting in urban centers. Considered opportunistically, however, this his-tory provides extremely rich sites for building another kind of intelligence among networks. When the interstate became an intercity network diverging from the railroad outside the city and coinciding with it inside the city, it reduced its potential to develop a variety of exurban ports of exchange out-side the city. Though the coincidence of rail and automobile infrastructure inside the city intensified the potential for urban switching, rather than take advantage of this proximity, the various carriers fought to be the most domi-nant method of transport even when that fight created inefficiencies or rigid-ities that ran counter to their claims of fitness and superiority. Most urban landscapes are layered with overlapping corridor and networks, including canals and piers, passenger rail, working and abandoned freight rail, mass transit, surface streets, and expressways. Like the redundancies that are inten-tionally built into an electronic network to amplify its intelligence, these sites potentially support a kind of parallelism that, through connection, strength-ens all of the associated networks, and they might be understood as switch sites or sites for some kind of differential exchange among carriers.

Similarly repeated fittings potentially recondition and recircuit longer segments of the network. The suburban interchange too has this potential for building switching and meaningful redundancy. There were optimistic projections, even as early as the 1940s, that airplanes would enter into the mix of carriers, creating the need for air strips in subdivisions and office parks.[2] This vision never fully materialized and airplanes certainly were never in any position to completely usurp any of the major modes of transport. Still new hub organizations of air freight carriers and new intermodal superhubs in free trade zones in America are rearranging patterns of production, stor-age, and distribution for national and global commerce, and these new hubs provide air links at critical junctures along the highway network.

The sites of adjustment that lie between networks in the cities and suburbs are often treated as vacancies or as places that fall between jurisdictions. Similarly, the roadside outside the city limits is often regarded as a kind of residual right-of-way that is fused to the purposes of the highway. The scenic highway landscape is modeled not after the activities of the landscape but after traffic engineering's own "natural" contours. That land, when beautified or adopted by communities, is still usually directed by visual protocols originating from inside the vehicle. The roadside offers a site of adjustment that is constituted differently from the urban switch. As a linear site adjacent to a national network, it has several unusual qualities. It has a very large surface area and so contacts a large number of adjacent sites of different kinds, including commercial, agricultural, residential, and public properties. The site is constituted by many different legal designations that together form a fairly dense topography as prominent as any other landscape feature. The right-of-way also abuts many different kinds of land, including commercial, agricultural, residential, and public properties. The most recent advocacies surrounding the best use of the right-of-way portray it as a green preserve free from commerce, facilitating healthful exercise and extending nonvehicular connections to parks and larger land preserves. Although this use potentially links many expanses of public land and many organic ecologies, it is just one default position. The green program proposes a powerful possibility for the roadside site in that it implicitly projects the accretional growth of the site as a separate parallel network that is potentially national in extent. The idea of a national web of sites, however, that lies between different linear networks, including waterways, rail lines, and roadways, suggests possibilities other than those strictly related to green landscape. The diversity of sites and uses that might occupy that land are positioned to build parallelism and intelligence among several networks. Most critical is the perception of this roadside not as a vacancy in the traditional use of the word but as a site that has been partially cleared of dominant programs and is overlain with a topography of not only terrestrial but legal and commercial features. These sometimes invisible factors may provide some of the most pliable means of adjusting or reconditioning highway sites for different uses, thus facilitating another series of intelligent national and local networks on the back of the midcentury interstate highway system.

Notes

1. For instance, Rem Koolhaas's new town of Lille is an example of this kind of mega-program where the most provocative space was created by simply subtracting the separations among the several infrastructure networks at their crossing. Called the "Piranesi" space, it is largely a visual, aesthetic cross-reference between these different transportation networks, though it functions as a passenger exchange.

2. Stanley McMichael, *Real Estate Subdivisions* (New York: Prentice Hall, 1949), 5–6 and H. McKinley Conway, *The Airport City and the Future Intermodal Transportation System* (Atlanta: Conway Publications, Inc., 1977) passim.

Part 3

3.0 SUBDIVISION PRODUCTS

Considered to be among the most banal and simplistic development environments, the subdivision, in league with both the market and the military during this century, has also been one of America's most powerful spatial
protocols. Though we have often simply labeled residential formations of
single-family houses, "suburbia," and often also rushed to a sociological critique of this fabric, a great deal of intelligence resides in the logistical and
organizational constitution of its many distinct formats. In fact, the assemblage of residential subdivision formats is perhaps best described by organizational expressions. For instance, the design of a single house or platting
plan does not convey critical information about the spatial character of the
aggregate. Rather, the typical postwar suburb would be best described by a
series of sequential operations performed on a repeatable dwelling. Residential fabric is typically arranged in generic formats with varying degrees of
neutrality and differentiation, and either by design or default, their financing,
ownership, and construction protocols differentiate or add complexity to
them. The house and all its attending elements, however, are also commercial
destinations, and the various fittings, which attend the building and refur-
bishing of a house, though seemingly discrete agents are powerful factors in
formatting the overall organization. Subdivision products are adjusted by yet
more products. Moreover, as an organization that commodifies space, the
subdivision is a precursor to many contemporary "real estate products" serving retail, workplace, and global commerce.

The subdivision has been treated as not only a commercial instrument to
organize consumption but a cultural instrument to instigate social or political
reform. Many well-meaning cultural engineers have been convinced that
they could systematize or aestheticize residential fabric in a way that would

have a remedial effect on American urbanism. During the first half of the century, these practitioners assumed various roles in partnerships with business and the federal government. They were engaged as "associates" from the private sector during World War I and later as technicians, engineers, and social planners during the Hoover and New Deal years. The episodes in part III examine one crucial moment during the New Deal period when many of the new technicians of "subdivision science" were present in Washington at the same time. They were all vying to influence postwar policy on residential fabric until by the late 1930s, in a conservative political climate, the rules of the game shifted and private enterprise ascended to or returned to its position as the de facto architect of the dominant postwar subdivision format. Not only does this moment invite comparisons between different residential organizations but because this "subdivision science" was essentially appropriated by a merchandising strategy, the episodes examine the way in which architects managed to exclude themselves from the game.

In the early twentieth century most planners organized residential fabric into one of several prevailing forms—suburban satellites, autonomous towns, or subdivisions. These forms evolved from a variety of property organizations in America's urban history—from the grids of colonization and westward expansion to specialized enclaves and company towns. The leafy railroad suburbs were arranged as satellites outside the cities, whereas the more densely platted streetcar suburbs inhabited a middle ground on the urban periphery. During the last half of the nineteenth century, both had already begun to make a generic commodity of lots of an acre or less with houses set against a street populated by trees. Since most of these forms subdivided the territory into lots, the word "subdivision" was often used to describe new parcels of residential and nonresidential properties. This generic term began to describe not simply a process but a distinctly different residential format used as a means of tiling urban land into municipal neighborhoods. It was easy to commodify. As a neighborhood it had the fewest political responsibilities since no separate sponsor had to finance it and make prescriptions about the character of its community. Though not originally designed to be separate from an urban context, over the years a combination of factors, including growing municipal boundaries, gave the subdivision the position, but not the composition, of an autonomous community. Gradually, the subdivision was giganticized. Its housing options and production protocols were made more uniform, and it was given less access to the city both because of its boundary conditions and its distance from the urban core. The distributive organizations or architectures of marketing, merchandising, banking, and publicity campaigns formed a group of unifying protocols directing the merchandising and distribution of the individual house and lot as a repeatable commodity, and subdivision would become a common label for the generic tract-house development on a separate parcel of land outside the city.

The "science" of subdivision design was created in part by the willingness, even eagerness, of some designers to systematize their formulations. They had begun to call themselves "planners" a title that had previously been associated with scientific management of industry. Early in the century, a small number of these newly self-appointed planners, serving on various committees for professional associations or for the federal government, developed guidelines, codes, and numerical formula that attempted to optimize subdivision layouts. These formulations were usually accompanied by telling forms of representation, including some specialized drawings and diagrams that were not only representations of architectural arrangement but also more abstract graphical tabulations of the interdependence between numerical and spatial relationships related to, for instance, infrastructure runs or economies of density.

While, since midcentury, the subdivision has been associated with imagery related to home ownership, at the beginning of the century subdivision protocols were often treated like practical inventions. For instance, the functional schematics of the Garden City in Ebenezer Howard's *To-Morrow: The Peaceful Path to Real Reform* (1898) read like a somewhat effusive yet practically detailed patent application. To small acclaim, Howard actually did invent several physical contraptions (the Remington typesetting typewriter being perhaps the most notable), but Lewis Mumford likened the Garden City diagram to the inventions of Leonardo da Vinci or the introduction of airplane fight.[1] Howard illustrated his idea with diagrams depicting simple phenomena associated with magnets or with commonplace devices like keys and locks. The main Garden City diagram that designers misread as an actual planimetric representation was notation for a new commercial and cultural economy that repositioned and recombined both the elements and activities of town and suburb. It was a shorthand embedded with intelligence from sources as far ranging as Taylor's systems studies to the anarchistic writings of Kropotkin. A network of small autonomous industrial cities would more equitably redistribute property and population and finally replace the large city. Though capitalized in traditional ways these communities, under a different organizational protocol, would support cooperative, socialist groupings. Howard was fascinated with America's western expansion and its many hybrid urban formations that were instrumental in shaping land use on a telescoping scale from the lot to the region. In fact, the Garden City wards were not unlike the wards of Savannah, Georgia. In both ward systems, green, private, public, and semipublic space as well as space in the regional periphery were expressed as quotients or functions of each other. These specialized interlocking functions established different but complementary protocols for both predictable and unpredictable growth in agricultural, residential, or civic space. Although each of these programs governed the other, their interdependent relationship did not control the shape or extent of the overall formation but rather the contents of its unit of growth. Another invention, Unwin's diagrams of housing densities in *Nothing Gained by Overcrowding* (1912), demonstrated that for a twenty-acre lot, doubling housing density increased roadway infrastructure, so that the cost of developing land almost doubled with only a small reduction in the final price of each house. A smaller number of houses were not only more economical to build, but they also provided a great deal more open space. Unwin's planimetric graphs demonstrated the interdependent ratios between houses, roads, gardens, and cost.[2]

Early twentieth-century metropolitan and federal planning projects galvanized the new profession of planners, many of whom used the British Garden City as precedent for a community-building movement in America. During World War I, the federal government's U.S. Housing Corporation consulted a number of planners in the design of ship-building communities. These "war towns" as they were called, were the government's first attempts at subsidized housing. The U.S. Housing Corporation, for planners, like the War Industries Board for the industrialist, engaged the subdivision-housing planner as an associate and organized the housing industry within a managed framework. Comparative data from the financing and building of the ship-building communities lent credence to the idea that subdivisions were quantifiable organizations. Many of the planners were in the process of replacing their City Beautiful ambitions with a new conviction about the healthy and "scientific" city, and they looked now to public sponsorship of that effort. As a consequence, new residential planners set up private practices that specialized in the making of fabric for new Garden City satellite suburbs and subdivisions. Many also began a practice of tabulating comparative land-use percentages between open space, infrastructure, public building, and residential areas. They also developed a variety of protocols for regulating the balance between public and private space, and they shared their findings in publications, conferences, and collaborations. Most of these techniques involved rules-of-thumb about streets or housing aggregate that were potentially highly complex when differentiated by the timing of successive growth phases. Conventional subdivision design, as practiced in the 1910s and 1920s used the neighborhood as a unit of metropolitan expansion and annexation. The informal arrangements of the street operated as intermediate organizers or functions, while lot sales provided a more anarchical and distributed differentiation of the fabric.

During the early days of the Depression, the Hoover administration enlisted planners who, like the new experts interested in the systemic management of industry, attempted to engineer optimal subdivision protocols. The administration lay on the cusp of change from the essentially conservative positions surrounding the roles of engineer, liberal, and planner to a more radical double of those terms that emerged during the 1930s. The term "liberal," which prior to the New Deal was associated with laissez-faire, would soon be synonymous with radical reform and state control. Planning too would become a dangerous word to some during the New Deal, associated not with civic or national boosterism but with five-year plans or the central direction of nationwide economic and social patterns. The politics surrounding individualism versus state control that maintained an ambiguous coexistence within the politics and ideology of the Hoover Administration would grow into distinct often opposing positions.[3]

During the New Deal, subdivisions and houses were political pawns and economic indicators. Industry and community were paired not only because planning goals linked home and work but because small communities were a component of the industrial order, one that was not only tied to a decentralized pattern of growth but was also, at midcentury, to become the product of America's chief industry—home building. The government sponsored several different approaches to the use of the subdivision as an economic and social instrument, and it was the landlord of such experiments as the subsistence homesteads and the greenbelt towns. Many of these experiments borrowed from the Regional Planning Association of America (RPAA), a tightly integrated, often holistic, prescription for interlocking organizational agents like the neighborhood unit, superblock, and the cul-de-sac. These functional agents had a very specific spatial repertoire that significantly altered the arrangements of the typical subdivision.

Eventually, the government reversed its previous support of the earnest planning ideas of the 1920s and 1930s, delivering a mandate to private enterprise instead.[4] The subdivision, like the highway, was organized according to a product mode that made not only the house but also its surrounding space a distributed commodity. The National Housing Act (1934) and the Federal Housing Administration (FHA) established the house and lot as an economic indicator or unit of currency that could be used to tune or adjust social and economic systems by influencing consumption or employment. Private enterprise became not only the government's associate but its board of directors, and the subdivision became a major U.S. industry. Under the guise of conservative politics, this extreme version of managerial capitalism ironically resembled something like central statist control or state capitalism.

Depression era and postwar housing developments mixed the techniques of traditional real estate development with vague planning notions and garbled persuasions about futuristic modernism—thus the "all new scientifically modern Cape Cod house." The FHA published guidelines and issued approvals for mortgage insurance, so naturally developers conformed to those guidelines and even began to streamline the process by submitting large tracts of similar houses for approval. The FHA also preferred "prebuilt" subdivisions, ones that were built all at once before the owners arrived thus constraining those factors that typically differentiated the fabric. Borrowing military procedures for prefabricating housing or turning the entire site into an assembly-line organization provided few means of differentiation and few functions of growth other than accumulation. Traditional development protocols were replaced by protocols for product distribution or financial structures. They were often expressed not as functional relationships, developing over time, but rather as templates that formatted the entire organization at once. The intent over the coming years was to establish the subdivision as relatively inactive organization, one that achieved financial stability by establishing a single static relationship among its parts and maintaining that relationship over the life of a mortgage. The subdivision was primarily formatted to absorb products, and these products would be its chief source of differentiation.

Some residential formations in the episodes discussed here were explicitly designed. Others were unplanned improvisational organizations that resulted from a series of default relationships related to real estate protocols, housing aggregates, changes over time, or multiple designers. Some of the subdivisions examined here were shaped by global maneuvers or batch summations across many similar elements or fittings. Alternative subdivisions established some kind of intermediate organizer that behaved like a function to group variables in space and time or use the changes in one variable to trigger or initiate change among another set of variables. For instance, some functions established encoded units of growth to direct an ongoing development process. Simple streets were used in this way to modulate growth, density, calibration, or other relationships within the fabric. Some of the smartest street networks were either unplanned, developed in periods of both planning and neglect, or developed as a relaxed version of more controlled formulations. These unplanned arrangements often achieved the greatest complexity, either within an anarchical pattern of growth or after a few simple relationships established some means of cross-reference and integration among its parts. Those arrangements controlled by planning and styling or those ruled entirely by property and finance usually resulted in the dumbest and most neutralized street volumes and networks. Repetition and banality within unpredictable patterns of consumption, not aesthetic reform, have been the subdivision's most powerful means of adjusting itself, and the fabric is usually most complex when the wild cards have outnumbered the rules.

The following episodes sample planning publications and projects, government documents, and commercial artifacts as a means of examining the various forms of subdivision engineering and their attendant promotional campaigns. The episodes begin by looking at early cooperative efforts between planners and the federal government in organizing subdivisions.

Notes

1. Lewis Mumford, "The Garden City and Modern Planning," introductory essay in *Garden Cities of To-Morrow* (Cambridge, Mass.: MIT Press, 1965), 29, 30.
2. Sir Raymond Unwin, *Nothing Gained by Overcrowding! How the Garden City Type of Development May Benefit Both Owner and Occupier* (London: Garden Cities and Town Planning Association, 1912).
3. Documenting shifting ideologies in New Deal liberalism, Alan Brinkley, references Ronald Rotunda, "The 'Liberal' Label: Roosevelt's Capture of a Symbol," *Public Policy* 17 (1968): 377–408. Brinkley and Rotunda discuss the dual meanings of the term "liberal" during the early 1930s.
4. Jordan A. Schwartz, *The New Dealers: Power Politics in the Age of Roosevelt* (New York: Vintage Books, 1994), xi.

3.1 FUNCTION AND TEMPLATE: WAR-TOWN SUBDIVISION SCIENCE

Early twentieth-century residential planners articulated a new responsibility for architects that involved not only the aesthetics of landscape and building design but also the logistics of larger building and landscape organizations. Though most of these planners advocated the design of separate communities after the Garden City model, in the end, they almost always designed neighborhood subdivisions or satellite suburbs some of which only referenced the Garden City through radial street geometries or English-country styling. Most of the planners were experienced, however, with techniques for differentiating the fabric over time with simple, functional relationships between, for instance, streets and housing aggregates. These planners managed to find various public and private sponsors and situations to rehearse their techniques, and, finally, the logistics of sponsorship and financing would often prove to be among the most powerful means of formatting the entire organization.

Two studies, one sponsored by a private municipal organization, the 1913 Chicago City Club competition, and the other sponsored by the federal government, the *President's Conference on Home Building and Home Ownership*, provide a comparative sampling of their early twentieth-century attempts to optimize subdivision planning. The graphics accompanying these two studies, one before and one after the war-town projects, also marked a tendency within the profession to record very complex spatial relationships with a planimetric notation. Although this kind of notation was often not simply plan but rather a graph of subdivision data registered as plan, these graphs did not necessarily convey the functional, temporal expressions that were critical instructions in the organization.

In their design prototypes, the new subdivision technicians typically organized residential fabric by establishing limited design controls within the default protocols of real estate development. Most municipal subdivisions were developed with a grid of streets platted for incremental lot sales. The planners typically established a few simple functional relationships that created not comprehensive control but selective interdependence between separate sets of residential elements. The tree-lined street was one of the primary functional expressions or organizing agents against which other variables were balanced, and it was at once durable and fragile. Planners often designed a graduated set of tree-lined streets extending from the smaller scale of individual residential lots to the larger scale of public territory. Specialized in this way, the network was to create private areas and filter traffic volumes. The streets were differentiated by many components, including housing, infrastructure, and vegetation as well as the circumstantial contributions of many individual designers and owners over time. Many of the new subdivision and community planners were trained as landscape architects and so knew how to design mixtures of tree species and vegetation that would resist disease over time.

Another complex of constraints involved housing aggregates. Among planners of the day, group housing was a practical science unto itself, a housing puzzle that inspired a number of inventive solutions. The group house was a cross between apartment house and row house. Units could be stacked or interlocked across what would have been row-house party walls, and multiple entries replaced the corridors and stairs of an apartment building. Houses were grouped in multiples as mixtures of double houses, row houses, or stacked apartments, and they might form a continuous wall along the street or create a series of detached groups. The group house was used in combination with specialized street formations and architectural controls as a means of timing and phasing growth. The grid often deformed into closes or special residential squares to accommodate the denser grouping, and the housing was usually styled to reference some quaint historical tradition. Formations like these were typically built in the initial growth phase as special architectural assignments, and they might contain properties for sale or rent. These special groupings were used as promotion for lot sales, since they were believed to provide the necessary domestic imagery and density to create a recognizable place around which the rest of the less intensely developed lots would gradually crystallize.

Metropolitan Sponsors

In 1913, as part of its larger metropolitan planning vision, the Chicago City Club held a competition for the subdivision of a quarter section of residential property. The competition attracted Garden City designers, designers of romantic suburbs, urban reformers, and even visionaries like Frank Lloyd Wright. The neighborhood-sized quarter section of land provided an identical palette for comparative study of the prevailing practice in subdivision design. Wright's late entry rehearsed Broadacre City arrangements of suburbia. Another entry, by a physician, demonstrated important factors in solar orientation. All of the entries were evaluated according to careful tabulations of such things as housing density, infrastructure costs, and open space. Though some of the entries may have exercised slightly different subdivision options, most contained no new organizational protocol but were rather street-pattern compositions that looked something like obsessive subdivision mandalas. One exceptional entry, however, by William Drummond proposed new protocols for developing networks of "neighborhood units." Rather than simply subdividing the quarter section, in his scheme, the quarter section itself became a kind of intermediate organizer or a function of larger metropolitan growth patterns. Each of these neighborhood units would have central open space allotments that would also serve as points of linkage for a citywide network of such neighborhoods.[1]

The neighborhood unit idea was usually credited to Clarence Perry and an article he contributed to the *Regional Plan of New York and Its Environs* (1929), another metropolitan regional planning project. Perry used his own community of Forest Hills Gardens (sponsored by the Russell Sage Foundation) as a model neighborhood, and he defined the unit as a quarter-acre radius of development around a school. Perry also calculated an optimal quotient of open versus developed land and speculated about various planning and real estate protocols for the propagation of these neighborhoods into interconnected neighborhoods.[2] His version of the neighborhood unit was referenced both by the World War I planners and the regionalist planners (figure 3.1.1).

The President's Conference on Home Building and Home Ownership

The Hoover administration targeted the individual house as a commodity useful in stimulating the economy and home ownership as an economic tool for maintaining property values and a cultural tool for stabilizing the work force. Hoover had been honorary president of the 1929 "Better Homes Campaign in Rural Communities and Small Towns," one of several private efforts after which the federal government would later fashion its own New Deal home-ownership campaigns. Leaflets, films, and educational publications provided primers on such things as plumbing, decorating, curtains, cleaning, and convenient kitchens, and services like The Architect's Small House Service Bureau provided boilerplate house plans.[11] Different from the engineer as technocrat, engineers like Hoover associated with Taylorism and industrial efficiency. Hoover himself resembled the new professional "associate" of the government who used central authority not for statist control or economic cartelism but "voluntary association." Within the associationist political fraternity, old style laissez-faire capitalists, while still maintaining a stance of independence, could systematically reform inefficient industries and safeguard against monopoly. The state could be used as a clearinghouse for information and promotional publicity, and the new standards authored by professional associates would influence the independent contractor within a kind of "managerial capitalism."[12]

Once president, Hoover assembled his own conferences to collect intelligence from practitioners of the new planning science. In 1931, The President's Conference on Home Building and Home Ownership engaged personnel from most of the early planning efforts, and the reports from its two committees—*City Planning* and *Zoning* and *Subdivision Layout*—were interesting artifacts of the profession's attitudes toward residential subdivision. Consistent with the sentiments of its leadership, those who had helped to lead metropolitan planning organizations, the Committee on City Planning and Zoning, endorsed a "centralized" pattern of municipal growth. Neighborhood development should not be "based upon some fanciful theory of reorganizing our processes of urban growth," but rather follow what had long been the "natural form of city growth, opening territory between main traffic highways." Now, the neighborhood unit would be the appropriate increment of both municipal and suburban growth and an instrument for the redistribution of population. The neighborhood unit was also seen as an increment that, unlike the ever-expanding grid, would generate definite boundaries around neighborhoods thus ensuring stable property values. The committee also endorsed public regulation of subdivisions and consultation with "experts" to promote consistent "scientific" planning.[13]

The landscape architect has turned naturally with the evolution of our times from the planning of estates to public parks, parkways, and

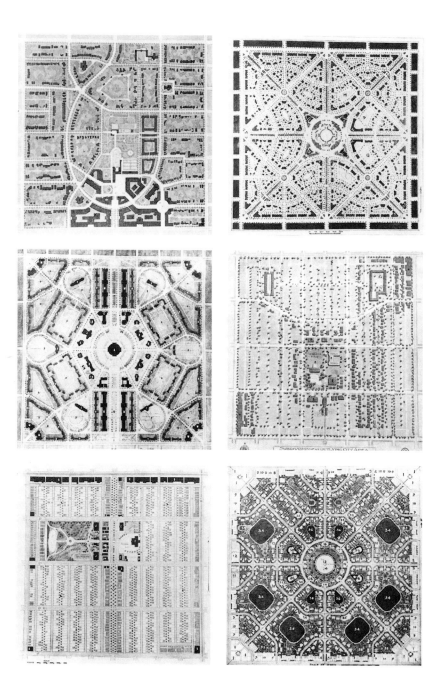

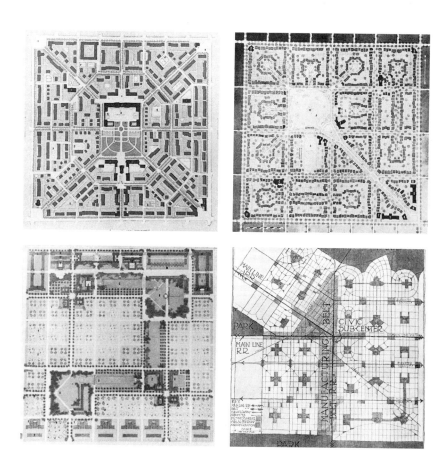

3.1.1 Chicago City Club competition, 1913. Competitive plans for subdividing a typical quarter section of land in the outskirts of Chicago. Plans by: (a) Wilhelm Bernhard, (b) Louis H. Boynton, (c) Brazer and Robb, (d) G. C. Cone, (e) H. J. Fixmer, (f) Edgar H. Lawrence and Walter B. Griffin, (g) Albert and Ingrid Lilienberg, (h) Albert Sturr, (i) Frank Lloyd Wright, and (j) William Drummond. Alfred B. Yeomans, ed., *City Residential Land Development, Studies in Planning: Competitive Plans for Subdividing a Typical Quarter Section of Land in the Outskirts of Chicago* (Chicago: University of Chicago Press, 1916).

boulevards; from boulevards to suburban development and land subdivision; from land subdivision to neighborhood unit development and new towns; and from new towns to the orderly improvement of whole states and regions, and there has been a development, step by step, in the professional technique of planning to meet the requirements of wider and still wider fields.[17]
—*John Nolen*

We invite anyone who may contemplate housing enterprises, to confer with us in regard to our method of conducting such work, according to the most advanced modern practice.... Booklet of Modern Industrial Housing sent on request.[18]
—*the firm of Ballinger and Perot*

In addition to the "rugged individualist" and Christian capitalist, there was Hoover the "organization man," the master administrator and organizational genius who had early embraced the gospel of efficiency and the values of order, rationality, and planning. His experiences, both in the business world and the war government, had made him a leading member of the new managerial and scientific elite.[19]
—*Ellis W. Hawley*

The Committee on Subdivision Layout intended to demonstrate that engineers, planners, and professional subdividers engaged in the artful science of "modern subdivision practice" could now provide a "technical service" by coordinating streets, sidewalks, open space, and housing within the residential fabric.[14] Included in the report was a study conducted for the Harvard City Planning series that, like the Chicago City Club competition, depicted various subdivision strategies on a identical palette of 200 acres. The study encapsulated subdivision science and real estate conventions as they had been practiced since World War I. It arrived at fairly predictable conclusions about the relationship between density and infrastructure: 40 percent of the land was reserved for open spaces and streets with 60 percent buildable area. Tabulating cost of land, numbers of houses, utility runs, paving, and other factors, the study scanned numerous arrangements of street, lot, and building. The plans represented spatial arrangements but also served as graphic tables of these various financial and spatial economies (figure 3.1.2).[15]

The study diagrammed arrangements with single, double, and triple building lines, cul-de-sacs, loops, square versus hexagonal blocks, and cross-access superblock grids. Perhaps most unusual were the diagrams of double and triple building lines that suggested the possibility of accessing more than one row of houses from a single street. The double and triple building line developments, by necessitating a cul-de-sac extension of the street were essentially approaching some of the RPAA's special planning techniques. In fact, the committee featured Radburn, New Jersey, as a frontispiece to the report and noted it favorably in the text. The final diagram was of a "model" neighborhood that, unlike the other diagrams, mixed multiple unit dwellings with single family houses and achieved the greatest efficiency. While the neighborhood supposedly followed some larger city planning directive, there was no graphic depiction of the relationships between the neighborhood units themselves. Rather there was an intensive study of quantifiable formulaic relationships at a much smaller scale, thus lending credence to the idea that leadership was largely being provided for conventional real estate practices and municipal annexation by subdivisions.[16]

For many of the planners, the Harvard study's abstract graphics would have been treated as a kind of notation for a much more complex process, one that could only be guided by years of experience. The graphics as well as the treatment of the subdivision as a discrete element unto itself, however, supported changing attitudes about residential fabric as an organization whose relationships were as elementary as the shorthand used to represent them. More importantly, the graphics did not convey information about timing. The functional relations of street and housing aggregate relied on incremental growth or partial control of the fabric for their complexity. Establishing all the relationships at once created a planimetric template rather than a number of interdependent functional expressions with temporal variables. Subdivision designs included far fewer of the sectional, volumetric, or experiential relationships between house, infrastructure, and topography. The plan also lent itself to the kind of financial tabulations that became the real governing order underlying subdivision arrangements, as they became tools of banking and employment in the ensuing years. For the subdivision's new banking sponsor, these representations of building footprint facilitated the idea that the subdivision and its houses formed an organization that could be optimized for maximum economies of space and profit.

In recent years the whole science and art of subdivision design has been developing rapidly; on no account would a good subdivider now be guilty of the ugly and uneconomic type of subdivision that underlies most of our cities; such experiments as Radburn, New Jersey, and many others are testing out new and valuable principles.[20]
—*President's Conference on Home Building and Home Ownership*

War-Towns

In addition to being the first government-subsidized housing projects, the so-called "war-towns" were laboratories for experimenting with subdivision and housing protocols, addressing in particular various means of capitalizing and structuring land acquisition, management, and ownership. In 1918, the U.S. Shipping Board established the Emergency Fleet Corporation and the U.S. Housing Corporation to manage the building of new shipping communities to support defense efforts.[3] Upon entering World War I, the United States inventoried its productivity, resources, and infrastructure. An endemic housing shortage exacerbated by the mobilization of new military bases and the need for expedient war time production prompted an extensive federal appraisal of American housing.

Just a year earlier in 1917, in response to the petitions of "thousands of American citizens," the U.S. Senate had held hearings on the feasibility of the Garden City in America.[4] Most of the testimony centered around timing and sponsorship, and indeed these factors would be strong determinants of subdivision organization throughout the century. Though the testimony explored several funding strategies, "copartnership" or "limited dividend" were usually quickly inserted into the discussions to replace the word "cooperative." In government-

DIAGRAM 12. THE SINGLE BUILDING-LINE IN THE GRIDIRON PATTERN

DIAGRAM 13. SINGLE BUILDING-LINE IN IRREGULAR PATTERN

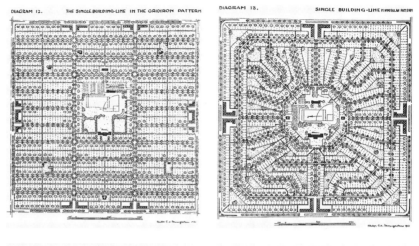

DIAGRAM 14. DOUBLE BUILDING-LINE IN IRREGULAR PATTERN

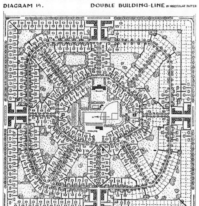

DIAGRAM 15. TRIPLE BUILDING-LINE IN IRREGULAR PATTERN

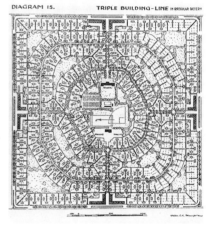

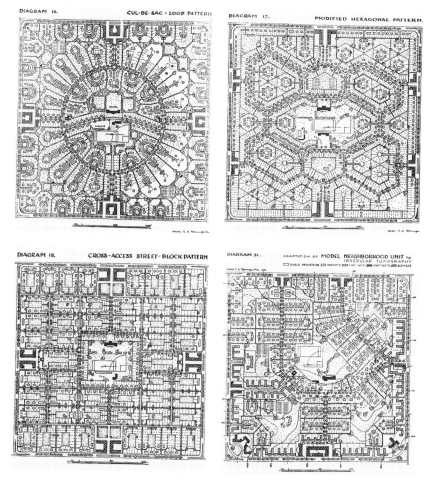

3.1.2 Diagrams from study conducted for the Harvard City Planning Series: (a) single building line in the gridiron pattern, (b) single building line in irregular pattern, (c) double building line in irregular pattern, (d) triple building line in irregular pattern, (e) cul-de-sac-loop pattern, (f) modified hexagonal pattern, (g) cross-access street-block pattern, (h) adaptation of model neighborhood unit to irregular topography. President of the United States, *President's Conference on Home Building and Home Ownership, Vol. 1 Planning for Residential Districts* (Washington, D.C.: U.S. Government Printing Office, 1932) 100, 101, 102, 103, 104, 106, 109.

supported British Garden Cities, inhabitants did not buy their individual property, but rather became stockholders through the payment of rent. When the individually owned stock equaled the value of the property, inhabitants could become owners of that property. The senators noted that even this copartnership plan differed from the "ordinary American plan" that "Americans seem to think is still the best plan." They noted the "distinct advantages to those of the laboring or operative class in buying, paying for, and eventually owning" their own property.[5] The Senate also heard testimony concerning special industrial towns in America that had managed the initial investments of capital to include provisions for employee-owned housing. (e.g., Pullman, Illinois; Gary, Indiana; Fairfield, Alabama; and Goodyear Heights near Akron Ohio). Most of the company towns also provided evidence of the importance of ownership by allied industries as well as asset management by an intermediate land-holding company. Testimony included several suggestions that the government follow in the footsteps of England's Parliament, establishing a Garden City experiment with an initial loan outlay of federal funds.[6] Though there had never been communities developed with direct subsidizes of federal funds, by the next year, a year marked by America's entry into the war, there would be several.

Since building houses involved a number of trades, professions, and industries, in building the war towns the government presided over projects affecting a broad domestic economy. Consequently, the war towns contributed to the inclusion of housing concerns on the nation's agenda in the ensuing decades. Since most of the projects were funded with a mixture of federal and private sources, the effort was in some ways, a rehearsal for the federal government's later involvement in community building and public housing in the 1930s and beyond.

Though critical, the physical arrangements were perhaps not as important as the financial arrangements that capitalized and maintained the war towns. Unlike some later federal community-building projects, these war towns delegated both financial management and land ownership to several different private entities who invested the government contribution, often using it to return value to the community or initiate its self-maintenance.[7] The organizational architecture of these financial arrangements, with all their redundancies and safety nets, was particularly intelligent and sturdy.

Having seen the benefits of government management and allied private interests through their association with the World War I ship-building communities, a number of planners began to solicit federal and private support for what they considered to be a new planning science. From July 25, 1918, to the end of the war on November 11, 1918, the U.S. Housing Corporation completed the plans and specifications for eighty-three projects.[8] Wishing to give the appearance of a movement, John Nolen's 1927 address to the National Conference on City Planning reported seventy such "war towns" and at least thirty-five "new towns, garden cities, satellite towns, or garden suburbs" had been built as part of this effort.[9] After the war, one of the most prominent members of this generation of planners, John Nolen wrote, "A new town can be built for $1,000,000. We are waking up to this fact. We are coming to see that if a battleship costs $42,000,000 and we have been able to build a fleet of them, the actual building of an entire city is a mere incident in terms of dollars but of the most momentous importance to the present and future welfare of every citizen."[10]

Mariemont and Kingsport

Two notable examples of the war-town planning science, Kingsport, Tennessee, on the Kentucky border and Mariemont, Ohio, a satellite of Cincinnati, were the work of John Nolen's office. Both were in the planning stages before World War I, but completed the first stages of their growth between the postwar "business as usual" period of the 1920s and the Hoover years of the Depression. Critiques of these two towns have usually focused not on their organization but on their appearance. Considered together, these two towns provide a comparative framework for assessing both the deliberate and default protocols of residential subdivision development during the interwar period. In both, the simple grid of streets developed by lot sales was adjusted with intermediate organizational agents, related to sponsorship, timing, and housing aggregate (figures 3.1.3 and 3.1.4).

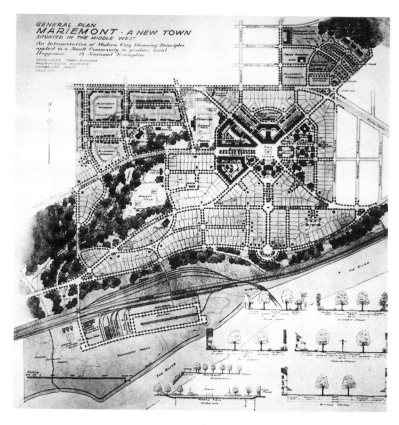

3.1.3 Plan of Mariemont, Ohio. John Nolen Papers, The Department of Manuscripts and University Archives, Olin Library, Cornell University.

Kingsport was an American mongrel, an industrial "city functional," initially sponsored and directed by railroad executives. Mariemont, on the other hand, was a pastoral, landscaped satellite, sponsored by a philanthropic organization. Mariemont was developed by members of both the Commercial Club and the Municipal Art Society in carefully tended steps. Inspired by Letchworth in England, Mariemont, like other American versions of the Garden City, was styled after a picturesque English village. Kingsport, on the other hand, was developed by the members of the Chamber of Commerce and the Boosters. The town's history was not chronicled and celebrated by an adoring citizenry as it was in Mariemont, but rather understood through real estate artifacts and the publications of the Rotary Club. Mariemont was comprehensively planned, whereas Kingsport received the most minimal planning treatment and was developed in the midst of a less genteel and more anarchical pattern of growth. At 365 acres, Mariemont was a self-contained satellite that has remained true to its initial plat and boundaries over its several decades of growth and has served as a kind of time capsule of the spatial volumes associated with vintage 1920s planning science. At 1,100 acres, Kingsport was almost three times the size of Mariemont and comparable in size to other small American cities. Throughout its several decades of growth, the town has become a museum of various twentieth-century approaches to subdivision design.

Neither town was a garden-variety American small town like Sinclair Lewis' fictional town of Zenith, though Kingsport more closely resembled "the old Zip City." Mariemont was one of Nolen's favorite examples of town-planning arrangements, while Kingsport was a kind of problem child over which the office had little control. Touted as a "national exemplar," Mariemont was internationally recognized as a successful model of the Garden City as urban satellite. In 1924, the *New York Times Magazine* called the town, "The City Set at the Crossroads: A New Experiment in Town Planning to Fit the Motor Age."[21] Soviet planners inspected the town. Raymond Unwin also visited and praised Mariemont. Cited in books and articles as a noteworthy American variation on the Garden City idea, the town stood as precedent for federal experiments during the New Deal period. Kingsport also drew many visitors during the building of neighboring TVA experiments. But the leadership of both towns, particularly Kingsport, steered clear of all associations with social experiments to maintain the character of a traditional financial venture.

Kingsport's land was bought by railroad executives for reduced rates because of their advance knowledge of the railroad's route. Different from its company-town predecessors like Pullman, Illinois; Alcoa, Tennessee; or Kohler Village, Wisconsin, Kingsport was sponsored by allied industries, including glass, dyes, synthetic fibers, charcoal briquettes, and textiles. The town congratulated itself as a modern model community with well oiled, Taylorized industrial

3.1.4 Early aerial views of Kingsport, Tennessee. John Nolen papers, #2903. Division of Rare and Manuscript Collections, Cornell University Library.

arrangements, motivated businesses, diversified industry, access to railroads and resources, and inexpensive labor. Avoiding the mistakes of other industrial boom towns, Kingsport provided housing as a means of settling and pacifying its workers. In 1916, Nolen was asked to consult on an initial plan for Kingsport. The plan bluntly outlined the essential elements of conservative southern civilization: industry, transportation, business, religion, and family. In the plan, which had been designed by a railroad engineer, a business boulevard rolling up-hill from the river, connected factories, a railroad station, and a rotary called "Church Circle" that radiated out into the residential districts on the hills above. Nolen and his associates, Philip Foster and Earle S. Draper, worked on various refinements of the scheme's street design and platting, though difficult communications and the client's occasional disregard for professional advice distanced Nolen from the proceedings. The office completed an initial plan in 1916, but the most familiar early plan for which Nolen is often given full credit was published after the war in 1919. It primarily refined the street hierarchy in the central business district and added some new residential districts.[22]

In Mariemont, Nolen was allowed to construct an elaborate exercise in 1920s town-planning techniques. At the turn of the century in Cincinnati, Ohio, Thomas J. Emery, a first generation American from Wales and his wife Mary Muhlenberg Emery commanded real estate interests in Ohio that by the 1930s rivaled those of the Astor estate in New York. When Mr. Emery died in 1906, Mary Emery established the Thomas J. Emery Memorial, a nonprofit philanthropic corporation among whose chief projects was to create a country village outside Cincinnati for the workers who had helped build the Emery empire. The Emery's two sons, Albert and Sheldon, had both died at an early age, and Mary Emery summoned one of their college friends, a young man with the appropriately Dickinsian name of Charles J. Livingood, to come to Cincinnati to manage the design and construction of her model town. While traveling in England, Livingood had visited Letchworth which, as stylistically rendered by Raymond Unwin and Barry Parker, portrayed the Garden City as an English country village with a bucolic blend of Ruskin and Morris and an apparent appreciation of craft and rural cottage industry. The aesthetic appeal of the Garden City idea and its association with the progressive ideas of British and American intellectuals perfectly suited Mary Emery's rather beatific dream of reforming the housing of city dwellers.[23]

Preliminary plans for Mariemont were made as early as 1914 before American involvement in World War I.[24] In 1920 Livingood formally retained Nolen as the town's designer. Land was purchased in the early 1920s and construction begun in 1923. The announcement of the town appeared in the *Cincinnati Enquirer* in 1922 with the headline "Lady Bountiful's [Mary Emery] wand is to wave over tract near Madisonville."[25] The Mariemont company offered both rental properties and lot sales. Citizens could buy stock in Mariemont and would benefit from increases in land value through their own investments, or, if the company enjoyed excess profits, the addition of extra amenities to the town. The George Babbitts of Cincinnati, however, would read on to find that Mariemont was not to be a: ". . . laboratory for sociological experiments in the problem of housing. It, therefore, does not follow the English plan of copartnership building and ownership . . . The people in this country are still individualistic in their attitude and action and do not readily take to cooperative housing schemes. It is a real estate development, pure and simple on normal American lines. . . ."[26] On the evening of Mariemont's announcement, John Nolen spoke to the businessmen of Cincinnati's Commercial Club about the need to increase home ownership as a means of generating worker stability and contentment. "No longer are we a nation of homeowners. We are mere renters, and therefore, drifters and floaters—at least 60 percent of us." Nolen claimed.[27] He was courting a partnership that he hoped would create a Garden City movement.

Kingsport and Mariemont incorporated both specialized and default arrangements of the street. At Kingsport, Nolen did little more than help to shape the main streets. He designed a hierarchy of five business streets ranging from 50 to 100 feet wide in the down-town area.[28] Elms were planted down the length of Broad Street, the central business spine. Steeples from the Church Circle were placed on axis with the residential streets and could be seen from the hills above. The Mariemont plat blended radial and curvilinear grids to ac-commodate topography as a geometric reference to both Howard and the City Beautiful. Considering approximately 250 of the total 365 acres, a little less than 50 percent were given over to lots, 20 percent to parks, approximately 10 percent to other public and semipublic areas, and 23 percent to streets.[29] He planned for a population of 5,000 that would eventually grow to 10,000. Nolen designed a minor street (40 to 20 foot roadway), secondary street (50 to 24 foot roadway), main street (60 to 82 foot roadway), streetcar line street (80 feet), a business street (100 feet), and the concourse street which ran along the bluffs at the edge of town. Most of the residential streets had 20 to 35 foot setbacks. The largest street, Wooster Pike, was a grand boulevard which extended the space of the village into the city of Cincinnati. The central square receiving Wooster Pike was 150 feet wide.[30] All the streets were lined with trees as a matter of course and to resist disease, a variety of trees were used in landscaping the town.

In both Kingsport and Mariemont, the group house, like the street, served as kind of intermediate organizing function. At Mariemont, Nolen devised a scheme to both ensure variety in the fabric and support an incremental phasing plan. The housing was accomplished through assignments to different architects. The more densely platted subcenters and special formations around squares or closes each received an architectural assignment. In Kingsport, these specialized residential districts were intended to anchor sections of town with a neighborhood of recognizable character. Two of them, "the Fifties" and "White City" were intended to house the bosses of the industry and they contained double, triple, and group houses in specialized formations. Platting by quarter-acre lots and separate subdivisions filled most of the remaining area of the town.

In 1937, the federal government publish a supplementary report to a larger study entitled "Our Cities" that inventoried planned communities in America. The report looked at approximately 150 communities in America and selected 29 to survey in detail. The thorough surveys studied physical planning issues like street size and hierarchy, sponsorship, maintenance, governance, size, and aesthetics. Perhaps most interesting was the fact that the study arranged its catalog of communities according to the sponsorship and financing that was so critical to the organizational character of residential formations. Both towns appeared in the report. When representatives of the National Resources Committee visited Kingsport in the 1930s, they found areas of boom-town blight and uncontrolled growth that the Depression had only exacerbated.[31] Unions organized during the Depression and, though there were some serious episodes of labor unrest, wartime industry in both World Wars I and II created an intensified demand for labor that temporarily masked growing problems surrounding the town's facilities. The town preceded Mariemont, but developed through the growth booms of both world wars and acquired a subdivision during each successive phase of suburban growth from the Depression to the present. During World War II, several FHA-financed subdivisions were developed: Cherokee Village, Bayview, and Forest Lawn. Some contained good brick housing stock, well-platted lots, and well-sized roadways. Other war-time housing stock ranged from wood and brick structures to less expensive wood-frame conscript houses or simple barrack-like boxes on streets with no other components besides the roadway itself.[32] The house and street were considered separately. The streets were usually designed to absorb a generalized quotient or "peak load" of traffic that often rendered them too large to sustain spatial relationships with small housing stock. Housing was sized and shaped to constraints associated with affordability and the developer's financial protocols. Some of Kingsport's annexed areas were larger than the entire town of Mariemont. The pattern of development called for large roadways sometimes 60 feet in width without sidewalks or planting. Most also had set backs of over 20 feet or larger. The Elm trees died of blight after World War II, and many of the sites were turned to parking lots in the central business district. Mariemont on the other hand was a storybook town for a community of "joiners." Livingood carried out his duties like a gentleman overseer "curating" the main public buildings and other public fixtures (e.g., bell tower, church, hotel, and theater) that were also funded by the Mariemont Foundation. Paradoxically, preservation of the quaint styling of the town has served to neutralize changes and new relationships between the house and street almost as effectively as postwar subdivision protocols.

Arguably, the most complex spatial organization occurred on the mongrel streets of Kingsport or Mariemont where some accident in the design protocols or the anarchies of lot sales and consumption laid a richer bed of spaces. Both towns were affected by their method of sponsorship and eventual self-governance. In the ensuing decades, the method of finance and sponsorship as directed by bureaucratic government agencies would prove to be one of the dominant protocols shaping residential subdivisions.

John Nolen: Planning Rotarian

John Nolen (1869–1937) was planning's Rotarian and dean. His career spanned from the City Beautiful movement to the period of regional and greenbelt town planning in the 1930s, and he was a leader and founder of conferences and professional associations. In the 1910s and 1920s, an investor interested in establishing a suburb based on Garden City principles could choose from a number of practitioners, but John Nolen was among those from whom one would surely seek consultation. Nolen was at once the City Beautiful aesthetic consultant, the Garden City reformer, and the small town booster. He kept the movement and his practice alive by changing the tenor and scope of his agenda to address any opportunity. Whether the sponsor was public or private, he was always there, presenting his resume and indicating his eagerness to serve in the making of a town, parkway, or region. In fact, he often tailored his advocacies to win the support of the reformers as well as the powers that be.[33] By the end of his career, he had designed 27 new towns in America and been involved in a total of over 400 planning projects of various kinds. Nolen chronicled the planning movement in various books, pamphlets, studies, and public addresses.[34] In addition to organizing his colleagues by leading the early conferences, he also established a city planning curriculum at the Harvard School of Landscape Architecture. A number of planners, among them Earle S. Draper, Tracy B. Augur, and Jacob L. Crane, who led significant careers during the New Deal period and after worked in Nolen's office.[35]

Having studied under Frederick Law Olmsted Jr., Nolen inherited expertise from the late nineteenth-century landscape tradition. Landscape design, often involved organizing vision and experience in the contours of space between architectural objects and so perhaps sponsored an experiential rather than purely formal approach to planning. Like others who began their careers in the incipient phases of a planning movement, Nolen did not specialize. He and his colleagues often took a broad approach to the enterprise of arranging land. He knew how to juggle the interdependent details of platting, promotion, and the bottom line. Promoting planning "science" as a repeatable and quantifiable phenomenon, Nolen's office led the profession in the practice of tabulating comparative land-use percentages between open space, infrastructure, public building, and residential areas for selected communities.

While conservative enough to seek the support of capitalists like Henry Ford, Nolen's writings and speeches echoed many progressive ideologies and traditions. He campaigned for the Garden City as a unit of development in America, and as part of a comprehensive plan regarding labor, land use, and quality of life. In the course of his career, his discussions of the Garden City expanded to support regional planning goals, and his experience in the making of urban and suburban streets expanded into the realm of parkway design.

In the 1980s, Nolen was revived by neotraditionalist planners who were trying to associate the idea of "town" with their subdivisions, as that idea evoked associations with a broad range of planning Americana from the Colonial settlement to the Kansas gridiron. Nolen's towns in particular were valued in this revival in part because he merged several traditions within the garden-variety real estate format associated with small municipalities. That basic format had grown out of a longer tradition of land subdivision by grids and plats, but curiously Nolen's very specialized designs for the fabric of small municipalities were treated by revivalists as having a kind of authenticity, even with the full knowledge that America has no authentic urbanism, only a long history of diverse and hybrid models. For those accustomed to postwar residential arrangements, the work from Nolen's office exercised an incredible variety of different aggregates and formations for housing and real estate sales. These planning methods were, to some degree, successfully revived in the marketplace because their cosmetic charm was as bankable in the 1980s as it had been in the 1920s.

Notes

1. Alfred B. Yeomans, ed., *City Residential Land Development, Studies in Planning: Competitive Plans for Subdividing a Typical Quarter Section of Land in the Outskirts of Chicago* (Chicago: Chicago University Press, 1916), passim. Gwendolyn Wright's *Moralism and the Modern Home* also contains a discussion of the competition.

2. Clarence Arthur Perry, "The Neighborhood Unit," *Regional Plan of New York and its Environs, Volume VII Neighborhood and Community Planning* (New York: Regional Plan, 1929), 73.

3. U.S. Department of Labor, *Report of the United States Housing Corporation, Volume II: Houses, Site-planning, Utilities* (Washington, D.C.: U.S. Government Printing Office, 1919), 15–18.

4. Senate Subcommittee of the Committee on Agriculture and Forestry, A resolution authorizing and requesting the Senate committee on Agriculture and Forestry to hear and consider testimony relative to the Garden City and Garden Suburb movement, H. R. 10104, S. Res. 305, 64th Congress, 2nd Session (Washington, DC: U.S. Government Printing Office, 1917), 1.

5. Ibid., 6.

6. Ibid., passim.

7. For instance, in the development of Union Park Gardens in Delaware, the Wilmington, Delaware, Chamber of Commerce organized the contributions of several local industries involved in war-time production to capitalize the Wilmington Housing Company. The development was then managed by an operating company, the Liberty Land Co., which bought a parcel of 58 acres and gave it to the government. The government loaned the construction costs and was repaid 5 percent per year with balance used toward the amortization of the principal. John Nolen was the town planner. Ballinger and Perot, designed twenty different group house types for the 554 units. Even in this small neighborhood, Nolen incorporated a hierarchy of four different street types, including a large parkway. For Yorkship Village in Camden, New Jersey, the government provided $10 million for the building of a town. The land was already owned by the New York Shipbuilding Corporation residing in Camden which set up a subsidiary agency, The Fairview Realty Company, to run the town. This company repaid the government at 5 percent interest and 3 percent principle per year. The rest of the profits went into the maintenance and improvement of the town. Although they were attached dwellings, the ship workers owned their houses. U.S. National Resources Committee, Urbanism Committee *Urban Planning and Land Policies: Volume II of the Supplementary Report of the Urbanism Committee to the National Resources Committee* (Washington, D.C.: U.S. Government Printing Office, 1939), 67–69.

8. U.S. Department of Labor, *Report of the United States Housing Corporation, Volume II: Houses, Site-planning, Utilities* (Washington, D.C.: U.S. Government Printing Office, 1919), 23.

9. John Nolen, "Twenty Years of City Planning Progress in the United States, 1907–1927," *Planning Problems of Town, City and Region Papers and Discussions at the Nineteenth National City Planning Conference* (Washington, D.C.: National Conference, 1927), 15, 16.

10. John Nolen, "A Demonstration town for Ohio," *Journal of the Town Planning Institute of Canada* 2 (May 1923): 6.

11. Better Homes in America, *Guidebook for Better Homes Campaign in Rural Communities and Small Towns* (Washington, D.C.: Better Homes in America, 1929).

12. Alan Brinkley, *The End of Reform: New Deal Liberalism in Recession and War* (New

York: Alfred A. Knopf, 1995), 9; Elis W. Hawley, *American Forum Series: Herbert Hoover and the Crisis of American Capitalism* (Cambridge: Schenkman Publishing Company, 1973), 4, 14.

13. President of the United States, *President's Conference on Home Building and Home Ownership, vol. 1 Planning for Residential Districts* (Washington, D.C.: U.S. Government Printing Office, 1932), 8, 9, 26, 5. Membership in the City Planning and Zoning Committee included Frederic Delano as chair, Charles W. Eliot II, Harland Bartholomew, and Thomas Adams. Delano and Eliot had served on the National Capital Park and Planning Commission in Washington, D.C., and both would later serve as chairs of the National Resources Committee. Delano and Adams had administered the regional plan of New York and its environs. Mumford's critiques of this plan perhaps alienated the group from planners like Adams and leaders like Delano, who would hold positions of power during the New Deal period.

14. Ibid. 47, 51. The committee was composed of a familiar group of planners, including Harland Bartholomew, Henry Hubbard, chairman of City Planning at Harvard, the developer G. A. Nichols, John Nolen, Robert Whitten, and RPAA member Henry Wright.

15. Ibid., 85–124.

16. Ibid.

17. John Nolen. "The Landscape Architect in Regional and State Planning," *Landscape Architecture* (July 1935): 2.

18. Advertisement, *Architectural Record* (1919), reprint, Nolen papers, #2903, Division of Rare and Manuscript Collections, Cornell University Libraries.

19. Elis W. Hawley, 9.

20. *President's Conference on Home Building and Home Ownership*, 52.

21. Brock, H. I. "The City Set at the Crossroads: A New Experiment in Town Planning to Fit the Motor Age," *New York Times Magazine* (August 24, 1924), 7–8.

22. Ibid., 31–57; and Margaret Ripley Wolfe, *Kingsport: A Planned American City* (Lexington: University Press of Kentucky, 1987), 44.

23. Warren Wright Parks, *The Mariemont Story* (Cincinnati: Creative Writers and Publishers, Inc., 1967), 12, 62.

24. Ibid., 17.

25. "Model Town to Arise Over Mound Village; Mariemont Likened to English Garden City," *The Cincinnati Enquirer* (April 30, 1922).

26. Anon. *A Descriptive and Picture Story of Mariemont, A New Town 'A living Exemplar'* (Cincinnati: The Mariemont Company 1925), 13–15.

27. John Nolen, Abstract of speech delivered to the Commercial Club of Cincinnati, April, 1923, Nolen papers, #2903, Division of Rare and Manuscript Collections, Cornell University Libraries.

28. Minor residential streets were typically 40 feet wide, including planting strips and sidewalks and were flanked by 20 foot setbacks. Secondary residential streets were typically 50 feet wide, including planting strips and sidewalks, and were flanked by 30 to 40 foot setbacks.

29. U.S. National Resources Committee, Urbanism Committee, *Urban Planning and Land Policies: Volume II of the Supplementary Report of the Urbanism Committee to the National Resources Committee* (Washington, D. C.: U.S. Government Printing Office 1939), 18.

30. Parks, *The Mariemont Story*, 27–28.

31. National Resources Committee, 38, 37.

32. Wolfe, 145; and *Kingsport, Tennessee* (Kingsport: Rotary Club, 1938).

33. John Loretz Hancock, *John Nolen and the American City Planning Movement: A History of Cultural Change and Community Response 1900–1940*, Ph. D. diss., University of Pennsylvania, 1964, 37.

34. Most notable among his books and collected writings were *City Planning* (1916) and *New Towns for Old* (1927).

35. Hancock, 37. Other planners who worked for Nolen's office include Russell Van Nest Black, Philip W. Foster, Justin R. Hartzog, Hale J. Walker, Irving C. Root, Harold A. Merrill, Max S. Wehrly, and Howard K. Menlinick.

3.2 FUNCTION: NEW DEAL DEMONSTRATION PROJECTS

Advocates and practitioners reporting for duty in Washington at the beginning of the New Deal period espoused various strains of communitarian planning ideology associated with, for instance, regionalism, industrial decentralization, employment relief, population redistribution, experimental agriculture, or the virtues of home ownership. Many of these planners used their wartime experience to form a broader and politically more radical critique of the metropolis and its satellite suburbs. New Deal community-building programs incorporated some of these ideas in their demonstration projects. The RPAA's specialized residential planning devices were widely admired among the planners in Washington. A few of these planners were, or had been, RPAA members, and some of the demonstration projects borrowed RPAA techniques. Two of these demonstration projects, Norris, Tennessee, and Greendale, Wisconsin, incorporated RPAA techniques; due to different constraints of timing and site, however, they resulted in relaxed or hybrid versions of the more holistic RPAA prototypes. They also were among the few New Deal community projects to use single-family detached housing, which became the dominant dwelling type after the war. Consequently, these more informal projects provided a rare glimpse of the generic postwar housing commodity arranged under very different terms.

RPAA

The RPAA was not only intent on replacing the city's suburban satellites with a network of smaller regional cities, but also intended to turn the typical subdivision grid inside out, making it dependent on a set of relationships between house, pedestrian network, and vehicular network. The two main RPAA prototypes, Sunnyside Gardens, Queens (1924), and Radburn, New

Jersey (1928), were explicitly governed by specialized interlocking functions—the neighborhood unit, superblock, cul de sac, and greenbelt—organizational expressions for local as well as regional-continental relationships.

The foundation of the Sunnyside experiment was a financial organization—one that had typically been used for urban apartment dwellings. Alexander Bing, Clarence Stein, and Henry Wright funded Sunnyside through the City Housing Corporation, (CHC) which they established as a limited-dividend corporation. Limited-dividend corporations typically invited investors (Eleanor Roosevelt invested in the CHC), to contribute to affordable housing by agreeing to receive a limited return, usually 6 percent on their investment. Bing was the financier while Stein and Wright handled the design, but the trio had complementary skills and treated the project as a kind of "laboratory," thus, both the physical and financial planning were highly integrated.[1] The partnership itself was a notable organization. Wright was an ingenious technician of the group house, who could single-handedly juggle adjustments to utilities, room sizes, corridors, stairs, and interest rates. A fellow planner later wrote that, "Henry had the most delicate feeling for contours; he could walk over a fifty-acre tract and go home and sketch its contours with uncanny accuracy."[2] At Sunnyside, Wright proposed a different framework and orientation of houses within the block system wherein remainder spaces in lots and roadways could be put to use in group houses and community street networks. While the row house on a city block was typically narrow and deep, Wright's adjusted configuration turned the row houses ninety degrees to form a more continuous, though not unbroken wall along the street. As a consequence the houses received more light, shared a slab, saved on party-wall construction, and provided area for an interior green. They also reduced maintenance costs for corridors and common internal staircases and contained a mixture of different dwelling types and sizes (figure 3.2.1).[3]

In the Radburn prototype, the cul-de-sac, superblock, and neighborhood unit were used as interdependent functions in a larger expression of growth. Radburn was to have three neighborhood units, each a unit of growth determined by a half-mile radius around a school and containing a quotient of private residential space, public green space, and circulation space. Within each neighborhood unit, the housing would be arranged in thirty-five to fifty acre "superblocks," penetrated by cul-de-sacs, leaving an open spine of green park in the center of the block. This interior green formed a large park with long views to replace the traditional backyard. Just as the neighborhood unit

3.2.1 Advertisement for City Housing Corporation showing Sunnyside Gardens, Queens, New York. *The Survey Graphic.* Regional Planning 54 (1925): 125.

was a function of the walking distance surrounding a school, the cul-de-sac was a function of both an interior pedestrian network, a reoriented house, and a system of vehicular networks. The roadways were service lanes, and a separate network of pedestrian paths used underpasses to avoid crossing these and other vehicular networks, giving children a safe route to school. Thus the cul-de-sacs were not dead ends or terminations of the network. Rather, the house was a point of transfer between the vehicular and pedestrian networks. Houses also turned their more formal entry and rooms toward the pedestrian path and the interior green, thus reducing the cost of street improvements but requiring cooperative control. In a sense, strands of the typical grid network had been pulled into a reserve of open green space and then platted with small lots to accommodate a specialized dwelling with two types of entry.[4] The fourth component of the RPAA formula was the greenbelt, a land preserve that would buffer the community from excessive growth either from the inside or the outside. The group was disappointed that as a satellite suburb of New York City, Radburn was not a true regional city and

3.2.2 Plan of Radburn, New Jersey. Clarence S. Stein, *Toward New Towns for America* (Cambridge, MA: MIT Press, 1957), 50.

therefore not an emblem of their larger political program. Radburn not only had no greenbelt, but it was also developing housing on agricultural land that effectively served as a greenbelt for the larger metropolitan area of New York City (figure 3.2.2).

Though the RPAA's experimental prototypes marshaled private funds and managed them successfully within cooperative structures, they concluded that most private corporations were simply incapable of taking risks associated with the large expenditures of capital that community development required. As some evidence suggests, the group also wished to pursue its holistic goals of regional reorganization unencumbered by the compromises associated with market pressures, especially since Radburn had been crippled by the crash of 1929. Though private industry was also serenading the government for subsidies, the planner's call for public funding would eventually alienate community-building projects within the conservative Congresses of New Deal.[5] The RPAA's antimetropolitan bias and nostalgic sentiment about the authenticity of the New England settlement rarefied its approach. In addition, the prototypes were often self-referential, only reluctantly inviting circumstance or contamination from prevailing organizations of land and housing. For instance, the RPAA's eventual position about government funding did not engage any of the conventional protocols of real estate and financing, so that when the cul-de-sac and superblock were borrowed by developers of postwar tract housing, they were always quoted outside the context of the RPAA's specialized planning calculus. As RPAA formats were adopted by federal community-building projects and later by private enterprise, they were transferred into organizations of an entirely different character. In some cases, exposure to more anarchical forms of real estate development added intelligence to the organization. In other cases, as in the context of the postwar FHA subdivisions, use of these formations as planimetric templates erased their functional relationships entirely.

Norris, Tennessee

In June of 1933, Arthur Morgan, one of the TVA administrators, proposed a model town to house the workers for Norris Dam, one of several dams within the river system. Norris, with its large greenbelt and small internal community, was to be a demonstration town illustrating Morgan's utopian ideologies about community, worker, and craft.[6] As the first completely hydroelectric community, however, it was also associated with new technological goals. For instance, the housing was based on vernacular types found in the Tennessee hills, but the coop grocery store was styled as a gleaming, modern socialist experiment. The houses also fashioned a folksy modernity out of new and old materials, including brick, plywood paneling, aluminum showers, and steel windows, but they had efficient demonstration kitchens, modern plumbing, electric wiring, and contemporary furnishings as well (figure 3.2.3).[7]

Since Norris was a divergent negotiation of both regionalist and postwar residential arrangements, the same small boxy houses that would be so prevalent after the war were positioned within an eccentric organizational context. Because Norris was an emergency employment project, workers were on the job before the plans were complete and planning perpetually lagged behind the construction work in the field. In fact, due to the speed with which Norris had to be built, many houses were sited and built before roads were cut, so siting was not determined by planimetric orders but rather by vistas and topographic contours. The groupings were not intimate but afforded the view of a population of houses that appeared to stand together in the land rather

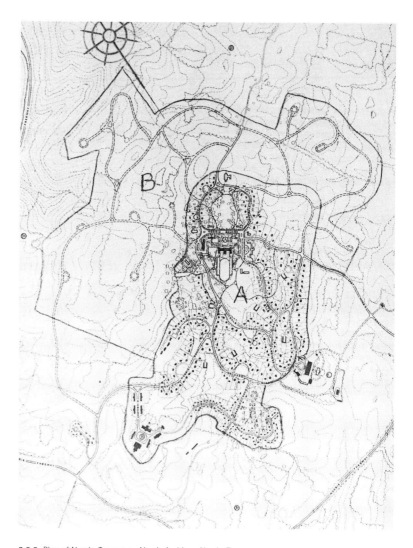

3.2.3 Plan of Norris, Tennessee. Norris Archives, Norris, Tennessee.

than on individual lots. A common version of these looser superblocks and cul-de-sacs grouped houses around a semicircular drive or semicircular green. In some cases, the loop was enlarged to a diameter of approximately 300 feet and sited along a topographical ridge. The houses were then spaced along the rim of a large arc surrounding an enormous shared green space. These variants of the superblock and cul-de-sac were further manipulated by schedule and site constraints creating in many cases unplanned, yet more precise spatial arrangements.

Norris and Oak Ridge, Tennessee, shared the same sponsor, and they were thirty miles and roughly a decade apart, yet they were vastly different organizations. Whereas topography dictated certain design expedients in Norris, planimetric systems controlled the arrangement of Oak Ridge. As a massive plant for building the bomb, the design of Oak Ridge was an expression of an efficient distribution of elements necessary to complete a military mission. The town was a long highway thickened by residential and commercial areas. Perhaps the town defined a more expansive form of urbanism. Nevertheless, there were a few special groupings or arrangements. The residential streets were primarily sized as secondary streets and only deviated from straight lines to negotiate topography. Most of the homes were typical of the boxy prefabricated conscript housing found in many defense projects all across the country. Oak Ridge was a special case, however, design was not the foremost consideration. For security reasons the designers, Skidmore, Owings and Merrill, were barely given enough access to documentation to provide a reasonable site plan. At Norris, over thirty-five different housing types were developed for a comparatively small number of houses (a notable figure compared to the same ratio in postwar times when, as in the case of Levittown, Long Island, 17,000 homes were designed after only four models). Despite its pedigree, Norris would not be a precedent for suburban housing in America. Rather, Oak Ridge and other military projects and protocols would influence the design and construction of the postwar suburb.[8]

Greendale, Wisconsin

Rexford Guy Tugwell, a close advisor to FDR, member of "brains trust," and assistant secretary of agriculture, was among those in the New Deal administration who skewed liberalism toward left-wing plans for comprehensive economic restructuring, decentralization of industry, and redistribution of population. He remained more strident than some New Deal liberals who, courting favor with the political power of private enterprise, softened their notions of comprehensive reform in favor of more traditional business practices. For Tugwell, the revitalization of agriculture and industry were interdependent, and his views were a prime target for conservative members of Congress looking to expose leftist tendencies in the Roosevelt administration. When he became director of the Resettlement Administration (RA) he inherited a number of agricultural and industrial demonstration towns that were underway, and he also inherited all the political suspicions associated with them.[9]

The RA was ostensibly concerned with the rural poor as well as the inner-city slums that had been collecting refugees from failed farms. Reversing patterns of urban blight and encouraging home ownership were generally accepted goals in Washington at the time, and Tugwell convinced FDR of a project that would swap populations between blighted urban areas and suburban new towns. These towns would partially depend on the city for employment, and the urban land that was vacated would, in theory, become city parks. Tugwell's direct line to the president helped gain approval for the project, and he was eventually authorized to administer what was called the Greenbelt Towns Program.[10] Tugwell thought there should be 300 greenbelt towns, yet of the twenty-five potential sites only four were finally chosen for development and assigned chief planners. Two of the four were planned for the east coast, with Greenbelt, Maryland, near Washington being perhaps the best known of these, and a cross-section of America's most prominent professional planners were quickly enlisted in the project.[11]

One of the three greenbelt towns, Greendale, Wisconsin, as planned by Elbert Peets and Jacob Crane, was distinct in that it rearranged the regionalist functions and hybridized them with conventional residential street components. Many of the Greenbelt, Maryland, housing blocks were built of brick, painted white, and detailed with imagery faintly expressive of early twentieth-century modernism, biological determinism, and the heroism of New Deal technocracy. Considering the International Style and the group housing employed in the other greenbelt towns to be European affectations, Peets based Greendale on American urban hybrids. He created a grid of cul-de-sacs and superblocks, and while one half of the town contained group housing the other half contained detached housing and so was, along with Norris, one of the few public projects to incorporate the single-family detached house within an organization eccentric to the dominant postwar formats.[12] Peets also developed a significant alternative to the Radburn house by developing not two fronts but one side court like the side garden house of colonial times. More importantly, by treating the house as not simply one volume but a group of three volumes, the number of possible housing arrangements increased dramatically. The garage, the house, and the yard formed a compound of three elements in the landscape. With these elements, Peets made large back yards, eliminated the front yards, and used the mass of the house to create a wall along the street. A variation on that arrangement positioned the garages for a pair of houses parallel and adjacent to the street edge. These were not simply new generic rules or plan arrangements but rather new organizations that altered a more fundamental chemistry of multiple houses and street (figure 3.2.4 and figure 3.2.5).

Mimicry and misquotation have been responsible for some of the most durable urban formations in America. There was certainly nothing to revere or preserve about the RPAA's original holistic conception. In fact, its more relaxed or degraded versions were as complex if not more complex than those that strictly adhered to the formula. From an organizational perspective, a critical distinction could only be made about the shift that occurred when these devices of subdivision were referenced as templates or planimetric expressions rather than interdependent functional relationships, especially when they were adopted by a building industry that increasingly organized housing assembly as a summation or repetition of successive operations across identical pieces. For instance, defense-housing additions to the greenbelt towns often managed to completely neutralize the functional relationships among house, cul-de-sac, and superblock.[13] The FHA reproduced images of cul-de-sacs and larger blocks as tools for solving platting formations in the subdivision. For instance, cul-de-sacs reduced infrastructure costs and maximized development on awkwardly shaped parcels of land. Over the years, this "dead-end" form was also enlarged to more than double the size of the Radburn cul-de-sacs to accommodate the turning radii of large vehicles and fire trucks. In the 1950s, luxury suburbs adopted the cul-de-sac and superblock, replacing the interior green with a golf course. When that form was mass marketed as luxury "planned communities" in the 1970s and 1980s, a particularly large version of the cul-de-sac was used as a device for phasing large fields of suburban development. Rather than building a specific network of streets all at once, the main arterial could be incrementally extended, with cul-de-sac offshoots along its length. These cul-de-sacs were as long as

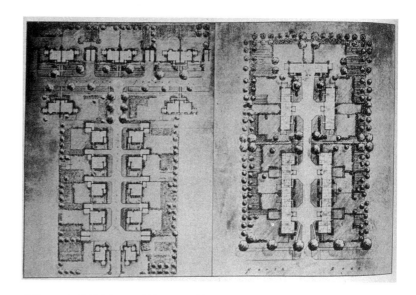

3.2.4 Plan of Greendale, Wisconsin. Library of Congress, Prints and Photographs Division, Washington, D.C.

3.2.5 Greendale, Views of Residential Streets Library of Congress, Prints and Photographs Division, Washington, D.C.

necessary to access developable land, thus balancing infrastructure costs over the gamble of housing sales. The golf course was not a public interior green and when not surrounded by parks and crossed with pedestrian networks, the cul-de-sacs were not exchange points between vehicular and pedestrian circulation but rather very quickly formed isolated pods of development connected only by arterials sized for large volumes of cars. The same planimetric reference, without precise temporal and functional expressions, was capable of describing two entirely different organizations.

Elbert Peets

In the course of his career, Elbert Peets witnessed a diverse gallery of America's cyclical housing fixations and fashions from the City Beautiful period to the 1960s, so that even though Greendale was loosely based on Williamsburg, Virginia, and some buildings were vaguely colonial in appearance, the reference was not nostalgic. In one article, comparing the newly restored town of Williamsburg, the Century of Progress exhibit, and his own town of Greendale, Peets' wry commentary on the cloying, instant history of Williamsburg would be perfectly suitable for application to our own fictional community developments of the late twentieth century. He wrote, "Williamsburg complete with 'Ye Olde A. and P. Foode Shoppe' is crowded with happy nostalgic visitors. . . . The stores are frantically picturesque and various. . . . There is no design value in these weak deviations from alignment, merely an affectation of unmechanicalness which, since we know it is not modern, we are intended to assume is colonial." In the same article he claimed that the quaintness of Williamsburg was really no different from the antihistorical "chic of science" at the Century of Progress.[14] Even into the 1960s, Peets continued to invent streets and organizations for the arrangement of detached and group houses. Later in his career, when asked what he considered to be the main problem in contemporary planning, he replied that there were not enough "specialized streets."[15] Rather than "shady superblocks," the street network of the subdivision had become generic or "all purpose." "The only apparent change since the 1920s is that the houses are smaller and the streets are wider."[16]

Though President Roosevelt said that Greenbelt, Maryland, was "an experiment that ought to be copied by every community in the United States," the greenbelt towns appear to be destined for bad press and socialist labels.[17] Greenbelt citizens were labeled "'long-haired New Dealers' conducting a 'dangerous communist experiment.' Some residents were even dismissed from their government jobs as security risks."[18] Comprehensive planning was economical in that it reduced infrastructure costs, but schedules, weather conditions, and the added agendas of employment relief sent the project over budget. The towns were criticized for their expense, for competing with private enterprise, and for encouraging social regimentation. Detractors even raised questions about the collective structures of the town like the cooperative grocery store. All these factors gave the conservative private enterprise lobbies ammunition to defeat the greenbelt idea as a model for suburban development after World War II.[19] Calling these projects "socialistic" experiments was code for the complex of agendas advocated by lobbies like the National Association of Real Estate Boards (NAREB). Speaking on behalf of the NAREB, Herbert Nelson said: "We have had a number of demonstration projects erected and are somewhat at a loss to know what has been demonstrated."[20] Everyone was interested in slum clearance, perhaps most of all the NAREB. The group was in Washington to fight against blight and to oppose government management of property on the grounds that it compromised popular control. For the NAREB, the greenbelt towns diverted attention from possible government subsidies for their own interests and defeating them was simply a good precedent against all public housing projects.[21] Ironically most of the social regimentation in the greenbelt towns was probably no more extreme than the *de facto* social constraints of postwar residential fabric, the exaggerated or hyper-capitalistic versions of traditional real estate practices that were packaged in an all-American form and endorsed by the FHA.

Notes

1. Clarence Stein, *Toward New Towns for America* (Cambridge, MA: MIT Press, 1957), 22.

2. Henry Churchill, "Henry Wright: 1878–1936," in *The American Planner: Biographies and Recollections*, edited by Donald A. Krueckeberg (New York and London: Methuen, 1983), 216.

3. Henry Wright, *Rehousing Urban America* (New York, Morningside Heights: Columbia University Press, 1935).

4. Lewis Mumford in the introduction to *Toward New Towns for America*, 11. Mumford pointed out that the "admirable device" of the superblock had been used in Cambridge and Longwood, Massachusetts, since before the middle of the nineteenth century. He continued, "Longer blocks had been used in subdivision, but superblocks held public space that was not accessed by vehicular networks. Curiously it never attracted any later attention, not even from nearby planners like Olmsted and John Nolen, though the latter had his office in Cambridge and must have repeatedly visited these very superblocks on friendly, if not professional errands."

5. Stein, *Toward New Towns for America*, 73.

6. Michael J. McDonald and John Muldowny, *TVA and the Dispossessed: Resettlement of Population in the Norris Dam Area* (Knoxville: University of Tennessee Press, 1982), 19–20.

7. Tracy Augur, "The Planning of the Town of Norris," reprint *American Architect* (April 1936), 1.

8. Charles W. Johnson and Charles O. Jackson, *City Behind a Fence: Oak Ridge, Tennessee 1942–46* (Knoxville: University of Tennessee Press, 1981), passim.

9. Paul Conkin, *Tomorrow a New World: The New Deal Community Program* (Ithaca: Cornell University Press, 1959), 105, 114. The Federal Emergency Relief Administration (FERA) also began a community building effort, but by 1935, the Division of Subsistence Homesteads had spent only a small portion of its budget and FERA had built only two communities. Meanwhile, foreshadowing future conflicts, this activity attracted debates in Congress about whether the government should be in the town-building business. The Division of Subsistence Homesteads was required to set up a more centralized disbursement of funds through the Treasury. In the ensuing year, even the constitutionality of the FERA would be overturned.

10. David Myhra, "Rexford Guy Tugwell: Initiator of America's Greenbelt New Towns, 1935–36," in *The American Planner: Biographies and Recollections* edited by Donald Krueckeberg (New York and London: Methuen, 1983), 236.

11. Conkin, *Tomorrow a New World*, 306, 173–74. In 1935, New Jersey citizens in Franklin Township, the site of the Greenbrook project, filed injunctions against the Resettlement Administration and against Tugwell himself that eventually resulted in a decision on May 18, 1936, from the U.S. Court of appeals in Washington, D.C., ruling that the Emergency Relief Act was unconstitutional. Among their list of grievances was the threat of reduced local revenues resulting from the fact that the RA did not have to pay taxes as well as fears that the new community would result in bad neighbors. They also anticipated architectural developments similar to that which had been planned for the Jersey Homesteads, a subsistence homestead project that had been criticized in the area. The controversy was fueled by Tugwell's lack of support in Washington. Tugwell's towns had been accused of creating socialist communes. Eventually, while the other towns were allowed to go forward, the New Jersey town was scratched and legislation was passed that would required the RA to make payments to and be subject to local authorities. The National Association of Real Estate Boards issued a statement saying the decision set a good precedent that

would bring many public housing projects into question. Hale Walker was Greenbelt's planner. Greenbrook near New Brunswick, New Jersey, was headed by Henry Wright. The other two were planned for the midwest: Greenhills near Cincinnati planned by Justin Hartzog and Greendale near Milwaukee, Wisconsin, planned by Jacob Crane and Elbert Peets. To send a message discouraging federally managed community building projects, local and federal politicians and lobbyists, including the National Association of Real Estate Board (NAREB), sued the government and successfully blocked the construction of Greenbrook on the grounds that it was unconstitutional. The planners began work on the remaining three towns as arrangements for land acquisition began. Joseph Arnold, *The New Deal in the Suburbs: A History of the Greenbelt Town Program 1935–1954* (Columbus: Ohio State University Press, 1971), 49.

12. Joseph Arnold, a greentowns scholar, has noted that Greendale was the first and "... remains the only public housing program that built the detached houses most Americans apparently prefer." Arnold, *The New Deal in the Suburbs*, 99.

13. Clarence Stein describes how the Radburn arrangement was employed in Greenbelt, Maryland, and compared those original developments with the town's later war-time defense homes developments. The defense model provided housing grouped around a dead-end car court and with major rooms facing toward the outside. Though the arrangement seemed similar, the activity sponsored by the arrangement is almost the inverse of that in Radburn or the other Greenbelt cul-de-sacs. The car court was a "dreary" and widened version unbounded by landscape hedges which would contain the yard area near each house. In addition the pedestrian paths, the only entry into green space and underpasses, were not developed and the entire arrangement, in the end, did not separate children from automobile traffic but rather drew them into the vehicular area of the car courts. In fact, Stein noted, a child was even killed in an automobile accident within one of the car courts. The "uninspired" almost barrack-like housing was unrelieved by trees or shade and was overexposed to automobile noise, since its primary entry was on the courtyard. Stein, *Toward New Towns for America*, 137–148.

14. Elbert Peets, "Washington, Williamsburg the Century of Progress and Greendale," *City Planning-Housing*, Werner Hegemann, ed. (New York: Architectural Book Publishing, 1937), 396, 398, 410.

15. John Loretz Hancock, *John Nolen and the American City Planning Movement: A History of Cultural Change and Community Response 1900–1940* (Ph.D. diss., University of Pennsylvania, 1964).

16. Peets, Elbert, "Studies in planning texture for housing in Greenbelt towns," *Architectural Record* (September 1949), 131–137.

17. *New York Times*, 14 November 1936.

18. Mary Lou Williamson, ed., *Greenbelt: History of a New Town, 1937–87* (Norfolk, Va.: The Conning Company, 1987), 148.

19. Arnold in *The New Deal in the Suburbs* traces the demise of the greenbelt towns in Congress.

20. Conkin, *Tomorrow a New World*, 193.

21. Mark Gelfand, *A Nation of Cities: The Federal Government and Urban America 1933–1965* (New York: Oxford University Press, 1975), 115, 117.

3.3 SUMMATION: SUBDIVISION MERCHANDISING

While the earnest planners were hard at work on federal demonstration projects, elsewhere in Washington the subdivision had become not a tool of political and economic restructuring, protected from the evils of the marketplace, but a product traveling as quickly through the marketplace as much smaller or more temporary objects of desire. This time, rather than engaging the rather pink notions of the planners, the war towns used their own military protocols and building techniques. The only other architect was the "invisible hand" of commerce formed by a giant cast of characters in the trades and home-building industries. Since a distributed set of products would, one by one, recondition the suburban fabric, it was their distribution and the promotional campaigns that were the critical organizational sites. The FHA's mobilization of the home-building and real estate industries as well as the reorganization and retooling of the construction industry to respond to a population of homes also formatted the space of the subdivision.

Housing Currency

Financial protocols have always influenced subdivision invention, but the 1934 National Housing Act, which was responsible for the most familiar and pervasive subdivision organizations of the twentieth century, clearly established a subdivision protocol within which the design of the individual home was less important than the architecture of its consumption and financing. New Deal reformers were beginning to favor not comprehensive restructuring but rather adjustment of the economy by, for instance, altering patterns of consumption. The Federal Home Loan Bank Act (1932) and the Home Owner's Loan Act (1933) were two early experiments of this kind that used tools like banking insurance to regulate commerce and generate confidence. The house was treated as a stationary form of durable goods that engaged banking interests, and it was second only to agriculture in the numbers of workers and trades it employed. Like these, the National Housing Act (NHA) of 1934 and the Federal Housing Administration (FHA) which the bill established were intended to address the housing shortage, stimulate the economy, reduce unemployment, and increase confidence in the banking system. It did away with multiple mortgages and set up a federally insured long-term, low-interest single mortgage system with low monthly payments that were often cheaper then rent.[1] Despite private enterprise's claims of greater fitness, there had always been shortages of affordable housing. The federal government would insure the lending institution, not the individual, against mortgage default, and the low-priced home would be the vehicle of that insurance. Consequently the first determinations about the new house involved appraisal value, and all housing expressions would have to exist within the limit of $16,000. An individual wishing to "modernize" a house or build a new house would get an estimate from a contractor and receive a mortgage for that amount from the bank. The bank would then pay the contractor to begin work and since the loan was insured, the home owner would be able to pay off the mortgage with a low monthly payment. The insurance premiums paid to the FHA would make it self-supporting.[2]

The authors of the NHA-FHA legislation were not proponents of "subdivision science" or community planning but rather were experienced primarily in business, finance, insurance, and government.[3] A number of individuals who worked within the FHA were developers or members of the NAREB who traded on old watchwords concerning the stabilizing influence of individual home ownership. Though touting laissez-faire politics, the group was angling for government subsidy of more traditional real estate practices. Subsidies were un-American unless in service of conventional practices of private enterprise, especially those practiced by real estate professionals themselves.[4] NAREB lobbyists were banking on more generic and streamlined processes of development based on extreme versions of selected stylistic and real estate traditions. Ironically the habit of gathering statistical data practiced by planners in Washington ideally suited the new goals of the FHA bureaucracy (figure 3.3.1).

The distributive protocols associated with financing, banking insurance, and merchandising as well as the statistical study of consumption, industrial relocation, and property valuation would now direct home building. Within

3.3.1 Cartoon with caption, "How Can We Best Do This Job Together?" by John W. Morley. National Committee on the Housing Emergency, Inc. *Tomorrow's Town* (August 1943), 1.

this product model, the patterns of distribution might be complex but the product or repeatable unit could be controlled. Houses and entire subdivisions would, like cars, become a major United States industry. Since the suburban tract house was based on rent affordability, the subdivision was populated by the equivalent of distributed apartment dwellings, each approximately 800 square feet in size. Many of the sources of differentiation, changes over time, separate layers, or different directors were fused and neutralized into an ecology that treated housing like a kind of currency, valued, for instance, for the sheer numbers that could be produced.

Promotion

The NHA sponsored a Better Homes Campaign that was run like a cross between an ad campaign and a "war bond drive."[5] The earliest NHA promotional brochures deputized architects, contractors, building suppliers, and anyone else involved in the building trades to drum up enthusiasm and convey each profession's "responsibility in the National Housing Act." The bulletins were written with punchy boosterism and illustrated with pictures of parades, posters, buttons, and brochures that could be purchased from the government to kick off a local home-building campaign. In 1934, as part of this massive publicity campaign, "4,000 communities were organized, 3 million door-to-door canvass calls were made. More than a thousand newspaper carried better-housing sections."[6] The weekly newspaper, "Better Housing" had a broad circulation to home buyers and home builders, and it was joined by a number of other daily and weekly bulletins disseminating ideas and propaganda about the growing popularity of home building.[7] One cartoon appearing among the literature perhaps best illustrated the new architecture of federal-private sponsorship. It showed Uncle Sam gesturing toward a hilltop castle entitled "Better Housing Program." A crowd of men representing various industries stood to one side while banking and insurance representatives stood on the other. As Uncle Sam gleefully ushered them on, the caption read, "Thar's gold in them thar hills!"[8] The FHA also produced radio spots and movie shorts. Most of the radio programs, "Master Builder" or "Mrs. Homemaker" were fifteen minutes long and included orchestral interludes of patriotic or sentimental music played at soothing tempos. They dramatized the stories of young couples improving and purchasing homes to boost their physical and spiritual health. "Visomatic" slide shows with a separate audio recording were also available for showings within the community or even at the local hardware or lumber store. *Better Housing News Flashes,* produced for the federal government in 1935 by *Pathé News* were screened in movie theaters to over 35 million people.[9] The films dramatically depicted a campaign already underway, stimulating industry and putting men to work. Rousing trumpet fanfares and urgent narration accompanied footage of production lines, trains and automobiles mobilizing the country and distributing products. Home-buying couples entered charming sunlit model homes, and the camera panned back on a world where home ownership could lead to a "more happy and contented family life" as the official insignia of "Better Homes Campaign" was emblazoned on the screen (figure 3.3.2).[10]

The Federal Home Loan Bank Board also sponsored a homes campaign in which it solicited designs for exemplary small houses from architects around the country. Each design was submitted on one page containing a three-dimensional rendering and a plan of the scheme. The designs were coded according to number of rooms and their appropriateness to climatic and regional considerations and complied in a *Home Selector Portfolio.* A potential home buyer could visit a lending institution and review a portfolio that contained designs suitable to the area. The FHLBB also provided lending institutions with sample brochures and actual boilerplates for ads and other

3.3.2 Cartoon with caption, "Thar's Gold in Them There Hills," by Harold Talburt. U.S. F.H.A. bulletin for manufacturers advertising agencies and publishers (Washington, D.C.: U.S. Government Printing Office, 1934). RG 195 File "FHA."

promotional literature with which the lending institution could begin a Better Homes Campaign. These ads and pamphlets explained "how to own your own home" the "safe" and "insured" way (figure 3.3.3).[11]

FHA Technical Bulletins

An FHA loan was contingent on design inspection, and FHA underwriter's manuals and technical bulletins, which were distributed to a broad circulation of developers and builders, created the impression that there was a preferred arrangement of suburban fabric that was likely to receive mortgage insurance. The same graphic guidelines were reproduced widely in trade journals and other industry publications, and any developer seeking approval for FHA mortgage insurance was likely to follow them. Though the FHA guidelines initially did a great deal to improve housing standards, by World War II the agency was less interested in promoting good design and more interested in avoiding mortgage risk with formulaic standards for houses and neighborhoods. Two of these FHA technical bulletins, *Planning Neighborhoods for Small Houses* (no. 5, 1936) and *Planning Profitable Neighborhoods* (no. 7, 1938) provided subdivision guidelines by way of simple texts and pairs of drawings labeled "good" and "bad." In many cases, these simple cartoon

3.3.3 3MI15-Minimum House—Architect, Hyde and Williams. FHLBB-Home Selector Portfolios: 6McC1-Chosen as McCall's "Home of the Month"; National Archives, and Records Administration Pickett Branch, RG 195.

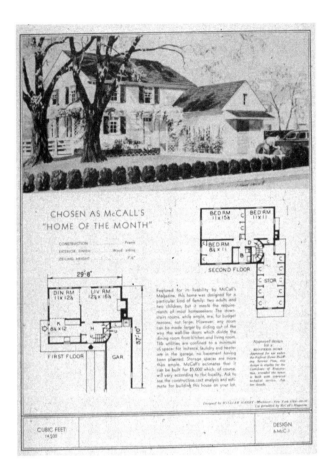

graphics outlined the design parameters of a postwar suburban landscape that would appear senseless and incomprehensible to ensuing generations. They explained why the roads swelled, the houses shrank from the edge of the street, and the entire organization was left blinking in the sun (figure 3.3.4).

Technical bulletin number 5 assumed the tone of a practical manual, selectively exhibiting some of the expertise of the progressive planning movement together with suggestions for what might be shared standards, but just two years later technical bulletin number 7 prioritized the developer's financial security and the government's mortgage risk.[12] The contrast between the two documents continued. Bulletin number 5 warned against

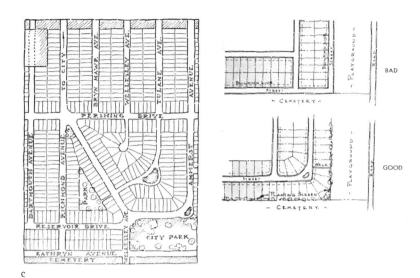

c

3.3.4 *Technical Bulletin No. 5 Planning Neighborhoods for Small Houses.* (a) The FHA's quotation of Radburn as a possible model of subdivision design; (b) street hierarchies: (top) typical court or cul-de-sac, (middle) minor residential street with planting strips, (bottom) minor residential street with sidewalks and curbs combined and street trees; (c) plan diagram showing typical neighborhood in relation to the city. *Technical Bulletin No. 7, Planning Profitable Neighborhoods.* (a) "Long Blocks Require Crosswalks Near Center," (b) "Plan Lots of Adequate Width," (c) "Protect Lots Against Adjacent Nonconforming Uses." U.S. Federal Housing Administration, *Technical Bulletin No. 5, Planning Neighborhoods for Small Houses* (Washington, D.C.: U.S. Government Printing Office, March 15, 1936). U.S. Federal Housing Administration, *Technical Bulletin No. 7, Planning Profitable Neighborhoods* (Washington, D.C.: U.S. Government Printing Office, March 15, 1938).

BAD

GOOD

a

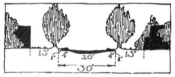

A section for a 50-foot right of way for court or cul-de-sac. This road provides a 20-foot paved strip graded to the center so that only one catch basin is needed instead of the usual two. The 4-foot walks are integral with the curb and gutter.

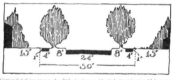

Conventional treatment of a 50-foot minor residential street having 24-foot paving, 8-foot tree strip and 4-foot walks. This road provides one lane for through traffic with parking space for cars on each side.

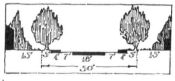

BAD

GOOD

b

dividing land into small parcels and urged coordination with city-planning authorities, while making size, however dependent on finance and timing, Bulletin number 7 suggested that the development be sized so that it could be "completed and sold within a period of time" that would "avoid the financial burden of carrying vacant land."[13]

Many of the graphics in bulletin number 5 quoted the RPAA's specialized functions and in one full-page illustration even reproduced a Radburn superblock. In bulletin number 7, platting in approximately quarter-acre lots was the default method of subdivision, and while superblocks and cul-de-sacs were not mentioned, longer blocks of approximately 1,300 feet were adopted, in part because they saved infrastructure costs. The larger block contained no spine of common green or pedestrian network, however, and all the land was private property. The cul-de-sac might be part of this arrangement, but it was used to plat additional lots in odd remnant spaces or irregularly shaped areas of a parcel.

While both bulletins encouraged street hierarchy, bulletin number 5 illustrated a range of residential streets with sectional drawings showing street trees and sidewalks. Bulletin number 7 did not provide street sections or mention street tree planting. Street hierarchies were discussed as a means of reducing traffic on residential streets but major and minor streets were the only options discussed. Bulletin number 5 recommended semi-detached houses on large lots (5,000 square feet with varying setbacks) since the land values decreased outside the city center. Smaller lots and group housing were only conditionally recommended, with landscaping and open play spaces offered as an appropriate use of the resulting extra revenues.[14] As a counterpoint, both bulletins suggested offsetting the increased costs of wider lots further from town with reduced land improvements that might involve the exclusion of sidewalks and trees. "To make wide lots possible for low-priced homes therefore, advantage must be taken of the simplification of land improvements that low density makes possible."[15]

Bulletin number 5 discussed various densities of housing and treated lots with wider frontage as a convenience to accommodate garages, but in Bulletin number 7, such lots with wide frontage for garages were presented as a standard.[16] Gradually shifting the critical dimensions of the lot reflected less concern for molding the space of the street and more concern for accommodating an increasingly uniform housing product.

The general remarks of both pamphlets emphasized the importance of the neighborhood's location and surroundings. Bulletin number 7 stated that, "The plan of a small subdivision will, to a great degree, be determined by its surroundings. In the case of a large tract, however, it is possible to establish a definite neighborhood environment and to protect it against unsightly outside surroundings and inside influences that depreciate land values." The bulletin also illustrated a way in which the subdivision could "protect against nonconforming uses" or "objectionable properties."[17]

The FHA also began to direct the temporal components of development as well, advising against lot sales and favoring "preimproved" or prebuilt subdivisions.[18] Though the term subdivision was still often used to refer to a neighborhood, more and more it began to describe a generic parcel of primarily residential development that was prebuilt in large numbers and maintained stabilized land values by means of strong boundaries. Particularly after the war, FHA's endorsement of prebuilt subdivisions paved the way for developments like Levittown that did not adopt the assembly-line house but rather turned the entire site into a giant assembly line. Holes were dug, slabs poured, and framing hoisted simultaneously in a stepwise sequence across the whole of the site within a huge choreographed machine that was several thousand acres large and produced fourty houses a day. Earth-moving equipment lined up and dug the holes for several buildings at once or planted a uniform number of shrubs on each lot. Even appliances were delivered to several houses at once. The balance sheet for this kind of subdivision was restructured as well. The bottom line did not only correspond to an individual address but to a process applied to hundreds or even thousands of homes. Thus, a developer might evaluate the costs of pouring a thousand concrete slabs, and as a consequence of this new tabulation of costs, find new ways to economize in the building process. Reducing the thickness of a slab or of structural members on an individual home would provide negligible savings, but within a summation process, alterations to several thousand slabs or beams provided significant savings. From prefinancing, prebuilding, and prefabrication evolved an entirely new residential fabric in which all the negotiations among the pieces occurred all at once and would be undifferentiated by iterative growth over time. In return for more predictable resale value, the home buyer bought the house lot together as well as accepting the simultaneous development of a very similar fabric throughout with more predictable resale value.

Real Estate Industry

Realtors, home builders, and subdividers recognized the authority of the FHA as a sponsor and a clearinghouse of information and reproduced many of its "good-bad" comparisons in professional publications. Since the last quarter of the nineteenth century, subdividers had, with the help of planners and designers, developed land and its infrastructure for lot sales, but since the FHA favored preimprovement, the subdivider became a home builder who also provided interior finishes and appliances. The homes substituted for street improvements. Often, sidewalks were built only on one side of the street and trees planted in the lawns rather than in planting strips. Alleys that previously allowed for smaller roadways were considered a thing of the past. An all-purpose street 50 feet wide replaced roadway variations. The garage had become an unquestionable part of the house, and shared garages were discouraged. New marketing studies demonstrated a clear preference for colonial homes on curvilinear streets subdivided into quarter-acre lots. The National Association of Homebuilders replaced the National Association of Real Estate Brokers, and this new quasiprofessional group portrayed itself as the architect of scientifically planned communities and the conveyor of all kinds of "modern know-how."[19] The subdivider would orchestrate the integration of commodities and infrastructure, distribute modern appliances, and provide new forms of transportation. Some even forecast the advent of airplane subdivisions. In the same way that houses and other commodities were likened to automobile manufacture in American, so was the subdivision. One subdivider wrote, "Just as automobiles passed through crude stages of design and mechanical construction over the years, so has subdivision planning emerged from a mere jumble of streets, alleys, and rectangular blocks."[20]

Federal Housing Administration/Veterans' Administration

World War II and the Depression had organized the housing demands of several years into a single large market. After passage of the Servicemen's Readjustment Act of 1944, the Veterans' Administration (VA) cooperated with the FHA by guaranteeing GI loans in lieu of equity. In 1946 the Veterans' Emergency Housing Act was passed, sanctioning VA and FHA cooperation and a loosening of FHA rules and regulations. A population of returning veterans with similar incomes and requirements also entered the home-buying market within a short period of time. This link between subdivisions and the military affected the constitution of the organization in other ways as well. Military

In the past five weeks, I have met with more than thirty groups from industry, labor, veterans, and government. I have listened closely to their recommendations; and I have examined the principal available data. Two sobering facts emerge from this study in bold relief. First, there is an urgent need for some 3 million moderately and low-priced homes and apartments during the next two years. Second, we can meet this need only by bringing to bear the same daring, determined and hard hitting team work with which we tackled the emergency job of building the world's most powerful war machine four years ago.[23]
—*Wilson Wyatt FHA/VA Housing Expediter*

War and its more sobering aftermath compel a new ap-

installations and procedures provided rehearsals for infrastructure, housing, and communication formats. While planners were usually interested in aesthetics and other static elements of the subdivision organization, military protocols often gave primacy to organizational expressions. The subdivision also required temporal expressions and logistical problem-solving techniques. Military techniques for streamlining the construction of barrack-like housing would be directly translated into private-sector building by war project builders like William Levitt as would the technologies of prefabrication and mobile housing units that had been used in various war installations.

Prefabrication

During the 1930s, private companies, research institutes, government agencies, and allied industries developed prefabricated housing prototypes, most of which were panelized systems of steel, concrete, gypsum, and plywood. The early prototypes like the Motohome came with a refrigerator full of groceries. The Ibec house was constructed in one pour of concrete. The Stran Steel house was constructed of steel rather than wood studs. The Higgins Thermo-namel and Lustron homes used panels made from steel coated with porcelain enamel. All of these, including Buckminster Fuller's Dymaxion, the Neff Air Form house, or the Palace Corporation suitcase house drew publicity as among the more experimental prototypes (figure 3.3.5).

By the 1940s, approximately thirty prefabrication companies in America worked primarily with panelized wood and gypsum systems. The industry's difficulty lay in balancing the promise of high-volume production against the gamble of building multiple plants across the country. Distribution of houses was not quite as easy as the distribution of automobiles. In fact, there were many reasons why the prefabricated house resisted the familiar analogy between house and car. Unlike the car, houses were complex, weighty, and bulky. Their assemblage involved plant labor as well as on-site labor. They did not receive subsidies like the transportation industry. The houses were also entirely dependent on land and property that was heavily controlled by local legalities. The dry-wall panel systems did not offer a product that was significantly different from conventional housing materials and they were regarded as less durable than conventional construction because of their light weight.[21]

The first large-scale application of prefabrication techniques was in mass-housing projects for World War II conscript housing and barracks at

praisal of family values that puts trivial, vapid, banal, and unsatisfying things in their true light. As a consequence, we are discovering that the instinct for ownership of a good home is not primitive after all but fundamental. The number of home-owning families in the United States jumped 40 percent between 1940 and 1947 to put that national ration of home ownership at the highest level on record—55 percent of all families.... However unmistakable the trend toward more home ownership, and however substantial its gains in recent years, it still is a matter of concern that it does not yet reach 45 percent of the families in the United States. There is no basis for a complacent assumption that things will advance to the best solution by themselves. There is a growing public utility-institutional attitude toward housing. It favors government built and operated housing for a large group of families. It is moving toward entrenched government control of privately owned rental housing. It encourages the institutional type of house production. There is still concerted, organized, and governmentally blessed effort to further this formula as an answer to the needs of a typical urban family.... Basic in

3.3.5 Interior view, the Higgin Therm-O-Namel House. National Archives and Records Administration, Still Picture Division, R6 31, Washington, D.C.

this antitraditional formula for housing America is the conviction that modern life—complex, urbanized, nervous, industry-centered as it is—does not permit the traditional home conceived as a man's castle to remain the dwelling norm.[24]

There was no national housing problem as long as a home was universally regarded as the stronghold of the oldest and most durable of governments; the citadel of that unit of society that demands and war production sites and military bases. A typical system assembled interior and exterior finishes within interlocking panels. The assembly-line house was useful high-security sites because it could be constructed without attracting attention. But in many ways prefabrication techniques ironically served as a model for the regimentation of the assembly processes in conventional stick construction. On-site construction was further rationalized by the manufacture of materials like plywood and gypsum board in four-foot modular dimensions. Since FHA approval was critical to the success of these prototypes, prefabrication companies avoided metals like aluminum or design features like flat roofs to make their housing look more normative in appearance.[22]

Though many of the individual prefabrication companies did not survive, since the chief protocol of subdivision composition would soon involve repeatability, the seemingly small determination of critical dimensions for prefabricated components and fittings would have enormous effect. The decision to work with 4 by 8 foot panelized sections formatted building calibration, assemblage, and transport. Three horizontal panels in this position produced a 12-foot section, while a single panel turned vertically formatted millions of homes for an 8-foot ceiling height.

Advertising Industry

Prefabrication, reconversion, and the coincidental return of thousands of veterans fueled the continued practice of suburban development as a major U.S. industry. Private enterprise itself was the architect of systems that the government only fine-tuned. It could no longer be entrenched against what it regarded as the threat of radical central control since by the end of the New Deal and for decades after, it was the beneficiary of the same concentrations of federal research and planning. This concentration of power was a kind of silent partner, providing official seals, guarantees, insurance, and expertise but never claiming authorship. Every piece of promotion characterized private enterprise as the pilot and the government as the servant. Home ownership, patriotism, and individualism were the persuasions that consistently adhered to the project of building homes even as that process became more and more uniform. As home-building campaigns took hold, most of the evidence shifted away from government documents and planning essays, and they began to mingle with pamphlets, newsletters, and ads of a second promotional campaign, now run entirely by private enterprise (figure 3.3.6).

Every maker, from shipbuilders to plastics manufacturers retooled their product to be part of this home-building effort. The same synthetic materials that made the bomber pilot's airplane would now make the veteran's easy chair. Advertisements incorporated patriotic political messages and garbled quotations of utopian modernism to sell the traditional Cape Cod house and all its accessories. Advertisements were loaded with political content during this postwar period. As if deputized to carry out political reorganization, utility and materials suppliers were almost evangelical about the "American way," portraying home ownership, "security," and "stability" as part of a world of light beyond the darkness of war. There were also giddy predictions about "postwar dreamitis" or "shangri-la 194x." Several ads confronted the choice between modern and traditional styling with wary ultimatums. One captioned a traditional house, "evolution" pairing it with a modern house captioned, "revolution." Most of the prewar futurism was reflected less in planning and building and more in the promotion of appliances. Dishwashers and toasters featured dynamic styling, turbojets, and roto-towers. Many ads

gets the highest loyalty of its citizens. The home came first, and other values fell into line accordingly. As individuals came to care less about homes, politicians came to care more about 'housing.'[25]

The man who owns and loves his home can usually be depended upon to practice the virtues of citizenship .... The discontented pessimistic elements in our citizenship for the most part come from the thousands who do not own their own homes. Other thousands of renters who deeply desire the advantages that come from home ownership and are entitled to its attainment need to be encouraged in habits of economy and thrift by the concerted action of industrial and commercial groups.[26]

To America's million homemakers. A home of your own! The dream of every true American! Your heritage from those hardy pioneers who wrought our nation out of the wilderness! Yours the goal they won! And yours the obligation to protect that nation against alien dockers that lead to chaos. This is the challenge of our times—a challenge being met with the sound common sense of our forefathers and the determination that America shall

3.3.6 Advertisement for Anaconda Copper and Brass, "Both are finding security in copper and brass"; advertisement for Watrous Flush Valve, "Keep 'em Flushing"; advertisement for Monsanto Plastics, "From a pilot seat ..." *Architectural Record* (February 1943; June 1942; November 1943).

of this period featured aerial views of orderly rows of dwellings as if to claim a market that would steadily absorb products through the end of the 1950s.

Like other durable goods, the house would be replaced or upgraded by new models. Refinishing gadgets and other extra fittings would relieve some of the indifference of the affordable homes via the same patterns of merchandising that had arranged the subdivision. In the late 1950s, after the peak of the home-building boom, Levittown began publishing its own home-improvement magazine called *A Thousand Lanes,* which featured the redecorating efforts of Levittown's home owners as the subdivision grew older. The magazine continued a trend begun in midcentury advertising. The first wave of ads pushed the materials of construction and infrastructure for the new subdivision, while the second wave of ads encouraged the home owner to update with new appliances, gadgets, and finishes inside the home. Each

grow by evolution not by revolution.

In this struggle to preserve American institutions, nowhere do we find sturdier backing than in the stability and good citizenship of the homeowner. For home ownership means safety, security, peace, happiness.[27]
—*Small Homes Guide, Builder Yearbook*

If modern design could be classed as a fad, the duty of

the insuring offices would be merely to eliminate it from eligibility. It appears obvious, however, that in spite of many faddish features displayed by it, the movement is one of more than a transitory nature, and that the basic elements which characterize it will in all likelihood sooner or later become characteristic of a large body of our stock of housing.[28]

—*U.S. Federal Housing Administration, Technical Bulletin No. 2 Modern Design*

model of refrigerator made last year's model obsolete, perhaps because of a new egg-tray feature, a new arrangement of the freezer, or a new color. Materials such as laminates, decorative self-adhesive papers, paint or wallpaper, and fabrics for interior redecoration were also featured. Most of the articles in *A Thousand Lanes* were about resurfacing and refreshing a home that had not been constructed of very durable materials. Decks, skylights, greenhouse windows, and other fittings and gadgets were also part of remodeling jobs. The only kinds of adjustments that could be made to this environment followed the same protocols that made the subdivision. The adjustment had to be a widely merchandised product with limited popular options. It had to be designed and priced to be sold by the existing forms of retail and sized for delivery in a car or small truck. Since they were largely cosmetic, the new gadgets and fittings of the suburban environment would reinforce rather than adjust the order of the subdivision while also initiating and formatting a giant do-it-yourself retail machine.

FHA Homes in Metropolitan Districts

The FHA also shifted the constitution of subdivision organizations by controlling their location and racial content. The agency's statistical division used the racial content of neighborhoods as an index of their bankability and so could "redline" or exclude entire areas of a city as mortgage risks. The FHA also mapped and rated inner-city areas not only for race but also for juvenile delinquency, foreclosure, and modern utilities among other things as a means of determining mortgage risk. Racial segregation was clearly directed from the technical bulletins, underwriting manuals, and other publications, and it was also part of a time-honored tradition that the real estate brokers and subdividers treated as sacred dogma in an otherwise unpredictable market. As a consequence of all of these factors, the FHA primarily financed homes in suburban areas. Responding to criticism, the agency conducted a study to determine whether it had unfairly biased its mortgage endorsements. The study, *FHA Homes in Metropolitan Districts*, reported a trend toward municipal annexation of outlying districts that allowed the FHA to include exurban tracts in its metropolitan designation. The FHA explained the large number of suburban subdivisions not as examples of its own preferences and rules but rather as a general American population shift from city to suburb—one that it had no choice but to follow.[29]

Technical Bulletin Number 2: Modern Design
In technical bulletin number 2, *Modern Design*, the FHA demonstrated its comprehension of modernism by evaluating it in relation to mortgage insurance risk. In fact, mortgage insurance was portrayed as the foremost cultural protocol against which modern architecture must reconcile itself. Regarded as another housing style, "modern design," since it constituted "a departure of a more or less marked degree from the character of housing that has customarily obtained," needed to be addressed in relation to "risk rating, particularly on the score of property rating and of adjustment for nonconformity."[30] Modern design was summed up as an approach that derived from plan and privileged materials and massing over exterior expression such as ornament. According to the FHA, balance, symmetry, and division of formal and informal spaces typical in other styles was in modern design often replaced by asymmetry, open plans, and reduction of room dimensions. Often the bulletin portrayed new real estate practices as "modern" simply because they were different from previous traditions.[31] Already broad and dilute as transplanted to American soil, "modernism" as applied to the FHA's version at the single-family house probably only inspired some liberty with the plan or some vestigial free-plan elements like half-height partitions or rounded kitchen counters open to another room. The FHA document supposedly reflected some consensus among practitioners that modernism's revision of tradition should probably be recognized as the inevitable hallmark of an unknown but possibly advantageous future. This bulletin like the other FHA technical bulletins was, though not regulatory, presented as a mixture of consensus and directive.

Notes

1. Kenneth Jackson, *Crabgrass Frontier: The Suburbanization of the United States* (New York: Oxford University Press, 1985), 196–197.

2. U.S. F.H.A., *Bulletin for Manufacturers Advertising Agencies and Publishers* (Washington, D.C.: U.S. Government Printing Office, 1934), 5.

3. The first Federal Housing administrator, James A. Moffett, had been a senior vice president of Standard Oil Company and transplanted business practices and personnel from the private sector to Washington. The idea of mortgage insurance was first proposed by Winifield W. Riefler who had worked for the Federal Reserve Board and the Central Statistical Board. U.S. F.H.A., *The FHA Story in Summary: 1934–1959*, 5.

4. U.S. F.H.A., *The FHA Story in Summary: 1934–1959* (Washington, D.C.: U.S. Government Printing Office, 1959), 4–7; and Marc A. Weiss, *The Rise of the Community Builders: The American Real Estate Industry and Urban Land Planning* (New York: Columbia University Press, 1987), 145–146 or Chapter 6.

5. U.S. F.H.A., *The FHA Story in Summary*, 9.

6. Ibid.

7. FHA Pamphlets, Box 18, RG 195, National Archives and Records Administration (NARA) Main Branch (Washington, D.C.: U.S. Government Printing Office).

8. U.S. F.H.A., *Bulletin for Manufacturers Advertising Agencies and Publishers* (Washington, D.C.: U.S. Government Printing Office, 1934), 3.

9. U.S. F.H.A., *Second Annual Report* (Washington, D.C.: U.S. Government Printing Office, 1936), 39.

10. *Better Housing News Flashes* (1935), RG 31, NARA Motion Picture Division, Main Branch, Washington, D.C.

11. *Home Selector Portfolio*, RG 195 Federal Home Loan Bank Board, National Archives, Pickett Street Branch, Washington, D.C.

12. U.S. F.H.A., *Technical Bulletin no. 5 Planning Neighborhoods for Small Houses* (Washington, D.C.: U.S. Government Printing Office, July 1, 1936), 1; and U. S. F.H.A., *Technical Bulletin no. 7, Planning Profitable Neighborhoods* (Washington, D.C.: U.S. Government Printing Office, 1938), 4.

13. U.S. F.H.A., *Technical Bulletin no. 7*, 4.

14. U.S. F.H.A., *Technical Bulletin no. 5*, 17, 28–29.

15. U.S. F.H.A., *Technical Bulletin no. 5*, 21.

16. Ibid., 28–31; and U. S. F.H.A., *Technical Bulletin no. 7*, 14.

17. U.S. F.H.A., *Technical Bulletin no. 7*, 5, 17.

18. Ibid., 4.

19. Stanley L. McMichael, *Real Estate Subdivisions* (New York: Prentice-Hall, 1949), 37, 5–6.

20. Ibid.

21. Kelly Burnham, *The Prefabrication of Houses* (New York: The Technology Press of the Massachusetts Institute of Technology and John Wiley and Sons, Inc., 1951), 49–63, 277–279.

22. Ibid., 289, 81–84, 34–35, 90.

23. Wilson Wyatt, *A Report to the President for the Housing Expediter* (Washington, D.C.: U.S. Government Printing Office, 2 February 1946).

24. *Homes for America*, published by the Washington Committee of the National Association of Real Estate Boards by Charles Steward, public relations director, 1948, 67–68.

25. Ibid. 66.

26. National Lumber Manufacturers Association, *Lumber and Its Utilization*, vol. IV

"Planning and Designing of Small Houses," 1923, 12. Quoted in John P. Deaned. *Home Ownership—Is it Sound?* (New York: Harper and Brothers Publishers, 1945).

27. *Small Homes Guide Builder Yearbook*, 1938–39.

28. U.S. F.H.A., *Technical Bulletin no. 2 Modern Design* (Washington, D.C.: U.S. Government Printing Office, March 15, 1936), 2.

29. U.S. F.H.A., *FHA Homes in Metropolitan Districts: Characteristics of Mortgages, Homes and Borrowers under the FHA Plan, 1934–40* (Washington, D.C.: U.S. Government Printing Office, 1942), 1, 5, 6, 7.

30. U.S. F.H.A., *Technical Bulletin no. 2*, 1.

31. Ibid., 3.

3.4 SITES

The inherent complexity associated with assembling multiple houses, architects, and attending industries into some kind of organization has attracted the interest of many cultural engineers. Planners and reformers of the subdivision, however, like those in Washington during the New Deal, repeatedly found themselves in the position of working on an organization arranged under different parameters than those of their initial goals. In many cases the new form was even cloaked in planning rhetoric, but the temporal site had been rendered considerably shorter and the means of production had entirely changed the character of the subdivision organization. Sanctioned by the implicity all-American efforts of private industry, many of the postwar subdivisions avoided questions of political restructuring by remaining commodities rather than municipalities. Most of the New Deal planning campaigns treated the federal government like a sponsoring client who would establish the financial and political architecture of community. Meanwhile, the government turned all the accumulated planning data toward a different purpose, and the merchandising campaign, with all the speed and power of advertising and marketing, took the reins and became the real architect of suburbia.

All of the statistical models of the World War I and New Deal planners might have more accurately represented the ephemeral qualities they sought to duplicate or control if their subdivision graphs and tabulations had been registered against time. The merchant builders who became the new designers of suburbia certainly understood the importance of temporal and logistical information, and they used those registers of time to create a housing product that could move more rapidly through the market.

Rather than a projected social or political site, the midcentury merchandising campaign found an existing practical site in a marketable product, and that product was the space of the house and subdivision. Within the history of the residential subdivision, the repeated dwelling as well as its accoutrement and construction techniques has always been an important site by which to adjust residential fabric. The house became a doubly powerful site when its assembly served as a model for the assembly processes of the subdivision as a whole. The techniques and materials associated with houses or cars dictated an approach to the site planning of the subdivision so that the entire organization was commodified. Any kind of fitting or gadget merchandised for this environment first entered the organization of the market, and therefore had the power to not only affect a single house, but also the larger subdivision.

Many reformers have not been interested in using the subdivision organization to adjust itself but have rather been interested in remaking the entire organization in a new image. For the nineteenth-century designers of suburbia, the turn-of-the-century Garden City planners, or even the late twentieth-century reformers aestheticizing an *organization* has been a tricky proposition. Just as some Garden City planners often merely provided a radial arrangement of streets, as if that would reference the complex financial protocols of Howard's invention, so the late twentieth-century reformers have also attempted to define the indeterminate complexity of historical urban organizations by referencing an historical aesthetic deemed to be more "authentic." Meanwhile, the dominant organizations of the marketplace have continued to effortlessly steal their earnestly crafted quasihistorical imagery in service of more powerful organizational protocols. The reformers long for an authentic model that does not exist and the market longs for a generic model that does not exist.

Comprehensive control of subdivision organizations often reduces their complexity. For instance, while the RPAA attempted holistic control through interlocking functional relationships, more relaxed situations in which these functions were used generated a more open-ended and complex calculus of relationships. In a more recent example, Christopher Alexander attempted to build mathematical models describing housing relationships. Using set theory, Alexander posited that the complex interactions of a limited number of housing factors could be mapped and controlled using semi-lattice structures. The semi-lattice structure recognized overlapping and branching populations of sets unlike a pyramidal or treelike structure that placed these components in a hierarchical arrangement. While Alexander's entire project was, in some sense, designed to demonstrate the unknowable complexity of community, he was also attempting to highlight principles that would eventually have predictable and holistic effects.

The Case Study houses and the Eichler homes were perhaps the most notable examples of projects that both critiqued and proposed to utilize the distributed housing market. One of the most powerful adjustments to the housing environment, for instance, resulted from the calibration of prefabricated construction materials. The Case Study houses proposed to adjust these very powerful protocols by reassembling into a home, prefabricated pieces that were not originally designed for domestic building. Borrowing protocols from media and from sources as varied as the aircraft and film industries, the Eamses, throughout their practice, found sites in many organizations operating outside the conventions of architectural design. The Eichler homes and prefabrication companies who survived into the 1950s, like Pease Homes, also found design sites in the processes of housing fabrication, and these companies designed not only the prefabricated pieces of the house but their modes of assembly. Perhaps the underexploited power of proposals like these lay in the possibility of adjusting not only the design aesthetics of the house but the spaces between the houses and the streets by means of a similar mechanism—a distributed product or assembly technique.

Following the Levittown precedent, other merchant builders developed subdivisions that were a great deal larger in land area than most municipalities. Luxury versions of these subdivisions, merged with security and recreational amenities like golf courses, began to call themselves "planned communities" during the 1980s. These were close cousins to the midcentury suburban subdivision in that they followed similar market protocols by selling imagery and obsolescence, but they offered both employment and housing enclaves without the inconveniences of municipal government. These edge city formats like the "real estate products" related to giant new retail and office organizations have become commodities which America also exports around the globe.

Optimization of the subdivision is not a meaningful desire, however, simple functional relationships and products potentially have enormous if not entirely predictable effects on the residential fabric that has been distributed across the country. An intermediate organizing agent might temporarily alter a residential organization for instance, by placing variables into interdependent relationships or by making batch summations of an alteration across

its repeated components. Similarly, while most of the gadgets sent to suburbia, from gardening supplies to decks to barbecues, were designed to reinforce its structure, it is also possible to imagine a fitting that does not remain
neutral to the larger organization but rather sends in an order to adjust interplay between the house and its surroundings or between groups of houses.
The midcentury subdivision inverted planning protocols by commodifying
subdivision space. Since these commodified formats were designed to absorb
the wild cards and jokes of the marketplace and are capable of tolerating
more circumstances than rules, they may continue to be more responsive to
salesmen and artists than to planners.

Afterword

The episodes, biographies, and models assembled here identify several different species of site within active organizations. Though these sites are part of many routine operations within the profession, they are not the official sites of architectural operation. They do not take their measure from geographical markers or geometric boundaries. They are part of an explicit architecture of generic programs and spaces for not only land, highways, and residential formations but offices, malls, and other franchises. An adjustment to these protocols may be expressed as a repertoire of constraints that utilize temporal, virtual, and physical strata of site. It might be a subtraction or a virtual adjustment that finds sites in the spin and makes space by reconditioning perceptions. It might be a dumb component that gains intelligence in multiples. All these switches or fittings are difficult to encompass within conventional representations of building or site. They are equally difficult to express as holistic visions, since their real intelligence may depend on a tactic responsive to temporary or circumstantial conditions.

Anarchical market forces or cultural persuasions that produce space in some cases format that space to be the means of its own adjustment as it absorbs both accidents and deliberate inventions. After a survey of the sites and episodes collected here, one lingering impression is of the potential power of these partial or tactical adjustments—these wild cards in the organization.

MacKaye's mediating lines, his trails, highways, landways, or "lanes of national development" are almost geological mechanisms for the subtraction and gradual redistribution of resources. They are something like giant differential partitions that change their own constitution over time, revaluing and recombining the ingredients inside their boundaries to revolve around different programs. In some ways they are the expansion of a single small detail into a gigantic field of influence. In other ways they are an evacuation, a subtraction, not only of physical space but of the dominant controls over a site—controls that reside within a legal or virtual realm.

The sites that remain from our attempts at the scientific organization of transportation networks are themselves quite dumb, in spite of all of their claims of sophistication. The number of networks that have developed separately however, in the fights for dominance between water, rail, highway, and air have laid the groundwork for potential intelligence within the networks. Those sites that lie between the networks as potential switches are extremely powerful, since joining one complex network to another increases their combined intelligence many fold. Similarly the roadside or wayside, now simply the vacant right-of-way for the force-field of traffic engineering or the strip of land vaguely associated with a landscape tradition is also a powerful site in a process of acquisition and site redesignation. The roadside is also a possible switch or a site for building parallelism and redundancy among several different networks. These slight distortions of the network are incredibly powerful means of magnetizing traffic and development both inside and outside the urban center.

The sites embedded within residential formations perhaps best exhibit the power of the small component to recondition a larger organization. The smallest decisions involving calibration or sequence in the construction of the midcentury suburb are extremely powerful in summation or when amplified across many multiples of houses by a global maneuver. Sometimes the simplest rules directing a functional relationship within a population also have very powerful effects. They potentially generate enormous systemic changes equal in power to the carefully choreographed protocols that have developed giant subdivision sites as a single assembly-line process. A repeated fitting affecting not only discrete details, but interplay among components, can potentially overwrite the existing protocols for street, yard, and other interstitial spaces in residential formations.

Finally, these episodes are only forays into the organizational strata of familiar environments that perhaps reveal new territory within them. The content of these episodes or the specific territory they describe becomes less important than the shifted perspective they intend to prompt. In fact that shifted perspective perhaps demonstrates the irrelevance of organizing this book into three parts with three different historical topics, since the most interesting sites are found by crossing between them.

In this book these sites are the territory of both individual artists and large groups. The most interesting artists and practitioners discussed here treat their work as inventions engaging culture's diverse and active agents of change. The most powerful inventions are often tactical adjustments fueled by larger associations and patterns of connection, so that however explicit the intervention, once released, it is flexible enough to absorb more and more circumstance and complexity for as long as it lasts.

Index